Pray for

Betty Maynard

IN AND OUT THE ANDES

◆ By the Same Author ◆
PACIFIC HOPSCOTCH

IN
AND
OUT
THE ANDES

MISSION TRAILS FROM YUCATAN TO CHILE

By Sister Maria del Rey OF MARYKNOLL

CHARLES SCRIBNER'S SONS

New York ◆ 1955

Some of the pictures in this book were taken
by Albert J. Nevins, M.M., and Sister Angelica.

◆ TO MY MOTHER ◆

CONTENTS

CONTENTS

THE PHOTOGRAPHIC ILLUSTRATIONS WILL BE FOUND BETWEEN PAGES 90
AND 91; 186 AND 187.

BOLIVIA

KEY

◆1◆

A PRETTY FIX

No doubt about it, we were in a pretty fix.

We were sitting in a brand new car. Nothing terrifying about that, to be sure, but the new car was in the middle of a mountain river up in the Andes, immersed in two feet of water. The engine was dead. Gaspar was mad. The river ran six inches deep over the floor. Our feet were propped up against the front seat, although why we bothered I don't know; every shoe in the car—and there were ten of them—oozed mud and icy water.

Worst of all our woes, Senorita San Benito kept on talking.

A helpful little soul, always ready to give advice to those in distress. She chattered to Gaspar,

"Why don't you pull that little knob? Maybe it will start the engine. Look, I'll hold it out while you press the thing on the floor. That ought to make the car go." And on and on. Gaspar maintained a stream of abuse at us, at Senorita San Benito, at the Indian who had enticed us into the river, and at Mother Nature who let hailstorms convert a trickling stream into a raging torrent.

I held my camera on my lap, supported my knees by the cord where ordinarily you hang the lap robe, and tried to still the awful thought of what was happening to the borrowed movie camera which was in the trunk of the car. I could shut out the sound of the San Benito voice and review a most awful day of calamities.

It was our first day in Bolivia. It started out fair enough.

We had spent the night crossing Lake Titicaca, that sapphire of blue-blue water in white-white Andes which God set gleaming on the top of the world. The overnight boats from Puno, Peru, to Guaqui in Bolivia are sizable vessels. So sizable, in fact, that the parts were brought up on muleback from the coast some 14,000

3

feet below, and assembled on the lake shore. You would appreciate the venture of the British company if you could see the half-pint mules there, and the size of the engines, cabins, hull plates and smoke stacks they carried over Peru's barren mountains.

Later, the railroad was put in and supplies like this now come by prosaic freight. But the boat we rode antedated the railroad.

We had a good assortment of passengers aboard, mostly young fellows going to study in Argentina. It seems that many Peruvians like the Argentine schools. Long before we saw the low squalor of Guaqui's dock—indeed, while we saw nothing but towering Andes whose dazzling crowns are first to blow a trumpet for the new day, —even then, the students' luggage was massed near the railing. Each lad was ready to grab his bundles and jump off as soon as we touched shore. It would be an interscholastic race to get a good seat in the La Paz train.

The baggage all looked like stuff we used to keep up in the attic because Grandpa couldn't bear to throw it away. Huge telescopic valises tied together with string or rope or straps or all three. Some with handles; some without. Paper bags bulging with clothes and trailing socks and ties out of the corners. Woven straw baskets packed to the handles and beyond; sheets with corners tied. But the prize was a hand-tooled leather affair, a cross between a trunk and a portmanteau which was definitely 16th century. Probably Pizarro brought his nightshirt and extra ruffs in it when he first came from Spain.

Guaqui is nothing but a dock and a train ending. The Bolivian immigration men came aboard and collected all passports. Like murder suspects rounded up by the police, we passengers sat around the stiff little salon. Off in one corner, the officials examined each passport and passed it on to the checker and double-checker.

We stood on the dock a moment surrounded by our baggage. A gentleman with sad eyes approached.

"You are Maryknoll Sisters, are you not?" he said in English.

We admitted it.

"I am Doctor Gonzales," he said, in a low tense tone.

"Oh, are you?" we said, seeing nothing to be so secretive about.

He looked around cautiously although not too conspicuously cautious. "May I speak privately?"

We cleared the baggage a bit and he came into whispering range.

"I am an exile," he began. "A year ago, the government saw fit to expel me from my native land. A cruel thing to do to a man!" He sucked in his breath in pain.

"Since then," he continued, "I have been living here and there, in Peru, Brazil, the Argentine, wherever I can find shelter. But now I have permission to return to La Paz to see my children once more. However," and his face grew hard, "the officials here at Guaqui will not accept my permissions. They are going to take me to the police station in La Paz. Probably, I shall not see my children after all."

"That's too bad," we said, all sympathy.

"Will you do something for me?" he asked. "When you get to La Paz, telephone my wife and tell her that I am in the Police Station. The telephone number is 3587."

I took out a notebook to write it down. "Don't let anyone see that," the poor exile said, as I jotted down the figures. "It is better to remember it only. 3587." Then he folded his arms across his chest and lapsed into bitter thoughts. "I do not know if I shall see them; but if they get word that I am at the Police Station, perhaps they can devise a means."

A suppressed whoop of delight interrupted this. It was Sister Angelica, come to meet us. A nurse from Idaho, Sister saw service in Manchuria before the war; she takes Bolivia in her stride. With her, was Senorita San Benito. She was talking even then—one sparkling stream of Spanish which cared not at all if it be understood, just so long as it filled the air with sound.

She was a good soul—the backbone of any parish, the instigator of a thousand good works, the most generous creature in the world. Indeed, when Senorita San Benito had a good work to do, you might just as well clear the tracks. Do it she would, come Hell or High Water.

That day, she was all set to give us a royal welcome to Bolivia. And she did. She certainly did. She hired Gaspar to drive us from Guaqui to La Paz in his new car. It was to be a few hours' run over the wide flat Altiplano.

A queer sense of timelessness fills the Altiplano. God has pushed back the tremendous Andes and cleared for Himself a wide play-

5

ground 500 miles long, and 12,000 feet nearer His Heaven. There are no trees to go past, no telegraph posts to whizz by, no roads to cross. The car keeps going and going and going, but still the horizon gets no closer. Only the coarse grass grows in tufts, and stunted plants struggle to breathe in this altitude. Your eye travels far, far, far out to the white mountains without a break.

Sister Angelica had brought a picnic, just a few sandwiches and fruit. But Senorita San Benito would have none of it. What! Welcome us to Bolivia with sandwiches? Indeed no! She knew of a *finca* nearby where they would prepare lunch for us. She chattered about the scenery; she chattered about the lunch; she chattered to Gaspar explaining how little out of the way it was. And still chattering she got out of the car and pointed out the faint evidences of a side road among the tufts of stiff grass. Had she stopped for just a half-minute, she would have heard three groans from the back-seat. We went, and that was our undoing. We drove three-quarters of an hour to the *finca;* on the way, the car wallowed through two shallow rivers.

The *finca* belonged to friends of hers. They and the Indian caretaker's family opened wide the door. Then they started on that grand luncheon. It took hours. I think they began the chicken dinner at the squawk stage.

In the meantime, we walked in the garden and patted the dogs and played with the children and admired the view and cocked an apprehensive eye at the grey sky. La San Benito was indefatigable. Sister Victoria Francis said she liked artichokes; the gardener was set to harvesting piles of them. I admired the flowers; a poor sleeping Indian was shaken awake and told to pick every flower in the place for me. I had armloads of them, enough to decorate St. Peter's in Rome, and all in the last stage of flickering life.

We started murmuring things about dark clouds and rain and the mud road and the two rivers we would have to cross, but to no avail. Luncheon was served and creaked through its inexorable courses. The thunder growled outside as we ended the custard dessert and unceremoniously hurried out to the car. But in South America, you don't get away without ceremony. The Indian girl server placidly brought the demi-tasse out to the car and we drank it. Anyway, where was Senorita San Benito?

6

Ah there she comes! Let's go now! Not so fast, my friend! La San Benito calls from the car window to the Indian girl, "Bring a drink for Gaspar!" and we wait until he gulps it down. Once again, all ready? Yes, yes. "But Gaspar has no flowers! We would want him to have a souvenir of this lovely place, wouldn't we?" I offer some of mine. "No, no, dear Sister. You keep all your posies for yourself, my dear. We will pick another bunch for Gaspar." Again we wait. "Now where are the artichokes for Mother Superior? In the back? Oh yes, there they are! Shall we start?"

She settles herself in the front seat. Like a concert singer to her accompanist, she nods to Gaspar to begin. He steps on the gas and the engine starts. Oh blessed sound! We go about ten feet.

"Stop! Stop!" cried Senorita San Benito. "Here comes an Indian selling fresh beans! I must buy some for the Good Shepherd Sisters in La Paz. The poor dears get so few good treats!" There's a deal of dickering but eventually the beans are dumped into the trunk. Good! Let's go!

Suddenly, blindingly, came the hail. Great hailstones drummed on the roof and wrapped the car in a blanket of whiteness. Road, fence, house and garden disappeared. Even the ornament on the radiator cap vanished. We might as well have been in the arctic wastes, miles from any human habitation. We started a rosary, but it was useless. Nobody could hear anybody else.

It lasted maybe twenty minutes. Then, just like the lifting of a curtain, the hail passed and the world came into view again and what a world! Dazzling white all over. Already our friends were in a dither about rescuing us from the car. It would have been so simple just to step out and walk the few feet to the house. But that would never do. No, a path had to be swept through the hail stones. Boards had to be laid out to the car. Two Indian servants had to support each one of us as we walked ten feet into the house. I felt like screaming with frustration.

We were back in the house. Indian girls and our hosts sat us on chairs and brought cushions for our feet. Each of us had her own chair and her own cushion. Senorita San Benito was now a whirlwind of energy. She was shouting for the servants to gather the hailstones before they melted. Why? To make ice-cream for the American Sisters.

7

"Oh, if only she had let us eat the lunch we brought!" sighed Sister Angelica.

Gaspar went to reconnoitre the rivers; they might be too swollen for the car to wade through. In the meantime, we sat on our chairs and rested our feet on the cushions and listened to Senorita San Benito tell us how brave we had been to live through the hailstorm.

The driver returned just as we downed the ice-cream made of hailstones. He wanted to take the chance and set out for La Paz even though it was late.

Once more—off to La Paz. The *finca,* with its low-lying mud brick walls, was like a Christmas card as we looked back on it. Impossible, that an hour ago we had wandered in the garden there gathering flowers and artichokes!

The first river was narrow, but hemmed in with steep banks. You could almost feel Gaspar grit his teeth as he tore recklessly down the bank and splashed through the water. He was bent on climbing the opposite side in one wild leap. Splash! We hit the water! Bump, bump, bump, we bounced on the river bed with water splaying out like the fire boats in New York harbor. Zip! Out of the water in a mad dash for the top of the hill. And Zrrrr! the wheels spun uselessly in deep mud. We slid back into the stream to try again.

A few more mad dashes like this and the river bank was little more than soup. We all got out and tried to fill the muddy goo with stones and tufts of grass, I searched the terrain frantically for something like a small bush to pull up. There was nothing but grass and a few stones which had to be dug out of the ground with bare hands. I remember noting absent-mindedly that my hands were bloody, cut by the rank grass, but so cold from the hailstones that I felt nothing.

On the twentieth try, more or less, the car came dripping out of the stream, waddled up that bank and—with a good shove from the three of us nuns—topped the rise successfully, Hooray! We picked up handfulls of hail and rubbed the mud and blood from our hands in an icy bath. At last! Our troubles were over.

Twenty minutes later, the second river was before us. Swollen and angry, it burbled in a muddy flood. Gaspar threw stones into it, testing the depth from the sound of the splash. He was an Indian and knew his country.

"It's deep, deep," he said dubiously.

Several hundred feet away, on the opposite bank, an Indian stopped his white horse, interested in the situation. Gaspar called over to him:

"How deep do you think it is?"

"Oh, not so bad," the Indian shrugged.

"Walk your horse into it and let me see how deep it is."

Slowly, inch by inch, the horse stepped into the river. He didn't mind the cold water on his feet, but when the icy flood reached his knees, he balked and scrambled ashore.

"I'll tell you what, then, my friend," Gaspar proposed across the river. "I'll put a mark on my car, right here"—as he plastered a piece of wet grass on the front mudguard. "When the water reaches that mark, let me know, and I'll stop."

Agreed! We all got into the car again and edged slowly into the water. The Indian on horseback kept waving, "Come on. Come on." Bump, bump, we eased over the stones in the river bed. The water rose higher and higher. At last it seeped through the door and spread over the floor. We picked up our feet and packages.

The tenseness quieted everybody. Even Senorita San Benito had nothing to say. Then Sister Angelica said, "All we need now, is to have the engine die."

And it did.

It's just as well I don't understand the high reaches of Spanish, for Gaspar's words were probably not in polite vocabularies. He yelled at the Indian who just laughed at him from the shore. He turned to Senorita San Benito. With one mighty gesture of scorn, he took the poor wilted flowers she had given him and threw them into the flood raging past.

"Get a lot of men!" he shouted to the Indian on the bank. "Get them to push us out of this river." The Indian leisurely turned his horse and ambled up the bank. He was in no hurry. What if we did have to stay there all night? Dawn would come eventually, wouldn't it?

Nothing to do but wait. Gaspar treated Senorita San Benito with kid gloves; after all, she was going to pay him. But we were anybody's target. Poor fellow, we could hardly blame him. Sure, sure, it was all our fault. It seemed not worth arguing about. Anyway you can hardly make a good case when your feet are tucked up and your lap is full of cameras, artichokes, suitcases and flowers.

Slowly we drew an audience. First one Indian and then another congregated on the river bank and laughed. It was the biggest joke in many a day. A brand new car, full of American nuns, sitting in the middle of the river, begging for help from the humble Indian. Soon the river bank ahead and the one behind were lined with Indians. They appeared from nowhere, for there seemed to be no homes nor fields around.

"Come in and help us," shouted Gaspar, purple with rage.

"How much will you pay?" they parried.

He promised them fifty Bolivianos each—about 25 cents in our money, at that time. With grins a mile wide, they rolled up their pants and waded into the icy water without a quiver. They surrounded us.

In Bolivia's Altiplano, the Indians wear a queer little cap. Knitted of bright-colored wool, it fits the head snugly and has two ear muffs. Hanging from the ear muffs are tassels or bright balls of yarn.

In no time at all, every window of the car framed laughing friendly faces of Indians. The tassels and balls swung back and forth in the mighty effort to move us. Most of them couldn't even get a hand on the car. They were pushing somebody else who had one hand on the car. A couple were tugging at the bumper in front. Ever so slowly we started, bump, bump, bump over the river bed. Happy to get 25 cents for just one icy bath, the Indians sang and joked as they scrambled to get place in the work-squad.

Lumbering slowly, quietly, the car began to heave up the river bank, dripping water from every seam. We opened the rear door and let out the flood. We clambered out, too, and let the Indians push it quite a ways up the river bank.

The Indians lined up and were paid. In spite of their red feet and half-frozen legs, they were as happy as larks and stayed around a good long time chatting about the affair. Our hostess was busy helping the chauffeur who had the hood up and was drying out the engine. It was getting dark, too.

Gaspar, for all his long line of Indian forbears, for all his childhood on the Altiplano where there is nothing more mechanical than a simple mortar to grind corn—Gaspar was an excellent mechanic. He took the engine apart and, within ten minutes, was able to start things up like a million dollars. We climbed in and started off—once again!—for La Paz.

Night was falling fast. Our water-soaked headlights would not work. In the half-light, it was impossible to see the ruts in the muddy road. We crawled along. We were leaving that wide, flat altiplano now and began twisting around the mountains which hem in La Paz. We climbed a hill in twilight; suddenly, at the top, the world opened like an oyster. A great valley, wide and deep, swooped down from the height on which we stood. Far, far over, it swept to the snow-crowned Andes shining in the last rays of the sun when all below was darksome. A terrific range of them, with a big tall one at the beginning and a great giant at the end, like a Mama and Papa Andes with all their white-topped children between them.

That was the last of the nice thrills. Three more hours of creeping forward in the dark followed. We were all for stopping right there and waiting for dawn, but Gaspar was determined to keep moving, even if it meant moving into eternity. Many times we slid, not knowing if we were sliding into a mudhole or off a cliff. We went off the road more than once, jouncing over hillocks and down gullies, as the ancient Fords used to do in Keystone Kop Komedies. I was thrown into Sister Angelica's lap; she often found herself in mine. Now and then, we passed a silent dark Indian hut. How I longed to cuddle down on its mud floor and wait for dawn! But something in Gaspar's hunched shoulders as he steered his craft through the muck of that road told me it would be useless to ask.

In the wee hours, we came into La Paz. The Good Shepherd Sisters with whom we were to stay, had shut up the house long ago. We knocked and rang the bell. We shouted and hammered on the door. Gaspar, now feeling like a Father Protector, helped at the rumpus mightily. We were looking for stones to throw at the upper windows when a light flared up in the fourth floor. Help was on the way!

At last, at last, we brought our mud-caked shoes, our dripping clothes, our tired selves into the rooms that had waited all day for us. Guess what was on the beds? Coverlets of vicuña fur,—that marvelous, light, elegant fur of the daintiest animal in Bolivia. It

11

looked like the Sleeping Beauty's chamber. So, after a cat-wash—
for the water in the bathroom was just one degree up from an ice
cream soda—to bed! The sleepy thank-you to my guardian angel
for a job well done, rose from under the vicuña coverlets. They say
in the holy books that prayers said in bed get no further than the
ceiling. That's all right, I'm sure my guardian angel was in no mood
to travel high up that night; he had probably bedded down right
on the floor beside me.

◆2◆

THE BULLS ARE DANCING

Man is a creature, the good books tell us, composed of body and soul. That's a good definition of the Indian, too, so far as it goes, but the Indian doesn't like half-way measures. He's all body or all soul at any one time. He can be so deeply spiritual, he puts you to shame. On the other hand—

Well, you should have seen Las Penas!

Father Foley had opened the parish two weeks before. Way, way out on the bleak barren dry and cold place the geographies call the Altiplano of Peru and Bolivia,—away out there on the mud flats which stretch to the mighty rim of Andes circling like the edge of a gigantic soup plate—in a tumble-down mud church and a non-existent rectory—there was Maryknoll's newest mission.

"There won't be anything much to see," Father McNiff apologized as he started out from La Paz in a rented car. "At most, we'll stay a half-hour and come back. It's more for the ride, I'm taking you. A nice peaceful way to spend Corpus Christi."

If we cold-blooded Anglo-Saxons are peaceful about Corpus Christi, the lively Indian is not. The central plaza at Las Penas was seething with color, music, dancing. The fiesta was in full swing—or perhaps I should say "full swig," for everybody there was completely and irretrievably intoxicated.

The plaza swarmed with dancers, most of them doing the Bull Dance. There wasn't much to the steps, just weaving up and down the field, but the costume made up for any simplicity in footwork. It was an entire cow-skin, complete with head, horns and tail, stretched over a frame. The dancer wore it around his waist much the way an Eskimo sits in a kayak. On his head was a conglomeration of Spanish stuff with lots of gold braid, but topped off with a tremendous sweep of feathers which towered four feet into the air.

I first saw one of these as we came into town. I scrambled out of the car and ran after the apparition.

"Let me take your picture?" I said in my best Spanish, eked out with eyebrows, hands, smiles and pointing to the camera.

"Naw! Naw!" he said and stumbled off, probably to sleep it off.

But I was mobbed in the plaza. The bulls came tearing from all sides. They pushed and jostled each other—and me too—to get into the picture. Other dancers in jaguar skins, made into a stiff cuirass like a suit of armor and finished with white skirts—accordion pleated, if you please!—marched by, piping on the bamboo flutes they have in the Altiplano. The orchestra—drums, drums, and more drums—made it a point to come close and play into my ear.

Poor things—they were so far gone! They danced until they could go not one step further, and then dropped in their tracks, unconscious before they hit the ground. The whole plaza was strewn with clumps of sodden men, their bull costumes at crazy angles, their fine feathers flung into the dust. Many a wife sat placidly beside her fallen husband with her children gathered round, making a neat little homestead-piece in the middle of the riotous dancing. Other women, much the worse for the fiesta, tottered round and round. Their derby hats—peculiar to the Aymará tribe—were set at an angle over one eyebrow. Then one by one, they too fell by the wayside to sleep it off. I remember one couple in particular who trailed after me. The wife held on to the horn of her spouse's bull costume. Together they swayed while I took their picture; together they followed me calling "Madre" every now and then so that I would at least click the camera at them. Eventually they swayed too far off-center and went down to slumber on the dusty plaza.

Father Foley found us there. He came out of what had once been the church, and rescued us from the hordes of picture-crazy Indians. Father is one of those mild-mannered Irishmen (if an Irishman can ever be said to be mild-mannered) who look conditions over and set about making them better. His two weeks at Las Penas had not been idle.

The church was all fallen down, all but the sanctuary and the front door. It's one of those exquisite church-fronts which the Spanish sprinkled all over South America. What builders they were! Here in this desolate spot, far out of the beaten track of civilization, they had erected what had once been a perfect darling of a church.

Between the front door and the sanctuary was—nothing. Big heaps of mud showed where the rains had melted the mud walls and goo-ed them over the floor. Father had cleared away some of these already and had put up wooden frames to build the windows around. It seemed so queer to see window frames set up with no walls or roof to support them. We picked our way over the mounds of earth and approached the sanctuary.

Since, for many years, this was all that remained of the church, the front of it had been walled up with wooden boards, making a dark little spot of the inside. But what an inside! As we stumbled across the raised threshold, we gasped. Here was a great altar sheathed in gleaming silver. Here was a reredos of gold leaf filling the entire wall behind the altar. Niches and statues were strung with colored stones and gold wire. A whole array of saints stood on an ancient vesting case to one side, looking pretty neglected. Just to cheer them up I took pictures of them. I had to take St. George's hair out of his eyes and set him upright on his horse. St. Mary Magdalen's ancient satin gown split as I tried to rearrange it. The perfume bottle she carried in her hand was sadly out of keeping. It bore the label, Pond's Honey and Almond Cream. I could almost see the woman's hand which had put it there,—big, dirty and work-hardened. She must have bought it in La Paz, figuring that only the Magdalen's spikenard could smell so glorious.

On the ragged remnants of a carpet, the Fathers prepared to baptize babies. And here we saw the Indian who is all-soul on Corpus Christi. There were eight babies lined up each with God-father and God-mother. The real parents huddled on the floor watching the process. Everybody was cold sober. When you thought of the Saturnalia going on in the plaza at that very moment, the fact was all the more remarkable. In all reverence, eight little Indian souls were made Children of God.

Paying no attention to the ceremony were two other worshippers. An old man knelt before the reredos, bearing in his hands a flaming torch. He knelt upright and stretched the flame up toward a statue of Our Lady, beautifully dressed, who reigned in dainty elegance in this ruin of a mud church. The old man, time and again, set his burning pot on the ground before him and prayed as though his heart would come right through his eyes. Then, once more, he lifted the flame to his lovely lady in supplication.

A woman crouched on the other side of the sanctuary. She, too, had brought a pot of flaming rags; but she sat back on her heels and let San Antonio, in the niche above her, do the talking. What he said to her, I don't know, of course, but it was evident that they were old friends. She kept looking straight at him with bleary eyes that had seen so much of poverty. He kept looking at her with the glassy eyes of a Spaniard's idea of heavenly joy, which nevertheless managed to be kind.

It was two-thirty as the last little bundle of Christian baby was carried out of the sanctuary. Father Foley took us to see what will be the rectory. It's right next door. Only a Maryknoll eye could see any rectory possibilities in it. The walls were half-finished, or rather, half-unfinished. They were in the process of melting down into the earth. But Father Foley stood in the middle of this desolation and pointed proudly to what will be the refectory, the reception room, the bedroom and—of course—the site for the convent-to-be. His eyes gleamed; he spoke quickly; his arm swung from mudheap to mudheap as he showed off the glories of the Las Penas rectory. I thought of Solomon taking some visiting satraps to the foundations of the temple of Jerusalem and pointing out the great halls and doctrine rooms. Solomon had nothing on Father Foley in enthusiasm.

Father was living at the *finca* fourteen miles away, until some sort of house can be built for him right there at the church. Father McNiff had packed five man-sized baloney sandwiches and we planned to eat them at the *finca*.

On the way, Father Foley was to stop at a cemetery where he was to bless a grave. Altogether it had been a very full day for him thus far. Besides a big Mass in the morning, he had had a funeral and a wedding, eight Baptisms and, now us, pestiferous visitors from the States who wanted to see everything possible. But no breakfast as yet. We tried to prevail upon him to eat one of the

16

baloney sandwiches but he preferred rigorous mortification until he could get a good cup of coffee. We would go to the cemetery and bless a grave; then off to the *finca.*

As the car nosed its way out of that screaming, highly exhilarated fiesta, the hullaballooing crowds gave us a grand send-off. A couple of horsemen escorted us on either side. Poor fellows, they were more horizontal than vertical; the horses had more sense than they had at the moment.

Along the road, were merry-makers on the way home. Many of them couldn't make it; they lay in heaps along the roadside. The rest of the family parked comfortably beside the fallen warrior to wait until he woke to cold reality.

When we stopped I couldn't see why. There was no cemetery that I could see. But, obediently, I trooped along with the others as Father Foley led the way across the stubbly Altiplano with its tufts of coarse grass and stunted little bushes. We ran down a gully in the dry earth and climbed to the other side. Here was the cemetery, an adobe wall maybe eight feet high, fencing off a piece of ground about as big as the backyard we had at home years ago. The dead were stored in holes in this wall, so that the inside of the cemetery looked rather like a room lined with file cases, each drawer labeled with the name of the occupant. A small group of men had just finished cementing up the newest file—that of the man buried that morning. As Father Foley approached, they snatched off the little woolen caps they wear and stood with bowed heads. Father blessed the grave, spoke a short while with the men in their own Aymará dialect, and turned to go. But not so fast! An Indian who was very very much the worse for fiesta barred his way at the cemetery gate.

"A *responso,* Padre," he asked. This is a sort of prayer that has become an abuse in the Altiplano. For a certain amount of money, the prayer is said or sung. Certain tribal medicine men have made a good thing of "responsos" so the Maryknollers are discouraging the practice.

"No," said Father Foley. "No *responso.*" He walked by.

The Indian ran up to Father McNiff. "*Responso!* See? Here is the money."

"No, my friend," said Father McNiff. "No *responso.*"

The poor fellow was desperate. He looked over the three of us Sisters. Sister Angelica, he passed over; me, he turned down. But he fastened on to Sister Victoria Francis as the holiest of us all.

"*Responso!*" he cried to her.

"No, no!" she said.

"*Responso!*" he begged. "*Madre linda! Madre hermosa! Mi querida Madre! Responso!*" (Lovely Sister, beautiful Sister, my dearest Sister, give me a responso!)

He was on his knees before her, grovelling in the dust. Then he raised himself upright, clasped his hands and implored her. "*Responso!*" he begged. "My darling Sister, a *responso!*"

Poor Sister, she didn't know what to do. She couldn't get around him to slip out the cemetery gate. The two priests stood around to see that no harm came to her. These men can be really dangerous when they get religion-mad.

As for Sister Angelica and me, I'm afraid we enjoyed it. It isn't often that a perfectly respectable Sister in her 60's has to walk out a cemetery gate over the prostrate form of a devout worshipper.

The priests lifted him gently and put him to one side. He muttered a little and then he, too, was a sodden heap of too-much-fiesta. We continued on to the *finca*.

Something happens to you on the Altiplano. You feel that you're on a treadmill getting noplace fast. The wheels go round, and tufts of grass go by, but you stay in the same place so far as the mountains are concerned. Only then, do you realize how vast a place the Altiplano is.

We left behind the colorful plaza, the dancers, the music, knowing that the backdrop to all this is sheer tragedy. The Indians have no amusement other than drinking. They don't play baseball, nor leapfrog, nor even tiddlywinks. They don't have a movie to go to. They have no hobbies; the women don't make patchwork quilts and the men don't play horseshoes. In their hard grind of a life, the only diversion is drinking—long term drinking that ends in oblivion.

On the way home, we stopped to do justice to Father McNiff's sandwiches. I must say that, for all his talents, the Maryknoll Superior is no hand at slicing bread. His baloney sandwiches must have been hewed from the loaf by machete. They would never have passed inspection at the Waldorf but missioners rarely eat at the Waldorf, anyhow. We had missionary appetites by then.

We hardly saw the sandwiches. We were feasting our eyes on the snow-crowned giants which hemmed in this great Altiplano. As we looked, they became whiter and whiter. Snow was falling up there.

Not all Indians are poor. In the market place or swinging up and down the streets which wind up the steep mountainsides of La Paz, you meet many Indian women in transparent velvet *polleros*— those full skirts of ten yards each. Over their shoulders are gorgeous shawls with long silk fringe. Earrings encrusted with gems dangle and shake droplets of gleaming color as the women haggle in the market or stop to chat with a friend. Gold teeth and well-brushed derbies bespeak the utmost in prosperity.

I saw two such *cholas* buying a radio one day. I happened to be waiting in a candy store while Sister Angelica was buying sweets for the poor children at our mission. The two Indian women, one old, one fairly young, walked into a radio store across the street. Their derbies were set at a determined angle; evidently they had already made up their minds. I crossed the street and edged in after them.

They knew exactly what they wanted. They walked over to a table-model radio.

"This!" they told the clerk. "Here!" and they handed him a roll of bills.

It was over in no time. The clerk was counting the roll as the younger *chola* lifted the radio and walked off with it.

I stood and watched them go down the street. At every step as they went down the steep grade, their full skirts swayed from side to side and their braids flapped against their backs. The two derbies were turned to each other in animated conversation. I wish I could have hidden in that radio and seen where they brought it.

Maybe then, I would know more about the heart and soul of the Aymará Indian.

◆ 3 ◆

CALVARY LIVES AGAIN

S-s-s-sh!

Sister's cautious hand wakened me. We dressed quietly, almost guiltily. We tip-toed downstairs and turned the key in the front door. We stepped out into the darkness of the garden path. The gate swung to with a subdued click. We began putting one foot in front of the other down to the rocky lane. As we passed under an infrequent street light, I looked at my watch.

It was 4 A.M.

I signed to Sister James Cletus and she winked solemnly. We were on time. We had two miles to walk down that black street, but we would be on time.

Then the great paschal moon lifted itself above the mountains of Cochabamba and showed the path distinctly. The trees were all silvered; the little puddles left from last night's rain were shining. The snow-crowned Andes gleamed far away. What a time for poetry and contemplation and deep, deep thoughts!

I was swimming in meditation, away beyond my depth, no doubt, when Sister James Cletus broke the silence.

"There's the Pink Elephant," and she pointed to a dark hulk of a house looming at the roadside.

At first I failed to make connections. Then I knew. The Sisters in Cochabamba used to live in a rented house that was a compendium of building troubles. The roof leaked, the plaster fell, the floors warped, the smells were incorrigible and the plumbing absolutely unique. It was a big place, painted a flamboyant pink with a fancy tiled court and fountain. We marvelled no longer as to why it was so cheap. We thought at first that Old Dolorosa, the Indian woman who owned the place, was so rich that she could afford to

20

give us a treasure of a house for a mere song. But after a month in the place, we realized that the songs she collected for her treasure of a house were what made her so rich. She wore sixteen *polleros* (those full skirts Indian women wear) and stuck diamond clips in her heavy grey braids of hair. Each *pollero* costs from $5.00 to $12.00. Old Dolorosa, like most Indian Hettie Greens, wore her bank account on her back or dangling from her ears. She herself would have nothing to do with so-called civilized houses. A mud hut was good enough for her, provided there was space to spread her sleeping mat on the ground over the hole where she buried her extra earrings, gold teeth, unmounted gems and hair-clips. More intimate acquaintance with the Pink Elephant told us that she was a wise woman.

In the Pink Elephant, frogs popped up from the bathtub drain. When water was run in the kitchen sink, a geyser broke forth in the tiled patio. Even a heavy step, let alone hammering or other she-nanigans, would send plaster spraying over the refectory table below. The roof leaked first, and then the floor warped so badly that feeble souls became seasick just watching the convolutions. Yet Old Dolorosa came faithfully for the rent each month. She lifted up six of her skirts to find the pocketbook secreted on the seventh and pinned the money inside with a smile of utter bliss. What was she to bathtubs, sinks, tiled patios and refectories? And what were they to her?

So, Sister James Cletus and I passed the Pink Elephant and struck along the main Avenida. Other shadowy groups were walking silently here, all bound in the same direction—that of the Hospicio.

It was Wednesday in Holy Week. We were to attend a *Via Crucis de Penitencia* during which a relic of the True Cross would be carried in procession through the streets and out to El Calvario, on the city limits, a mountain crowned with an immense statue of Christ. In order to have empty streets for the crowd of penitents—and also perhaps to add to the penitencia—we were to start at 4:30 A.M.

As we trudged silently along, I thought of what a good sport Sister James Cletus had been to agree to this expedition. Especially when you consider what I put her through on Palm Sunday.

We went to a procession. Sister and I had put on our best procession faces and sallied out. But I was cautious enough to bring a camera.

Sure enough! Right on the bus Sister sat beside a magnificent Indian woman with a big white hat. I fought with temptation as long as I could. Then I leaned over to the woman and spoke in my very best Quechua dialect. (This is second only to my Spanish; in both I am proficient in gestures, grimaces, lifts of the eyebrows and vivid facial work. Only the spoken language is still rudimentary.)

"How about posing for a picture with this Sister?" I asked. Being ignorant and not up on the finer points of Quechua, she failed to understand at first. But when I pulled out the camera, she was all smiles.

"*Si, si, como no?* What are we waiting for!" All eagerness, she posed. She jammed her hat down straight, threw out her chest, clenched her jaw, fixed her eyes in a glassy stare and froze her features in a true picture of Rigor Mortis. Nothing I said or did could unbend her. She stayed in the clutch of the The Grim Reaper until the flash flashed and the shutter clicked. Then she became human again.

By this time, the whole bus wanted to be photographed. The driver stopped his snail's pace over the rock-strewn road. There was nothing for it but to take one after the other, each one fixing himself as he would like to look in his coffin.

After other incidents like that, you can see why Sister James Cletus would look askance at any invitation to a Via Crucis de Penitencia with me. But she said at last,

"All right, I'll go. But this procession is *por piedad, no por fotografía.*"

So here we were walking down the dark streets toward the Hospicio Church, with an ever-increasing stream of people merging together on the way.

The church was jammed to the doors. We wormed our way in. One blinked at the bright lights. Usually in Cochabamba, the electricity leaves much to be desired. But at 4:30 A.M., the Church of the Hospicio could enjoy all the power it wanted.

Almost immediately, a tall Friar in Franciscan brown stood up in the pulpit and announced the streets we would follow. The crowd swarmed out into the street now, we with it. Some must have been there all night. Many had paper torches, merely candles stuck into the end of bamboo sticks and ornamented with crepe-paper shades. Blue, pink, red, purple, orange—all colors—they bobbed and danced over the heads of the penitents. Why somebody was not burned to death is a mystery.

We were a big crowd. I estimated it at 2,000; Sister James Cletus at 3,000. To tell the truth, we would be as hard to count as a mass of ants attacking a fallen beast in a jungle.

We all lined up very quickly and started off through the dark streets, surging over curbs and fireplugs like a stream of turgid water. The Franciscan Friar began the rosary in a high though pleasant voice. The crowd murmured the answers in unison.

We were a crowd. Not individuals, not people, not anything plural. We were singular in number—a crowd. Individual differences—oh, the thousand gradings and headings under which we classify people,—dropped off into the dark streets and were trampled to nothing by the multitudinous feet of THE CROWD. We were Penitent Humanity surging through the city to expiate our great common denominator, the fact that every last one of us had sinned.

We filled the street from wall to wall and stretched for half a mile up ahead and way behind. The friar's voice was strong and clear. Every few blocks we knelt on the street, elbowing each other for room for our knees. Then we sang a short, sad hymn—more like a contrite wail of sorrow than a song.

Up again and on through the city. The dark shops and homes were dead. I thought of crude molasses as I had seen it flowing through a trough in the Philippines, the turgid stream going at a snail's pace from the sugar mill to the hold of a steamer.

Or like a swarm of army ants. A car was parked in the street for the night; we engulfed it, as water engulfs a stone, and passed on. We swelled out at intersections and crowded together in narrow lanes. At the main plaza in town, we expanded joyously for the blessed chance of room to breathe in. Down through the city streets, usually so fretful with traffic; past the traffic cop's stand with its painted umbrella which said, "Use Shinola; El mejor por sus zapatos;" past the "Gloria a Stalin!" signs painted on house-fronts and stores; past the all night Estacion de Servicio FORD, whose big red and blue Neon sign was the one bright spot in Cocha-bamba at that hour. Past them all we went, a slow-moving compact mass of Penitent Humanity, praying our hearts out and singing our little wail of contrition.

Under the intermittent street lights, I took stock of the people nearby. I smelled their smells and rejoiced. The sharp smell of shaving soap from a well-to-do business man; the strong odor of garlic from an Indian woman; once or twice I was beside women with manicured nails who wafted perfume my way as they fussed with their black lace mantillas. The aroma of The Great Unwashed hung stagnant on the air as I walked beside poor laborers, still sweaty from a hard day's labor. I walked behind a fur coat for a while and smiled to think that she in her high heels was doing more penitence than the rest of us. An old Indian woman trudged beside me for a while; only when we knelt down for another station did I note that she wore no shoes at all. Most of the Indians here have sandals made from old automobile tires. There were some feet in the procession, however, so hard and horny that you could not have distinguished them from horses' hooves.

Two and a half hours praying in the dark streets! We walked all across town and, just as the blackness lightened, struck out along the broad Avenida which led to El Calvario. It's one of those beautiful Avenidas which modern South Americans are building everywhere. The mud-brick cities cannot handle to-day's traffic problems.

The army of penitents swarmed over the wide expanse of paving. I could hear an automobile trying desperately to honk its way through, but we were deep in prayer and "paid him no mind," as the Negroes say. He honked in despair for quite a while. Then acknowledging defeat, he made a U-turn and went back the way he had come.

The steady pace now quickened. The great processional cross came up from the rear and moved forward. It went before us now. We turned off the road and started the ascent to Calvario. I gasped at the sight. Here was a rubbled barren hill. A crowd like ants was swarming up the side of it. In the center was Someone carrying a great wooden cross. The cross stopped and we prayed the Ninth Station. We were back 2,000 years.

We surged up the hill, our feet curling in agony over the sharp stones, our faces pressing forward to follow that cross. I looked at the faces around me. They were the Jewish merchants; they were Roman soldiers; they were frightened women from Galilee. It was a public execution and One Whom we had hoped was the Messiah was to be crucified. That was He up ahead, carrying the great wooden cross. Why did He let this happen to Himself? Was He truly God, or had He fooled us with magical powers? Just last Sunday we had thought He was king, and now . . . now, we didn't know what to think of Him.

It was quite light by now. We knelt at the foot of the statue of Christ which crowns the summit, just as the sun's first ray touched his garments with red. With His Hands outstretched over the city, He appears to walk with masterful stride over the mountain top. We heard Mass, celebrated there on El Calvario, as the new day dawned. Then we walked home, a little jaunt of four miles.

I know right well that penance is not supposed to leave you with the comfy feeling of having suffered lots for your sins. All the spiritual books tell us that the truly contrite do not survey their worn-out shoes and fallen arches with smug satisfaction. Nevertheless, I highly recommended such a penitential jaunt as this for expiation of big and small peccadillos. Educators talk about Sensory Aids, but the Spanish missioners knew all about them centuries ago. They did not teach the life of Christ in classrooms. They plunged the whole person into living reality. Your eyes see the cross ahead; your nose smells the crowds, your feet ache from the rough street stones; your back and shoulders groan. There is real dust on your clothes and real perspiration on your brow. You are THERE!

Now, when I walk around a dimly lighted church in calm contemplation of the fourteen Stations of the Cross, I have no illusions that Our Lord proceeded majestically from one station to the next, attired in bright red robes banded with comely gold. Rather, I follow Him through the streets of Cochabamba and out to El Calvario. I brush away the flies; I breathe the dust; I wince at the stones. The smells of a crowd are in my nose; the jostling of many bodies touches me. And with the touch I know that I and the whole mass of human beings all over the world are one. We are sinners. We are sorry we are sinners. We follow Our Lord stumbling to Calvary under the cross ahead.

I went with Sister Barbara Frances to the public school where she teaches the Fourth Religion class to the little black-haired muffins who wriggle in the benches.

It's a good thing she took me. I'd never have recognized the place as a school. Rather it is more like a long-abandoned warehouse, well disintegrated. Yet they tell me, it is a school so new it has not yet been completed. They should hurry up and finish it so that it can fall down all in one piece.

As a school, the place is fantastic. Classes are held in mud-floored rooms where the wooden beams and nothing else bar out the bright blue Cochabamba sky. These are the better rooms, for they are light at least. Other classes are in tiny mud-walled rooms, with no windows, dark as the inside of a racketeer's conscience. The children sit in threes at shabby desks and benches, most of them falling to pieces. One desk with a leg gone entirely, rested a corner on another desk nearby.

The blackboards were two small pieces tacked to the front of the room. There are few textbooks, it seems, in Bolivia. The children take down every word the teacher says in notebooks and spend hours copying from one notebook to another.

Sister Barbara Frances stepped into the Fourth Grade and I edged my way to the back of the room. It was so dark back there, I was surprised to find myself between two little girls when my eyes became accustomed to the gloom. They paid half-attention to Sister and half to me. The lesson was on Adam and Eve, a story with which I am slightly familiar. I could follow it fairly well even though Sister did the lesson up in Spanish with fancy bowknots. I may have bogged down at times, but I caught up with her on the high spots; as when she handed Adam the apple, helped God to look for the guilty pair in Paradise and eventually closed and locked the gates of Paradise with as much finality as Michael did long, long ago.

The two little girls beside me hardly took their eyes from me. They were suspicious. I think they thought I was a stage-hand whom Sister had brought along to this particular lesson. At the proper moment, I would release Lucifero El Serpente and he would slither up to the front of the room with an apple in his mouth. Americans are great for visual aids, you know.

It was a wretchedly poor school. Any town would be up in arms at these conditions. In the gloom back there I thought of the beautiful public schools we have. Bolivia, at least, welcomes God to her schools. In the States, Sisters teaching released-time classes, have to take the children away from bright, airy, clean classrooms replete with teaching devices of all sorts and find some garage or neighbor's house where children may learn about God. Here, Bolivia may have little materially to offer Him, but she gives Him place in her curriculum.

The human head is fairly standardized. It is round on the top, bounded on the east and west by two ears put there by Providence for something to moor your glasses to, bounded in the back by a lot of hair and on the front by a strange arrangement of eyes, nose and mouth which we call a face. Given that set-up—the same for all of us—it is remarkable to see what mankind has devised as a covering for the head. In other words, hats are fascinating.

Hat styles in Bolivia are rigid. The La Paz Indian women wear derbies, as we've already noticed. They wear them straight; they wear them cocked; they wear them on the back of their heads. They wear them black, brown, blue, grey, orange and pink. But no Indian woman wears anything else than a derby. It simply isn't done.

The men wear woolen skull caps, equipped with a tassel at the top and two ear flaps. These can be any color and any knitted stitch. Many like to have the date knitted into the ear flaps; or a fancy design in colored yarn. But every man and boy wears a woolen skull cap, quite often with a Western-style felt hat on top.

On the other hand, no Quechua woman would be seen in a derby. Style decrees for her the tall white hat which makes Cochabamba the colorful city it is. It's a gorgeous hat, made of stiff white cloth, tall and clean as the one President Fillmore wore for his inauguration. A veritable stovepipe of respectability. Besides, it's a portable cupboard. Under the hat, you can carry on your head the little items which don't fit anywhere else, like the orange you're bringing home to the children or the burnt out flashbulbs you collected from the crazy American tourist who was actually going to throw them away.

The Sisters tell the story of Old Tomasa who made her First Communion when she was sixty. Tomasa had no idea of time. On the night before the big event, Sister gave Tomasa an alarm clock and set it for a half-hour before Mass. "When you hear this thing make a noise," she said, "you should start for Church right away."

Tomasa was so excited, she didn't wait. She put the clock on her head under her hat and came to Mass very early. And, as Sister was talking to her outside the church door, the alarm clock went off. The poor old woman nearly died of heart failure. In her panic, she threw clock and hat on the ground. The hat survived for it is very light; the clock was ruined for life.

◆ 4 ◆

BEGGAR ON A GOLDEN THRONE

Bolivia?

A volcano in the heart of the continent, still boiling and frothing long after the others have turned into green-clad mountains. The country follows no middle course, ever. Population, economics, politics and even the weather run to the extremes. Rich and poor, new and old, wet and dry, Communist and ultra-conservative, Indian and white, arid altitudes and rain-soaked jungles—the country is rent by opposites.

Bolivia? "A beggar seated on a golden throne," as the Bolivians themselves will tell you.

The energy of the Spanish in colonizing the place is amazing. They climbed two hundred miles inland and a couple of miles straight up into the air to found La Paz, the highest capital in the world. And this was in 1548, some seventy-five years before our Pilgrim Fathers set foot on Plymouth Rock. By that time, too, Sucre and Potosí, three hundred miles from the coast, were already towns of some years' standing.

And it wasn't as if they had the help of the Hudson River, or the St. Lawrence or Mississippi, where you could get food and water along the shore. No, the hundreds of miles were covered by putting one foot in front of the other over hard, sun-baked clay. In most places, it rains only once in ten years or so. Indeed, at Talara, on the coast of Peru, we learned that it had not rained there for twenty-five years.

Even with the help of abundant vegetation, colonists did not get that far into North America until two hundred years later. When western Pennsylvania was still a wilderness and Pittsburgh was only a log cabin called Fort Pitt, great cathedrals thrust their majesty into the sky in La Paz, Sucre and Potosí—indeed all over South America.

Bolivia is no mere bagatelle of land. It's a big chunk of terra firma comprising the heart of a continent. It is 416,000 square miles in area, bigger than all these States put together: Ohio, West Virginia, Kentucky, Tennessee, Indiana, Illinois, Michigan, Wisconsin and Missouri, and just about as far from the coast.

Three distinct areas are marked off. There is the Southwest around La Paz and Cochabamba, where both culture and geography hit the high spots; the Southeast around Santa Cruz, colonized centuries ago but just now being developed scientifically for agriculture; and the great North—humid, swampy frontier land with few inhabitants and little inducement for anybody to come. This whole jungle area has been settled in the last sixty years. Riberalta, population center for the area, was founded in 1894.

La Paz, 12,700 feet in altitude, nestles in a hollow which Dame Nature made in one of the highest ranges of the Andes, like a bird's nest away up on a cliff. This is the cultured Southwest of the country, the political and educational center, practically the only place that tourists ever see. La Paz looks with disdain on the rest of the country, and well it might. It has a corner on nearly all the beauty, wealth and learning there is in Bolivia.

Cochabamba, 150 miles away, is edging in on this exclusive circle. At a mere 8,000 feet, the mountains of this new city offer a respite for the people of La Paz who cannot stand the high altitude. Contrariwise, those in the jungles come to Cochabamba for relief from their oppressive humidity and heat. So Cochabamba is growing up as a midway spot where there is some hope of building up a Middle Class.

Santa Cruz is a case of arrested development. It is the center of a huge area in which New York, Pennsylvania and New Jersey could drop out of sight. As far inland as Detroit is from the Atlantic coast, it was settled in 1591 some thirty years before the Pilgrims landed. Not much has happened to it since. It reminds you of the Dodge City of sixty years ago in a Wild Western.

Santa Cruz is typical of the in-between section. Horsemen and ox carts go down the muddy streets and a hitching rail lines the sidewalk. We stayed with the Pontificianas. Just outside the mud-brick convent chapel is the main market street. During Mass the first day, I could not account for the commotion outside. It was the ox carts coming in; the drivers shouting and hallooing; the people buying the produce directly from the carts; the oxen straining and sloshing in the mud. This, together with the great stone cathedral dominating the adobe skyline, made a picture taken directly from the pages of early Spanish colonial history.

Yet, outside of Santa Cruz, is the best modern road I saw in Bolivia. It runs out for miles and miles, wide enough for 4-lane traffic, smooth and fast. We drove out as far as Montero, Father Burns' parish, where the Point-4 Program plans to put up a model agricultural plant. After jouncing through the mudholes in Santa Cruz's streets, this was a bit of heaven.

This road is part of the brighter outlook for transportation in Bolivia. The road to Cochabamba is almost done—after fifteen years or so! The road to São Paulo (near Rio de Janeiro in Brazil) will connect Santa Cruz with the Atlantic Ocean. A railroad to Cochabamba is under construction—and has been for many a long year. When completed, it will tie Santa Cruz with the Pacific ports of Arica and Antofagasta. To the "Crucenas" (as the folks of Santa Cruz call themselves), it is like the meeting of the East-West railroad when our great-grandfathers tossed their hats into the air and marvelled that you could go from the Atlantic to the Pacific by railroad. And, indeed, it *is* something to toss one's hat about. A great step forward will be taken. But the cautious people wonder how long a road will stay in good condition when ox carts can dig their wooden wheels into the surface.

All this talk about roads—and yet it was at Santa Cruz that poor roads defeated us. We hoped to get out to Cotoca, a national shrine of Our Lady. There are two trucks which go out there. Both were stuck in the mud somewhere between Cotoca and Santa Cruz. We waited all day for one to come into town. When it did finally limp in, the drivers said, not for love or money, not for kings, emperors or madres would they venture out on that road until it dried out a bit. So we didn't go, after all.

And now, let's look at the jungles in northern Bolivia. Here is the Maryknoll Vicariate of The Pando. Separated only by the Beni River, The Beni and The Pando are two of Bolivia's nine Departamentos, comparable to our States. The Pando, until a few years ago, was just a Territory like Oklahoma used to be; in the 1940's it was constituted a full-fledged Departamento. The Beni is older as a Departamento but it just woke up to importance in the last fifty years. Together they comprise 110,000 square miles of soggy jungle. On detailed maps, some of the rivers are marked in dots because the courses are not yet determined, and some few areas are still labelled UNEXPLORED.

The Maryknoll Fathers have spiritual care of the entire Departamento of The Pando, 23,000 square miles, but they, naturally, do not stop on one side of the Beni River. If they are going up the river, they stop and say Mass on both sides. Riberalta happens to be on the Beni side of the river. It is the biggest town in the whole area (7,000 people) and the most centrally located. So that is Bishop Danehy's headquarters, although Cobija is properly the capital of the Pando Department.

This is the frontier, a land still being wrested from primeval nature. It is one of the most sparsely populated spots in the world, 8/10th of a person per square mile. I went up 250 miles of river to Cavinas passing, in all, 67 populated places, that is, one in every four miles. Of 67 places, 21 had less than three families living there; almost all had less than ten families. It was rare indeed to see a town with twenty or thirty families. Only three had more than 300 as a population figure. So you can see why Riberalta with 7,000 seems like New York to Benianas. Riberalta itself was founded in 1894. The first settlers—agents of a European business firm—had come ten years before that.

Nearly all of this vast territory is in the hands of three "Casas" or business firms—Sonnenshein, Seiler and Suarez. They operate *"barracas"* where workers live in small groups in the forest, getting rubber, Brazil nuts, mahogany and other forest products. The small places are the *centros*. The bigger ones are the *barracas* where the stuff is stored, accumulated and sent to Riberalta for shipment.

In these river *barracas*, the big excitement comes with the launches. About eight or ten of these 35-foot boats ply the endless curves of the jungle rivers. A river settlement might be visited by a boat once in two weeks or so. When the river is low, or the channel is changing after the rainy season, a month or more often goes by without any contact with the big world of Riberalta. Sometimes, however, travelling merchants go from clearing to clearing bringing a small boatload of cloth, small toys, household stuff, cheap barrettes and bobby pins. They are like the old-fashioned tinkers.

We saw ample evidence of their visits. Everybody wears things made from the same two or three bolts of cloth. At Blanca Flor, our hostess had curtains of pink and grey stripes and her skirt was the same. Several little girls were running around, also in pink and grey stripes. A cushion on the bed was the same. Another favorite cloth had small red stars in it. I was overjoyed to see a little girl wearing something else, but she stumbled over while playing. I saw that her petticoat was pink and grey stripe and her panties had red stars on them.

For all the fact that they wear ordinary clothes and don't go around with ivory nose-rings, these people are wise in jungle ways. For instance, we went walking the four miles through the jungle to the new Blanca Flor project. A troop of townspeople, men, women and children, came along with us. We must have looked like a safari through Africa, strung single file along the jungle path. There were strange mud ant-hills, like tubes ten to twelve inches long, buried under the tall plants. The people showed us how to break them off and use them for horns when you are lost in the jungle. "Don't walk, for you won't know where you are going," they said. "Just stand still and keep calling through these ant-horns. Somebody will come and get you—probably." Many children will tell you that Papa's official occupation is *caimanero,* or alligator hunter.

It was here, however, that they made us a big dinner, complete with salad, fish, meat and even *suspiros,* a sort of cookie made of baked meringue. It was all baked in a big outdoor oven made of mud bricks and heated with wood. And yet it was food fit for the gods, beautifully served. Furthermore, Caruso sang for us throughout. The host has some old records—good ones. He cranked up the phonograph and produced magnificent music. The whole town jammed into the doorways and windows to watch the proceedings. This was not unusual; most of the time Don Juan's house is the

33

center of attraction. Everyone wanders in and out. Don Juan is well-liked by his workers. He has a fatherly concern for them.

Even religion depends on the administrator. It has happened that a change in administration meant that the padre had to leave because the new man made things so difficult for him.

The workers go out early in the morning to tap the rubber trees. Most of their time is spent walking from tree to tree as they are scattered through the jungle. We went out with one worker and spent fifteen minutes on the march before we reached his first tree. The second tree was ten minutes away. The third tree was quite close but he could not tap that for it was "resting."

When he brings home his collection of latex at night, it must be smoked immediately or it will go bad. So he and his wife and the whole family smoke rubber until late at night. The little girls take turns blowing a bellows on the fire; an older boy will pour the latex over the slowly revolving stick which papa pushes back and forth over the smoke.

The obvious question is, why don't they plant rubber trees closer? The answer is: nobody but nature planted Bolivia's rubber trees. And nature, as you know, doesn't go in for straight lines and solid coverage. She likes to mix her trees together.

Another thing to be reckoned with is the South American leaf blight. This factor, they tell me, ruined the Ford Rubber Plantation in Brazil. When trees are close together the blight travels through a plantation like a swarm of 7-year locusts. So, for the time being, the rubber workers of Bolivia must spend their day walking from tree to tree.

What kind of people live under such a system? Not very healthy ones, to be sure. Tuberculosis is very common, but there is no sanatorium where they may be sent. And if there were, who would care for the families left behind? *Espundia,* a type of tropical ulcer, produces conditions very much like leprosy. Worst of all the ills are malnutrition and intestinal parasites.

Medical people in the States scoff when I tell them that the average hemoglobin in the town of Riberalta is between 30 and 40. In our hospital there, patients come in with 15 and lower. I myself saw a boy there with a hemoglobin of 5,—Carlito, aged three. You're supposed to be dead, I know, when it drops to 15. But these are ignorant little children. They don't know any better. They stay alive for a long time after that, and sometimes we can help them pull it up beyond the danger line.

Intestinal parasites are rampant. To satisfy the cravings of these wretched worms, children chew on anything—sand, salt, soap, paper and even the dirt on the ground. With swollen tummies and heavy eyelids, the poor little tykes haven't the energy even to smile.

Most Beni-ites have gone to school through only the first grade, many for only a few months, and quite a few, not at all. Even the teachers in our schools have usually completed only the sixth grade, some have a year or two of high school and just a few have more. They are the best educated people in town, too. A girl in Guayara-merin applied for a teaching job to Sister Kateri. She had finished fourth grade and saw no reason why she shouldn't be teaching the third.

You can easily imagine how much our Sisters are able to give these people. Education in all the best things in life; a glimpse of something they would never know about if they did not see our Sisters as living examples of what they, too, can be; relief for their ills of mind, body, and soul; these are the stock-in-trade our Sisters bring with them to the Beni. Small wonder that they are beloved!

One of the minor blessings we brought is the Old-Fashioned Clothesline. Sister Marquette said that in the beginning she had a time explaining what a clothesline is to the laundry women at the hospital. "I had to go into such detail about the post and the rope and the clothespins. They used to drape the clothes over bushes or on the ground where, often, they picked up germs from the polluted soil." That was seven years ago. Now there are clotheslines all over Riberalta and even up the river. So civilization marches on!

And that brings us to the Vaca Diez family which did so much to send civilization marching into the Beni. Antonio Vaca Diez, an enterprising young man from Santa Cruz, packed his entire hopes for the future in his knapsack one day in the 1860's and pushed off down the river in a canoe. What he would meet, he had no idea. He opened up wide territories that had never seen a white

35

man before. He explored rivers that were dotted lines on the map. He started a rubber company, but remained chiefly an explorer and patriot. In return, the sub-province adjoining the Beni River bears his name, Vaca Diez.

The grandson of this pioneer is just as remarkable. A doctor, he was educated at the University of Paris in France and passed his internship in North Africa. With such a background, he could have settled down to a fine practice in any city of the world. But the thought of Bolivia's frontier jungle stayed with him. He returned to give his medical skill to the people of Riberalta. Besides the medical work he does for charity, he is in the forefront of every good civic movement in town. Dr. Vaca Diez and the Maryknoll Fathers and Sisters have a bond in common. We are united in doing our life's best for the Beni people, in body, mind and spirit.

Not many foreigners live around The Beni or The Pando. There is nothing much to tempt them. A few agents for the rubber companies, several Protestant missionaries, the Maryknoll Fathers and we Maryknoll Sisters—that completes the roll call, for the most part.

This accounts for some embarrassing situations. For instance, one day Sister Angelica found a can of talcum powder on the shelves of a little store. It was a find, indeed, in a humid climate which makes prickly heat a constant hair shirt. Sister was delighted.

"I'll take three cans of that talcum powder," she said fishing eagerly into her purse to pay for it.

"Sorry, Sister," the shopkeeper returned with a smile. "You're too late. The Maryknoll Fathers have beaten you to it. They bought all but that one can."

There are also a few other Americans interested in helping The Beni masses. These are the Point-4 workers. The one we got to know best is Paul Tobler whose rubber experiment in Riberalta may revolutionize the industry. As I said, up to now, crude rubber has been gathered from the raw forest.

Rubber companies keep their fingers crossed when there is talk of rubber plantations. Always, they face the danger of the leaf blight. Furthermore, the Bolivian rubber tree is forty years old before it starts producing. Nobody wants to wait forty years for the first return on his money.

But this young Paul Tobler (26 years old, I believe) has worked on rubber in Nigeria and in Costa Rica. He is growing trees which will produce in six years. You might say he is "making" them. The root is Bolivian so that it will grow in that soil. To this is grafted a stem from a Costa Rican tree which gives rubber in six years. The foliage is grafted on later. That, too, is Costa Rican, although of another species. This foliage is resistant to blight. So there you have a tree pieced together from three varieties. Paul regrets that only the big companies had foresight enough to help in his experiment. Together, they built the sheds and buildings he needed, and assigned young men to help him and to learn his methods. "I had hoped to benefit the common man," Paul said, "but none of them will believe me when I say that rubber trees will produce in six years. They think I'm crazy."

In return for their help, the three big rubber companies are to get each one-fourth of the trees produced. The other fourth will go back to the experiment and for other uses. This is where Maryknoll comes in. Maryknoll Fathers have ordered ten thousand of the trees to start their plantation at Blanca Flor.

We Sisters are thrilled about Blanca Flor. Here, the Fathers plan to have a boarding school for the children of those tiny hamlets, a model rubber plantation and a neat little Christian village. They hope to teach the children useful trades and a higher standard of living.

As Ben Franklin remarked once, "It is hard for an empty sack to stand upright." We are filling these empty sacks with right food, Christian principles, good housing, and a knowledge of Labor's rights.

There are few Indians in the jungles. Now and then you may see a canoe-full of wild Chacoba Indians with rings in their noses, as they paddle along the rivers. They speak no Spanish and do not even have a monetary system. For the most part the rubber workers are just plain Bolivianos—that is, a mixture of Indian and Spanish which has emerged as a real type.

Yet Bolivia is 75% Indian or mixed, a greater percentage than any other country of the continent. The streets of La Paz and Cochabamba are full of rich Indians and poor ones. They are the hope, as well as the despair of Bolivia, its color and its poverty, its great drawback and its greatest potential. The Indian constitutes Bolivia's past history and is shaping her future.

In North America, we simply eliminated the Indian. Our pioneer settlers wanted his land. The Spaniard, on the other hand, wanted cheap labor. He robbed the Indian, Christianized him and married his daughter. As a result, the Indian is still a factor to be reckoned with in South America. Many an election hinges on the Indian vote; the old antipathy against the White Man is played upon by one politician after another.

The poor Indian knows that somebody has wronged him, but he doesn't know how to right his wrongs. In his helplessness, he falls a prey to every wild-cat political scheme. Somebody is always promising to get his land back for him, but never does. Then the Indian gets mad and refuses to plant any crops. And there are what the newspapers call "incidents."

One day we went for a trip out of Cochabamba—a truckload of us Sisters, about eight of us. We were bound for a small town on the Altiplano, several hours away. We jiggled along over the rough road, trying to fool ourselves that sitting on the floor of a truck is an improvement over the humble donkey who takes his time to get you someplace but lands you there in one piece, not jiggled to pieces.

Suddenly around one of those mountain curves came a troop of Indians, armed to the teeth. They surrounded the truck. Plainly, they intended to commandeer the truck and let us walk home. The animus was against us as whites, for the political situation between the races was tense. However, by the time the leader had strolled up, the Indians were in a more lambent mood. Some of us could speak the dialect; they recognized us as harmless if not, indeed, beneficial to the Indians as a whole. So, with the leader's approval we went. They knew, however, that we would be coming back the same road later in the day.

That afternoon, as our truck came to the same spot, we saw a little crowd of Indians awaiting us. We were scared at first, as they blocked our passage. But the fear passed in a minute. The Indians had brought with them a woman who was, evidently, in labor, unable to deliver the child.

"Will you take her to Cochabamba?" the Indians asked.

We moved things and tried to make a sort of bed for the woman, to soften the jiggles as much as possible. Off we went. The driver did not know whether he should drive fast to get to the hospital quicker, or to spare her all the jolts he could. He decided on speed. We held on to the sides for dear life. The dust rose in a cloud—choking, blinding, gritty between our teeth.

The woman was moaning, but all of a sudden she gave a sharp cry. We called to the driver to stop at once. Almost before the wheels ground to a halt the baby had come. Luckily, one of us was a nurse.

The woman could see no use for going on to Cochabamba. The baby was born already, wasn't it? She asked to be left off to rest by the roadside a while. Then she would walk back home. We could not persuade her otherwise. After fixing her up well, we climbed back into the truck and proceeded at a more leisurely pace to Cochabamba.

Plainly, Bolivia is the most unfortunate country I saw. You feel the bracing air of progress when you step into Chile. In Chile, as the train stops at little towns, big packets of newspapers and magazines are thrown off and newsboys run to peddle the papers through the streets. There are daily newspapers printed in all the major towns, full of local and world news. Everybody seems to be going someplace with a definite aim, and getting there without too much delay.

Small wonder that one Bolivian revolution trips on the heels of the next, and Communism is always a threat. A United Nations report on Bolivia says, "No legally elected Bolivian President has served out his term in the last 25 years. There have been 7 presidents and 8 revolutions in the past ten years (1941–'51). There have been 18 Ministers of Labor in the past 4 years, and 8 Ministers of Finance within 18 months.

"In 125 years of independence, Bolivia has had some 60 presidents and 179 revolutions. They average one every nine months.

"Without stability and peace no responsible person could seriously recommend investment in Bolivia. It can be accepted as certain that under present conditions, risk capital will not be available in any significant measure."

Since this was written things have not improved. Governments totter after a few years of uneasy riding. The Boliviano has fallen. From 160 to an American dollar in May, 1953, it tumbled to 740 to 1. At that point it rose to about 450 but has since declined rapidly.

The hammer and sickle is all over Cochabamba with signs, "Gloria a Stalin!" or "Anti-Communism is the falseface of the Catholics," and even, "Death to the Catholics!" In La Paz, Communists took a statue of Our Lady from the Church at Obrajes (a suburb) and beheaded it. In Cochabamba, they held a big meeting advocating the nationalism of the clergy and the expulsion of "gringos."

A further sign is the silent departure of those "stateless" people who came to Bolivia as a refuge from Communism. Czecho-Slovakians, East Germans, Balkans, etc., they have fled before the face of Russia from all over Europe. One man is packing his things and taking an "extended vacation" in Argentina. He spoke as if he did not intend to return. "I know the signs," he said. "It was this way in those other countries before the Communists took over."

For all their frequency, Bolivia still does not take her revolutions yawning. They are bloody affairs. The public buildings in La Paz are pitted with bullet holes and they point out to you the spot in the plaza where the last President was strung up. Posters all over the city tell about the President, who, in 1946, was killed "sin piedad"; the posters advocate the return of his party to power.

How about the Church? What is going on there? Understand, this is the result of only a few months' observation and of questioning everybody I could get to answer. It is by no means a profound dissertation on the subject.

Before I came down here, I knew that religion in South America was mostly processions, candles and that sort of thing. I had an idea that the processions were lightsome affairs with the praying distracted and a lot of conversation on the sidelines. The processions in the Philippines are like that—the children trooping along with much excitement about lighting candles, and the Queen of the Procession expected to give a party for everybody. The big Christ the King procession in our town was very solemn but still there was a good deal of slipping in and out of line, and the bands-men had a good time of it.

But in South America, processions are real religion. In their mass demonstrations of penance and devotion, thousands of serious men and women show how deep Catholicism is. No one can take part in them and not realize that the people love their Faith. For many years and even now in the greater part of the country, processions are all that are left of the Church's ceremonies. Mass and the sac-raments are simply unobtainable.

In the large cities throughout South America, the churches are closed all week. Only for a few hours on Sunday morning are the doors open. It is sad to see crowds of Catholics passing by a down-town church in La Paz. It might just as well be a pile of bricks or a blank wooden fence. Contrast this with the streams of people going through New York's downtown churches—just dropping in for a short visit. Of course, churches are closed in South America for fear of robberies, a very real danger. In one city where our Maryknoll church is the only one open during the week, the taber-nacle veil has been stolen and the poor boxes wrenched off the wall, even with two priests living right next door. On the other hand, if there were people coming in all day long, there would be few robberies. And they can't come in all day, unless the churches are open. One of those vicious circles! It will take education to break it.

Ignorance is the rock this whole question breaks against. In all the churches of Bolivia there is a sign headed:

THE FOLLOWING ARE NOT TO BE SPONSORS AT BAPTISM:
1. Protestants, Masons and Jews
2. Communists, Piristas and Poristas (all political parties)
3. Divorced people and concubines; those married only civilly
4. Public adulterers
5. The parents of the baptized baby
6. Those who intend to commit homicide or suicide

But there is vigorous new growth in that grand old tree that has weathered so many hurricanes, so many droughts, so many floods—a tree that has been hacked at, torn down and left to rot a thousand times. I mean the Catholic Church.

Before the Maryknoll Fathers came in 1942, Riberalta was a parish in the Trinidad Diocese. There was a Franciscan there, an Austrian; he had thousands and thousands of square miles in his parish. About fifty old ladies came to Mass on Sundays. That was not a bad showing when the priest had to be away so much. But today you will find five Masses on Sundays crowded and even daily Mass is well attended. During May, the Fathers say evening Mass every night and the church is really crowded. I would estimate about 300 people every night. How would that compare with a town of 7,000 in the States? There were not all women, either. There was at least a third men.

So! There is no need to paint a despairing picture of Bolivia. The poor country has been trampled upon by all her neighbors. Every few months, the school children put on an "Acto Civico" to commemorate some "glorious defeat" in the national history. But there are strong green shoots coming up and that brings hope. If the nation could be induced to take the pledge, so to speak, and to swear off revolutions for ten years at least, something could be done to let the shoots come up. Then, perhaps, we will see a broad, peaceful land developing its natural and spiritual resources as God intends it to.

•5•

DOING TIME FOR JELLO

The rain hammered on the corrugated tin roof, dripped off the low eaves, splashed into the rain barrels and flooded the school's tiny play yard. The chickens huddled under an overturned bucket —that is, the hen and her family of eight. The chicks were in the molting stage; bald heads and scrawny necks peeped out from under Mama's feathers, to look around now and then and see if the weather had improved any.

Pepper, the Sisters' dog, a great big hound who can lick my face without half-trying, sat disconsolate with his chin between his paws. Susie the cat was bundled up in herself with her paws tucked in, in the ancient manner of all cats who detest wet weather but refuse to look perturbed by it.

Such is Cobija in a *"sur,"* as they call the south wind.

I looked up from the geography book I was reading and glanced at the barometer. It was marked from Very Dry down to Very Wet. But the needle was cuddled right down to the floor of the case in the blank space beyond the Very Wet area. Then I went back to the geography book. A rainfall map there showed South America in various shades of green and yellow to indicate relative dryness and wetness. Sure enough, there was Cobija well planted in the deepest green—the spot that has a yearly rainfall of 120 inches or more. It's part of the wettest land on God's green earth. As the old missioners tell you, "Cobija? Well, Cobija is a welter of mud that's always a little too thick to drink and too thin to stand on."

We arrived in Cobija by plane. You would think then, that it is quite a town. It is, in a way. It is the capital of the Pando Province, an area of 23,000 square miles, an area almost as big as the State of West Virginia, and three times the size of Massachusetts.

43

With all of 1,900 inhabitants it is the population center for a large slice of northern Bolivia. Three of the 1,900 are Maryknoll Sisters. The governor of the Pando and his office force live there. There is a garrison of soldiers—easily 40 of them. It's a town of 1,900 souls with hardly a dozen healthy bodies among them. If ever a town needed help, Cobija is it.

We came by plane from Cochabamba, 800 miles away. Cochabamba is 8,000 feet above sea level, high in the mountainous foothills of the Andes on the eastern side. We left the airport over a mass of treeless mountains tumbling over each other. In less than ten minutes, the plane skimmed over a vast flat sea of jungle. The rivers twisted and turned through the leafy green. In less than fifty miles, the geography books tell you, the level of land drops 10,000 feet.

The fetid jungle begins—a tremendous soup-plate 1,700 miles across, that drains out to the Amazon in the north. Twenty mighty rivers converge, each one a majestic waterway in itself, to form the Rio Madeira which escapes from Bolivia into Brazil and works its way through to the Amazon. Much of this huge basin is unknown; the river courses are uncharted. On a detailed map of northern Bolivia, you will find white spots bearing the word "Unexplored," a gilt-edged invitation to any adventurous Sister.

Airports in this kind of land are merely huge fields. The plane bumps on the soft earth, jogs up and down comfortably and settles to rest beside a small thatched hut which bears a flamboyant sign, LLOYD AEREO BOLIVIANO. This is the beloved "LAB" dear to all government officials, business men, Americans who are always in a hurry to get places, and even to small folk like missioners. They, also, are always in a hurry to get places but can't afford to pay for much speed.

Backwash from the propellers is fanning the tall grass as the plane door opens and you step out for the fifteen minutes' or so respite. You revel in the primitiveness. Ox carts are drawn up alongside the hut to load and unload the plane. Barefooted children run up and down the crude path; entirely bare youngsters nestle in Mama's arms or take their first wobbly steps holding on tight to Mama's hair which flows in a black cascade down her back.

You exult in it all. You pat the kiddies on the head and try out your Spanish on Mama. You edge close to the oxen and view with respect their long sharp horns. You stroll casually through the grass and wonder why the plane's crew and the other passengers keep rigidly to the path. And they, on their part, wonder how anybody could be so dumb as to walk in grass where the "Hopping Thomases" abound. But you—you have never met Hopping Thomas. You are happy in ignorance. Only when the welts rise where he and his tribe have dug into your skin and made themselves at home there, will you learn that in the jungle, grass is to be looked at, not walked in.

At Magdalena, 375 miles northeast of Cochabamba, my missioner's vocation got a severe jolt. While I reveled in the scenery and such, mischief was going on behind my back. The ox carts were loading on square packs of something-or-other tied up in rawhide.

I paid no heed. My Fairy Godmother was working overtime getting me good shots of oxen, carts, planes, children and trees. I could wish for nothing more.

But the plane had hardly left the ground before I was wishing on all eight cylinders. For what? Well, those square packs from the ox carts contained *charqui*. That's sun-dried meat which smells to high heaven. Some of the seats had been removed from the cabin, and a mountain of *charqui* confronted the passengers up in front. The sticky humid air did not improve matters, either.

I was wishing with might and main that we and *charqui* would part company, or else I was sure that I and my breakfast would. It was a short run to Guayaramerin, 225 miles further northeast. "Dear Fairy Godmother," I pleaded, "see what you can do to unload that *charqui* at Guayaramerin! Don't show me up for a squeamish American who can't stand the rougher facts of life."

Once more we bumped on the soft earth in a field grown high with grass. I made for the door. Horrors! The ground was strewn with hides, half-cured, waiting to be loaded. I came to terms with Fairy Godmother. "All right for you," I told her. "Either you get that *charqui* off, and keep those hides until the next plane comes— or I won't write a line about you, ever, anywhere. If you're publicity wise—and what Maryknoll Fairy Godmother isn't?—you'll do something to preserve my religious dignity. Now think it over."

Two Sisters are stationed at Guayaramerin. We were only passing through this time and would return later for a longer stay. The two came running along the road which led from the cluster of thatched huts, charitably called a town, to the airfield. They had counted on the plane being its usual two hours late; and here it was only an hour and a half behind time! Old LAB was being corrupted by American efficiency.

But the grapevine telegraph was on the dot as usual. The woman next door had shouted to the Sisters over the garden fence, "Hurry up, the plane's in already and there are three madres aboard."

My wobbly legs stiffened in the half-hour of happy reunion there in the small hut alongside LAB's airfield. I was ready to face the *charqui* again and even, if God asked it of us, those half-cured hides. But good old Fairy Godmother! She had seen to it that the *charqui* was unloaded there and the hides never set foot on the plane.

At Cobija, 250 miles due west, there were three white habits fluttering on the field in the backwash of the propellers. They were Sister Jeremie, Sister Alice Regina and Sister John Patrice. Father Garrity, Maryknoller, and a Mr. Copabianco were there too, offering the services of a jeep, painted a fire-engine red. Believe it or not, we eight people fitted into that jeep and off we bounced to town. That is an under-statement. I should say we wallowed into town. My respect for the jeep, always high, pegged up a few notches. That little gas-buggy was all but lost to view under the load of Maryknollers who overflowed the top and dripped down over the wheels. Nonetheless, it gallantly clambered up hills of gooey clay and paddled through puddles which sent out a spray like the old street-cleaning wagon of my young days.

Cobija is like a double exposure—the town is vaguely superimposed upon a meadow. There are wooden houses and, here and there, a bit of cracked cement, especially in the public plaza; but the streets are deep meadows or grass where horses, cows, oxen, pigs, chickens and ducks graze or wallow or scratch as their nature dictates. The town continues to exist for three blocks in one direction and six or seven blocks in the other. Then the jungle takes over and hems it in on all sides. The 1950 census credits Cobija with 1,950 inhabitants, but the Sisters here say that fully half of them must be hiding in the tall grass. There is no hint of paving on the streets; the tall grass is relieved only by puddles where ducks splash happily. At intersections, Simplicio, the handyman, who is the town's entire Bureau of Public Works, has laid planks from corner to corner. They reminded me of the old chalk line they used to have in Police Stations; if a suspected inebriate could walk on that chalk line, he was considered Not Guilty. Cobija's inebriates have a worse fate than two weeks in jail awaiting them, if they fail to keep steady on the planks at intersections. A good sousing in a mud puddle, inhabited day and night by all sorts of wild and tame animals, will sober them up in a hurry.

At night, the cows and oxen huddle up on the only strip of cement paving in town—the sidewalk that runs around our school and convent. Restless in sleep, they poke their horns into the building all night long. It is one of Sister Jeremie's major problems to plug these holes with cement every now and then.

Not that I don't like Cobija's animals. Far from it. They contribute spice to the liturgical life in town. It is nothing to stand up at the Gospel and unintentionally kick a dog spread out at your feet. The cows and horses drift in and out of church with charming simplicity. Ducks and chickens like to roost on the pews.

They tell the story of a hen who was really a liturgy fan. She took her stand on the missal up on the altar, determined to miss nothing of the Mass. When Father went over to read the Collects he swung his arm and brushed her off the book. Annoyed and indignant, she flew high up cackling like any old parishioner who has been pushed out of her favorite pew. But she had her revenge; for she laid an egg up there in the air and it dropped right on the missal. The Collect disappeared under the yolk. Which should be a lesson to any brash curate who disturbs a lady in her prayers.

Brace yourself for some statistics; just to show you the job missioners are up against in working in this territory.

Supposing, some fine morning, you picked up New York, Pennsylvania, Connecticut, Massachusetts and Rhode Island—that whole chunk of the United States—and dropped it into the Pando and Beni Departments of Bolivia. You could do it all right if you trimmed off Long Island and possibly Cape Cod. Then you could compare the population of 30,000,000 Americans who live in those states, with the 90,000 Bolivians living in the Pando and the Beni. Just 350 times as many.

That is what amazes one here. In Asia, there's always a crowd. People jammed together all scratching for a living from tiny plots of land. Too many mouths to feed; many hands grabbing for the same piece of bread. The endless bickering, scrambling, yelling of a Chinese waterfront. But here are great wastes of forest, tons of fertile ground, broad rivers with nobody on them. This whole Pando-Beni area has about eight-tenths of a person per square mile. Even Arizona which is just about the same size has about five people per square mile.

To give you another idea of the size. You can take New York, Pennsylvania, New Jersey and Delaware and drop them into the Pando-Beni district. They'd have plenty of room to wiggle their toes around in, too. Yet there are 300 times as many people in that area of the United States as in the Vicariate of the Pando.

Perhaps you will say that those are States of heavy population. True. To cite other States: The area is as big as Colorado, which has thirteen times the population; or two-thirds as big as California, which has a hundred times the population. It is twice as big as any of these: Florida, Georgia, Illinois, Iowa, Michigan or Mississippi. Also, if we go to Europe, twice the size of Czechoslovakia, or the unit of England and Wales. Korea could be dropped into the Pando-Beni district and would float around with 20,000 square miles to spare. The Philippine Islands are mighty big and there's plenty of water around them. The Philippines, too, are considered not too densely populated. Yet there, 165 people live on every square mile (land and water combined, remember); and here we have only eight-tenths of a single person scattered in every square mile of our jungles.

The Pando-Beni has one-fourth the area of Bolivia with only one-fortieth of her people. Small wonder the books tell you that this is one of the least populated spots on this crowded old world!

Little Cobija is trying to grow up. She takes her position in life seriously; she is a real capital city. Of course, most of the public things like sewerage, garbage disposal, water supply and all, haven't happened yet. They say Washington, D.C., took a while to grow up, too. But we do have a waver of electricity for four hours in the evening from 7 until 11. And the town makes itself responsible for putting boards across the biggest puddles in the streets.

And patriotic! We had a parade to celebrate the first anniversary of the current government. The entire garrison of forty men marched down main street. It was more like a snake dance; they weaved through the tall grass, in and out around the mud holes. But they ended up in good formation in the plaza, and Mass was celebrated attended by the Governor and his office force. At the Consecration, ten battered bugles sounded loud and clear, a salute to the King of Kings.

Afterwards, we had speeches—and more speeches. Folks leaned against the lamp posts and stood up on benches and clambered over the fountain, now defunct, and listened. It was like the old-time Fourth of July at home when oratory and good beer replenished the patriotic fires in our hearts. A good thing for the nation too!

The River Acre makes a sharp bend at Cobija so that it runs around most of the town. This is the national boundary between Bolivia and Brazil. You can take a rowboat and get to Brazil in about a minute and a half. Or, if you like to walk, there is "The International Bridge." This is merely a tall jungle tree which has fallen over the river so that one end rests in Brazil while the roots are still in Bolivia. The trunk has been flattened and the roots and branches lopped off, so that it is now a good firm bridge between the two countries.

The town of Brazilea in Brazil across the river, speaks Portuguese and adheres to its Brazilian customs. One of which is to build a concrete landing place for river boats, a nice little park and quite a few substantial houses. My word, they even have street lights!

We go back and forth to Brazil frequently, running over there for shopping or to get some special work done. The Brazilians come over to our Church for Mass on Sunday because there is no priest in Brazilea. An itinerant priest comes now and then, but even on Christmas Day they had no Mass of their own.

Oddly enough, on Sunday, you can see quite a style show pass down the church aisle—chiefly these Brazilians. Some stylish folks

49

from Rio de Janeiro seem to have originated in Brazilea, and they visit the old home town on occasions and give us a treat with their fine clothes at Sunday Mass.

Major tragedies often happen to our clothes so that we do not make such a fashionable appearance in Cobija. Pilar, who does the Sisters' laundry, came one morning bringing a habit but without the cape.

"Where is the cape, Pilar?" said inexorable Sister Alice Regina who is general housekeeper.

"The cape?" Pilar thought a moment. "Oh yes, the cape! Well, my Hugo ate it."

"Your Hugo ate it? If you're that badly off, Pilar, I will give you food for Hugo. I did not know that you were in such straits that the children . . ."

"No, Madre," Pilar explained patiently. "Not the children. Hugo is our goat."

Another time, she left a white habit soaking all night in a rusted tin tub. Sister John Patrice calls it her "Tigre habit." She is spotted like the jaguars round about—*tigre* in Spanish.

A circus was advertised in Brazilea and we took the children over to see it. While Sister Jeremie was "talking price" to the manageress the rest of us went to see the animals—a lion, two tigers and three jaguars. The tigers failed to stir much interest in the children; they were much like the jaguars which our children see too often for comfort. Interest perked up, however, when the keeper revealed that the bigger one had killed two men.

But Nero, the lion, thrilled and chilled them to bits. The keeper, a big black Negro the color of ebony, delighted us all by prodding Nero until he paced his cage roaring at the top of his lungs, shaking the bars and misbehaving in general. The manageress came along then and added further to Nero's glory when she revealed, casually, that he had eaten her first husband. She has traveled with her Big Tent for 27 years. Very agreeable, she gave the children front seats at half-price and let us in "for free."

A gong sounded and we trooped into the performance tent along with practically everybody we knew. Most of Cobija had come to Brazil for it. There was a trapeze performer, a strong man, acrobats, a trained dog, a clown and a comic dwarf. They all spoke

Portuguese—what speaking they did—and we applauded in Spanish.

A cloudburst came down outside—and inside as well. The tent was not much hindrance to it. We all were drenched. Then the sun came out. The entire circus personnel set to putting the tent to rights. The acrobats wielded brooms to sweep out the worst puddles; the strongman lifted the heavy canvas to let the water roll off; the dwarf and animal keeper sprinkled sand on the ring to dry it.

The show went on with undampened enthusiasm. From what I could gather of the Portuguese it was a Mack Sennett comedy.

At 7 P.M. we were back in Bolivia. Five hours after leaving it, we were climbing up the slithery mud bank of Cobija. It was a grand day for me. Not since the days when Papa put us all in the street car going home with our faces sticky from popcorn balls and our hands clutching balloon strings, had I been so surfeited with joy. Besides the performance, each child had been a circus in himself.

You never quite know what is in store for you on a Sunday morning. One day, set like two little butterballs of elegance in the drab spinach of our faded barefoot congregation, were two little girls with blonde curls and white dresses with pink ribbon. Believe it or not, they were Turkish. Four and two years old, they picked their dainty way to church, lifting their white shoes around the manure piles and mud, and edging carefully around the puddles where ducks were splashing happily.

Yes, the refugees from Europe and the East have penetrated even to Cobija. Jews forced from Germany and Austria in Hitler's day, Japanese, and Moslems have found a shelter here. In Cochabamba, there is even a larger proportion. The best photographer there is a young Jugoslavian who fled to Czechoslovakia when Tito came to power; and from thence to England. Refused a permanent refuge there and denied even the chance to land in the United States, he drifted to Bolivia. In a jewelry store in Cochabamba, the star of David stands solidly on the display case as if to re-affirm in this Catholic country, the faith of the Austrian Jew who had to leave his fatherland.

One afternoon in Cobija we went to see one of these wanderers. He is a Mohammedan, born in French Algiers. For this reason, he

51

is called Monsour Ali, possibly a corruption of Monsieur. We set out in broiling sun and walked for ten minutes, which brings you to the end of town. There we took a narrow, single-file path into the deep woods. Five minutes or so of this and we came to a small clearing, just big enough for an outhouse and a two-room shack. Four children were playing on the ground; a new-born calf was tied to one of the broken steps. The children looked up from their play and ran to greet us for they know Sister Jeremie.

"How is grandfather?"

Without a word, they led us to the second of the two rooms. An old man sat on the broken-down bed, his legs doubled up under him in a useless way. He had broken his hip falling from a mule some ten or fifteen years ago and could not walk except to swing himself, monkey-like, from bed to table to doorpost and, on rare occasions, outside in the sunshine from one support to another.

Ordinarily, the room would have been dark, but the entire side wall of mud brick had broken loose. The thick, heavy chunk of adobe was held upright by a table braced against it. Light and air —also wind, rain and cold—came in the wide crack at the side and top where it had once joined the thatched roof, now mangy and threadbare. Even so, with all this unintended light and air, it took several minutes for my eyes to adjust sufficiently to distinguish what was on the old man's head. It stuck up and it was dark in color. Then I saw that it was the weary remnants of a Mohammedan fez. I observed it with respect, for that scrap of felt must have sat upon that same head in Morocco, Paris, London, Hong Kong, Shanghai, Manila and Java. The old man had traveled far and wide before the bad temper of a mule tied him down to slow disintegration in Cobija's jungle. Now he lies crippled, deaf, half-blind and covered with sores waiting for the night when a jaguar will leap through that jagged hole in his wall.

We brought several things for him, but best of all to him was a letter from Sister Patrick Joseph in Riberalta. She used to be here and had not forgotten Monsour at Easter time. His delight to get a real letter, addressed entirely to him, was pathetic.

We also went over to visit two leper women who live not far off. These two are much more independent than poor Monsour. They are well able to get around, although Aurora's feet are so misshapen that she prefers to sit. The house is ramshackle, of course, but few houses in Cobija are not. Flowers planted in tin cans line the path; the bare ground is swept clean and neat; a new barbed-wire fence keeps out the animals who would otherwise eat the flowers and dirty up the yard.

Both these women are now arrested cases, most likely. One of our Sister-doctors, Sister Vivian, has been sending diazone and other Sulfa drugs from Riberalta. So the sores have healed and Aurora and Isaure are more bearable to themselves and to others.

Ten minutes after we left the leper women, we were lumbering through a heavy downpour. Just punishment for all the hard thoughts we had about the hot sun on the way over! This was a thousand times worse, for the road back to town was one slippery puddle, about three miles long.

Besides being capital of the Pando Province, Cobija is head-quarters for the Japutamus—pronounced very much like "Hopping Thomases,"—as wily a crew of bugs as ever plagued mankind, a relative of our chiggar. As soon as I stepped from the plane, word went around among them that the feast had arrived. Come ye to the banquet! It was like postulants the first time they get apple pie in the convent. The tribe just moves in and takes over.

I can't say that I blame them. It must have been a long time since the Hopping Thomases had seen such a bill-of-fare as I was. What a picnic! Mama, Papa, all the children and Grandma Japutamus attached themselves to my arms and legs and burrowed deep into the skin. They came to stay, too. After a week, I learned what every missioner learns down in this Insect Paradise—that one must live in a perpetual aroma of Skat. The Army insect repellant is the only hope. I hated to be mean to Mama, Papa, Grandma and all the baby Japutamuses, but after all, charity begins at home.

At Cobija, we Maryknoll Sisters have a school. One hundred and twenty-six little ragamuffins come every day, wading through the tall grass and puddles, to attend the only private school in the entire Pando Department, 23,000 square miles. The tuition is about 12½ cents a month. There used to be two public schools here in Cobija, one for boys and one for girls. But one rainy day the boys' school collapsed; the mud brick walls could stand it no longer. So now the boys and girls share the same building. One month, the boys come in the morning and the girls in the afternoon. Then, next month, the order is reversed and the girls have to get up early in the morning while the boys study late in the afternoon. Altogether, maybe ninety children go to the public school.

This leaves about sixty children in town who don't go to any school. This is always the missioner's ache—the ones he cannot reach. There are classes for public school children, but what of the little tykes who have nobody to see that they go to school for a few years at least and learn about God? One sees them on the streets. They are hewers of wood and carriers of water before they are old enough to know the words Social Injustice. But they feel its bitter tooth every day of their lives.

The task of helping children here in this jungle clearing overwhelms with frustration the good-hearted people who try it. I suppose you need a mission vocation to persevere at the job. A young Spanish doctor with splendid ideals came to Cobija a year ago. He was fired with the thought of bringing the Faith as well as bodily health to these children. He set up a clinic in connection with our school. Here, he exulted, was a fitting field for a medical apostolate. But after three months . . .

"It's useless," he protested. "I get a child all cleaned out of worms and, within a month, he's back again infested worse than before. Pedro is dying for lack of vitamins, and his mother won't feed him anything but rice and *charqui*. If everybody in this town who should be flat on his back in a TB Sanatorium were there, only the Sisters and me and a few others would be out of bed. I can't take it any longer."

So, he too went away.

All of which goes to show you that you need pity and compassion to be a missioner, but you also need patience and a sense of humor. If you took life too seriously, you couldn't last at a mission station in the jungle. Up and down the rivers, for instance, they are telling the yarn about Sister Jeremie's Jello.

Shopping is a bit difficult in Cobija, as you can well imagine. Sister Jeremie, knowing that Sister Victoria Francis and I were coming, wished to pamper us with all the comforts of home. So she ordered from a store in La Paz, a dozen packets of Jello in four flavors—chocolate, strawberry, lemon and plain. When the weekly plane landed at Cobija, four huge cartons labeled JELLO were deposited on the field. The store had sent a dozen cartons of a dozen packages each of each flavor. In other words, 144 packages of chocolate, 144 of strawberry, 144 of lemon and 144 plain. 576 packages of Jello for a household of three Sisters! Furthermore, the bill came to $125—all the money they were likely to have for a long time to come.

In the States, all you would have to do would be to sail down to the supermarket with a certain gleam in the eye and get things rectified. But it's a little difficult to hand a piece of one's mind to a grocer 800 miles away. Besides, the air freight back and forth is quite an item in the expense account.

Sister Jeremie is from New Hampshire. After the first stunning blow, her shrewd Yankee acumen began to click.

She let it be known here and there in the town. Indeed, it would have been hard to keep it a secret; everybody saw the cartons on the airfield. She met the governor's wife on the street.

"But I don't mind too much," she said. "We all love Jello. And it's so nutritious too. Just the thing you need for your children, Mrs. Lopez."

And Mrs. Lopez decided to buy a few packages.

Up and down the river, word got around that Sister Jeremie had Jello. The little stores stocked it. Traveling merchants who ply up and down the rivers introduced it to the far reaches of the Beni. And, to be sure, the other Maryknollers—priests and Sisters alike —were good customers.

This explains why it was that every convent we visited in the area served us whipped Jello, or Jello salad, or Jello-in-mold, or Turkish paste or, well diluted, Jello cold drinks. After seven weeks of this, we were back in La Paz and I felt that I had "done time" for Jello.

♦ 6 ♦

EMPIRE—CARVED BY MACHETE

The House of Suarez is a great bird; some call it an eagle, some call it a vulture. It's a moth-eaten old bird now; many of its proudest feathers are gone. Still it circles wide over a jungle kingdom of what the fanciful ones call The Green Hell of Bolivia. You can go up the river 500 miles or down the river 500 miles and ask the question, "Who owns this land?" The answer will be the same, "The House of Suarez."

The House of Suarez flies its own planes, runs its own little railroad, operates its own company stores. The Suarez river boats carry the Suarez rubber and alcohol; Suarez radio communications tie together the far-flung outposts of a jungle empire.

As the crow flies, Cobija is 400 miles from Cachuela Esperanza, headquarters of the Suarez empire. It is many more than that as the rivers meander along. There, our Sisters live on Nicolas Suarez Street in the solidest building in town, constructed by the House of Suarez as a warehouse and residence for its agents passing through Cobija on business up and down the river.

And here I was, typing in an old homestead of the great Nicolas Suarez himself—on a porch off his bedroom. Possibly, it was the room he died in. He was then, in 1940, an old man of 89 imperious years. Already his great rubber empire was splitting at the seams. The crest of the rubber boom had passed; his children were married to Americans and Europeans and living in villas in Switzerland and France.

His second wife, Judita, 28 years younger than he, lived here in this house after him. But she, too, died in 1951. Now, nobody knows what will happen to the house that Nicolas built for the family citadel in the lush days when rubber was a roaring king of industry.

56

The porch off the bedroom looks out on a garden where the parasites clamber thick over the grapefruit trees and the tennis court is moldy and sodden. Lichens grow slimy on the tiled terrace overlooking the rose garden. The pretty flower boxes are rotting apart. The complicated plumbing (English-made) allows for showers, sprays, tubs, hot and cold water and a hair-washing device. But thank goodness, buckets of water are placed strategically near the rusted faucets and you can dip out the water with *tutumo* gourds (like big coconut shells). As a final insult to fancy plumbing, a bathtub lies upside down under a mango tree in the yard. Propped up at one end, it makes a good shelter for chickens in the rain.

Sister Maura Kieran and I slept in the Nicolas Suarez bedroom, disregarding the large moldy spot on the wall where heavy jungle rains have seeped through the ornate wall paper. We ignored the ghosts of the past as they frolicked around the billiard room across the hall, and danced lightly among the swathed furniture in the old parlor downstairs. We decided that if they got too obstreperous, we could retreat to the porch. We slung up our hammocks there, just in case . . .

We had arrived that morning on the "Triunfo," a brave little river boat which is the "United States" to the wide-eyed little boys who watch on the bank for the great Triunfo to dock. Sister Maura Kieran and I had got it the night before by the skin of our teeth.

As we raced down to the "port" in Riberalta, as they call the simple mud bank where the boats tie up, the late afternoon sun was painting the Beni River a million hues. Pushed from behind and pulled from before, we walked up the single board which provided a gangplank from ship to shore. As Sister and I lifted the last foot from the board, it was unceremoniously hauled on deck. The whistle tooted, the rope was untied, and off we went.

The Triunfo itself was tied between two other boats. To my surprise, as we backed out into the river, the other boats came right along. They were lashed tight to the Triunfo which supplies the power for all three. We made an unbreakable unit of three boats which would sink or swim together.

The Triunfo is not much on looks. It's really a bit of decking built around a smokestack. About thirty feet long and eight wide, it could easily slip down one of our convent corridors and not even scratch the grandfather clock against the wall. The little Triunfo nonetheless can work up enough steam for all three boats, but it shakes all over from the effort.

We and the other seven or eight super-de-luxe passengers stood on the top deck facing the most beautiful sunset God ever painted. The low-lying jungle river bank was a band of black dividing the expanse of saffron sky from the equal expanse of the reflecting river. Every bright-rimmed cloud, every patch of purple had its counterpart in the water. After twenty years in religion, I have learned at long last that all earthly beauties fade. This sunset too faded, dimmed and darkened. But in my memory it flames eternally. This and other scenes of tremendous beauty God has given me are neatly filed away in my grateful memory like so many color slides.

We passengers stood around, talking in the cool blackness of the river air. We were a mixed lot but very chummy. Each of us had a different tale to tell. One was a woman in slacks with a cigarette hanging from her lip. She looked like someone from a trailer park in Florida. Why should she be on a tiny river boat in this primitive country? Her husband was a mechanic, hired by the House of Suarez for its machine shop in Cachuela.

Another told her sad tale; she had been born and brought up in Riberalta and now, married, was condemned to live in Cachuela far away from the bright lights, the night life, the gayeties of glittering Riberalta. Sad, is it not, *madrecita?* Another was a jovial woman, most generous. We had formed a little group at the bow of the boat. This woman had a fried duck in her baggage and, every now and then in the dark, you would feel her thrusting a greasy leg or a bit of breast meat into your hand.

It was lovely, there in the dark. The pilot stood silent at the wheel very close to us. From the lower deck a strong searchlight played on the water directly in front, picking up a floating log here and there, a bit of tree with branches and leaves intact, or a smooth place in the river which probably hid a submerged rock. I was so anxious to see an alligator, but none came to show himself off.

Then, the searchlight moved closer to the shore. It played on the bushes and trees, searching, searching. The boat edged closer, too, and soon the light stayed steady on one tree. A board was stuck in the cleft trunk. This is the sign that there was wood for sale in the jungle clearing near the river. We stopped here and two men ran ashore with a rope and tied us to that tree.

The searchlight beamed a path through the trees. Men leaped from the boats and ran up the path of light, barelegged and eager, splashing through the swampy places and up a slight rise where they disappeared into the dark jungle. Soon they began to reappear, each one with a load of wood on his shoulder, cautiously stepping down the slippery bank and wading through the swamps. The searchlight picked them up with a ghostly intensity. Each came aboard, dropped his load where others were stacking it and ran lightly back into the blackness beyond the trees for more.

In this way, we loaded on 22 cubic meters of wood—about 250 cubic feet. It took an hour or more. Then we put off again and once more the wide river engulfed us in darkness.

We set about more practical business. We de-luxe passengers, we elite travellers, we cream of the Beni populace—began to scramble for a place to sleep. Sister and I were vastly helped by Father Ralph Sylva (whom I had last seen when he was a high-school lad in Hawaii) and a Japanese boy named Zoilo Chuta, believe it or not. Moreover, Zoilo's sister is named Zoila and she is a Good Shepherd novice in Lima.

Zoilo was avid to help us. He found our duffle bag in the welter of cargo and fished out the blankets, pillows and two hammocks. Then he and Father Sylva elbowed a way up front and strung them from side to side of our little Triunfo. In no time at all, that upper deck was a corridor of hammocks. Six of them were stretched from side to side so that there was no place to walk. The men workers had to duck under the strings to move around at all. Father himself was wise to these river boats. He carried a canvas cot which folded up into a bundle of sticks. For the first part of the night I felt sorry for him on a straight cot; but in just a few hours, I envied him the chance to straighten his spine.

And so to bed. Nobody undressed of course; we stayed as we were. We wrapped ourselves up in blankets and, like two tight little cocoons, swung in our hammocks while the wet breeze from the river rocked us gently to and fro. What a life! No windows to open; no radiator to turn off; no curtains to draw; nothing to wash in; and best of all, no 5:15 A.M. bell!

I woke several times in the night, chiefly because my spine was twisted like a pretzel and the cold wet wind was soaking through the blanket. I could see the pilot still steering steadily while the searchlight played on the black water ahead. Sister Maura Kieran was dead to the world. As a missioner, she was used to hammock-sleeping. Beyond her, a woman made a big bulge in her hammock; a small boy, cuddled in a blanket at her feet, made a small bulge. Then our friend Zoilo and, beyond him, others sprawled half-in and half-out of their hammocks. Father was a dark lump on his cot and the whole floor was covered with similar huddles where the boatmen took their short rest. Behind us, the smoke stack was spewing out a shower of sparks. Then, the soft lap of the water lulled me back to sleep again.

We were up with the dawn. So was everybody else. We took down hammocks, stuffed them into duffle bags, folded blankets and put them away until the boat was shipshape. Good work, and none too soon, for in no time at all we were sliding up to the shore at Cachuela. Two men carried the heavy anchor ashore and hooked it around a tree trunk.

Cachuela isn't much. Don't look for it on any map. It's on the Beni River east of Riberalta and not too far from where the Mamore empties into the Beni. Cachuela means "rapids," and the full name is Cachuela Esperanza. The story of its name is part of the great saga of Nicolas Suarez.

He was a young fellow of twenty-one when he set out from Trinidad to the Beni country. Trinidad, even now, is a town of thatched huts with grass-grown streets which have never been paved. Suarez left it some eighty years ago—before the Bolivian rubber boom, before the planes put it in touch with La Paz and Cochabamba, before it really had any reason for existence. It must have been very primitive. Still, it was too civilized for young Suarez. He had been an itinerant merchant traveling in and out of Trinidad. He set out for the big white spots on the Bolivian map— the spots that were marked "Unknown."

Up in the States, Charles Goodyear had vulcanized rubber thirty years before. Down in the jungles of Bolivia, Nicolas Suarez gazed up at the great rubber giants of the forest and knew that he was seeing black gold. The problem was: How to get it from the jungle to those who would pay him yellow gold for it?

The rivers were the only way. Trinidad, center for everything in northern Bolivia, was on the Mamore. Running from south to north, the Mamore eventually meets the Beni which flows from southwest to northeast. Then it goes on to join the Madeira and eventually the Amazon. The road seemed clear. Float down the Beni to the Mamore, down the Mamore to the Madeira, down the Madeira to the Amazon. Simple! Suarez saw a way to get his rubber up to Manaos in Brazil, center of the South American jungle kingdom. Ocean-going vessels come to Manaos, even though it is a thousand miles up the Amazon.

Young Nicolas played no favorites when he set up his first rubber *barraca*—or headquarters for a rubber area. He named it *Todos Santos* (All Saints). He needed all their help, too, for the rivers proved to be very unsatisfactory roads.

At that time, nobody knew just exactly where the Beni River did flow. Nicolas was afraid to explore it and tried other means for some years. In 1882, however, just ten years after he began operations, he loaded several rafts with his black gold and started down stream. He was confident that, somehow, somewhere, the Beni would flow into the Amazon.

With him, in charge of one of the rafts, was his brother, Gregorio. The party was often separated for several days, because it was so frequently necessary to unload everything and carry both raft and cargo around the many rapids in the river. On one of these occasions, half the party was set upon by the wild Chama Indians. The chief fired a poisoned arrow into poor Gregorio. His companions fled in terror and joined Nicolas who had gone ahead a little way.

Nicolas returned to the scene to avenge his brother and recover his rubber. He found a wild orgy in process. The Indians were celebrating over the barbecued body of Gregorio. It was an easy matter to wipe them out entirely. But Nicolas saved for himself the satisfaction of personally strangling the chief who had fired the poisoned arrow.

When, at last, the party came to the site of the present town of Cachuela Esperanza, they were in despair. Ragged, naked and

61

hungry, they had brought their rafts of rubber through incredible hardships. Now, within 25 miles of where the Beni joins the Mamore, they met their biggest obstacle. The Beni waters, a half-mile wide, were boiling, churning, twisting, over rocks which would make mincemeat of anything that floats.

"This is the *Cachuela Sin Esperanza* (Rapids Without Hope)," his men told Nicolas.

They made one last effort. They unloaded everything and took the boats apart, carrying them piece by piece around the rapids. As they reassembled themselves on the other side, Nicolas named the spot.

"This is not The Hopeless Rapids," he said, "but the Rapids of Hope." And he decided to set up his headquarters at Cachuela Esperanza.

And *that* is why he built his railroad, if you can call it such. The rails are perhaps two feet apart; the engine stands maybe seven feet high. The engineer overflows his cab. The little thing runs only one kilometer (⅝ of a mile) and exists for the sole purpose of transporting cargo from one side of the rapids to the other. It is, nonetheless, the only bit of railroad in all of northern Bolivia, an area as big as Pennsylvania and New York combined.

With Nicolas Suarez, the railroad was a sentimental hobby. He loved the rapids and would suffer no one to mar their wild, imperious beauty. They say that an American engineer once said to old Nicolas, "If you gave me $10,000, I could blast those rocks in the river and make it passable. It will save you that much in a year, to have your boats go unhindered straight up to Manaos instead of being obliged to unload here and have the cargo transported by that silly little railroad."

Old tycoon Nicolas who spent millions like nothing at all, pulled his great handlebar mustaches and glared at the American. "I'll give you $10,000 to leave those rocks right where they are!" he thundered.

Cachuela is the end of the line, so to speak. No boat that plies the Beni can go beyond the famous rapids. They turn around here and go back to Riberalta, Cavinas, and away up to Rurrenabaque, some 800 miles up a river that backtracks on itself in one hairpin curve after another.

We picked up our duffle bags and went ashore with the small crowd. It was a very simple process; we simply walked down the single plank which connected the boat and the shore.

No sooner had we one foot on the shore when we were surrounded by a horde of children. They took our hands and danced around in front and back as if a delegation of fairy-godmothers had landed. But this is normal in Cachuela; you live in the middle of millions of children whose chief joy in life seems to be to gain possession of your little finger and to hold on tight to it.

The Cachuela children know the Maryknoll Sisters. Sisters Magdalen Mary and Anne Virginia once spent a month in Cachuela holding Summer School. Summer School? You might think it was a lollipop. The children here look forward to Summer School as we used to watch for notices that the circus was coming to town.

The children danced us up Main Street. First, we passed a good machine shop with burring lathes and shiny noisy machines. This was another Suarez installation. You marvel to think that all those things had to be flown over the Andes and then freighted laboriously down the river in such boats as the Triunfo. The technicians to put them together as well.

We passed the movie house; Wednesday and Sunday nights are movie nights in Cachuela. The place seats two hundred. On movie nights, the electric power goes off everyplace except for the theater; it's all needed there. Everybody's in attendance anyway. And even if you haven't paid your ten Bolivianos for admission, you can follow the action fairly well. Screams of the audience tell you that the hero is thundering to the aid of his beloved; yells, when it looks like the villain is winning the fist fight.

We passed the company barracks lined up on Main Street where the company men passing up and down the river can stay. Later, we were lodged in one of these rooms for a night—a bare but adequate room with pitcher-and-basin equipment. Then came the main company offices with a sign outside the door: "Pay Day tomorrow: Workers at 9 A.M.: Employees at 2 P.M." The difference is that employees wear white collars.

We were right opposite the rapids now—we and our horde of children. We stopped to admire the churning muddy waters rolling, twisting, tossing brown foam into the air. Right on the river bank was a small fenced-in area thick with flowering bushes and bright leaves. A bronze plaque on the gate said in tombstone style, "Esperanza, beloved wife of Nicolas Suarez." She is buried there beside the rapids whose roar hovers over the town. His first wife, —who loved him long before he became rich.

Then up we climbed on solid rock, a hill maybe thirty feet high. A tiny white church built like a miniature New England Congregational church—such a surprise in South America—sat like a cap on the top of it. Padre Jaime (Father James McCloskey) was just beginning Mass. We and our army of children swarmed in to fill the tiny place which at most can seat maybe forty people.

Cachuela is more like an army post than a town. It has no mayor; the *gerente*, or company manager, runs things. The hospital is fairly good—run by the company for its workers, and named "The Francisco Suarez Hospital" in honor of Nicolas' son. The school is nothing compared to what we Americans are used to, but the building is large and airy and the children well-disciplined. The name? The Judita Suarez School.

Of course, the social leader in town is the *gerente's* wife. It was she who accorded us the honor of staying in the old Suarez home. It's close to the rectory; indeed, the rectory used to be the Suarez children's playhouse, built in a corner of the big garden.

A parrot was perched on the old gate, sulkily blinking his eye. Father McCloskey called him Doctor and took him in his hand, smoothing down the indignant feathers, and the parrot did not dispute our entrance any more. The stones on the path were slippery with mold and the grass grew high on either side; the caretaker and his family who live in one of the small cabins were none too happy to open up the place, but we tried to win them over.

Sister Maura Kieran and I took a tour of the house. A perfect setting for a mystery yarn. Dampness is seeping through the walls, discoloring the rich wall paper and making the furniture clammy to the touch. The handsome stairway was once softly carpeted; screw-eyes are still on the treads; but it echoes now as the caretaker's wife slip-slops downstairs in her native slippers. I was amazed at the library. Not many books, but all in English, French, German or Italian. There was only one Spanish book, and that was "20 Easy Lessons in Spanish." Many were paper-backed mystery stories in English, but there was a complete set of twenty volumes in German, "Plants of the Tropics and How to Recognize Them."

Upstairs in our room there were three beds, two for adults and a small crib-bed in the corner. The furniture was inlaid, very well made. Even after fifteen years' disuse, the drawers did not stick nor was the metal work rusted. But there were marks where the caretaker had set buckets of water on the dainty bedside table. And we left footprints on the dusty floor, all of patterned hard wood.

I figure that the house must have been built around 1910–1915; it's that style. That was the crest of the rubber boom down here which swelled to huge proportions during World War I. The house is wired with lights everywhere, over dresser, beds, dining table and in the walls, but the wire is all exposed to view as if they were proud of it.

Ours was the only bedroom. But there were enough accommodations for guests. Hooks for hammocks were everywhere. They could be strung up in the billiard room, the library and out on the tiled terrace. On the porch six hammocks could be put up easily. I wonder if the Suarez children invited their school chums from England to spend the Christmas holidays here in Bolivia's Green Hell? Perhaps Judita, proud and happy in her first days as Rubber Queen of the Beni, threw open the house to visiting diplomats who were only too anxious to get the Suarez rubber for their countries' war machines. Did Nicolas bring here the men he trusted to run his business in the outposts of his jungle kingdom?

Nicolas was good to the white-collar men and women who served him. They risked life and limb for him. A woman in Cachuela told me the story of her parents.

"My father and mother came to the Beni in the early 1890's as Suarez agents. For seven years my mother ate practically nothing but *charqui,* and not good *charqui* at that. Food was such a problem down here in those days! All food was floated down from Trinidad on the Mamore. Boats with twenty rowers brought it down river, having to carry cargo and boat around many *cachuelas.* Often it took months to travel the 700 miles of river. By the time it arrived, the *charqui* was in no condition to be eaten.

"My mother was a real business woman. She used to go with the cargoes to Brazil where the British paid for our rubber in gold.

65

My mother was to carry the little box which held the gold and bring it back personally to Nicolas Suarez.

"In 1897, her health broke. She went to Europe and lived in the Suarez villas in Switzerland and in England."

In 1927, Nicolas Suarez made his will. He gave each of his six children an estate of 8,000,000 English pounds and considered himself free of any further obligations. His property he left to Judita, his wife.

"What sort of a person was she?" I asked.

"She just couldn't keep still. Judita worked day and night. She had her own *chaco* or farm-clearing at Santo Domingo, midway between Cachuela and Guayaramerin. Here, she was happiest, for she could make sugar and molasses in her own crude vats and raise flowers for her bees. Judita? She never stopped. Nor would she ever let anybody else stop!"

I think Judita was never quite at home in the Suarez mansion in Cachuela. We stopped later at Santo Domingo where she had kept her own *chaco*. It is a mere clearing in a 25-mile road of deep, deep jungle. Her house is a small three-room affair. The beloved sugar vat stands outside. For rest, she was content to sit on raw-hide swings, made from the skin of a cow's head, without any garnishing or decoration. Thongs of hairy raw-hide are tied through the eye holes stretching them so that the cow looks as if she had oriental eyes. The ears flop as the person swings back and forth. It's a gruesome sort of seat but Judita liked it.

I wonder if John Jacob Astor ever got used to luxury, either. In the splendor of his mansion in New York, did he yearn for the fur-trapping days of long ago? And Judita must often have looked at her children, educated in England and married to Europeans, and wondered what connection they had with her except the purely natural one of having been born of her in the deep jungles of Bolivia.

Nicolas and Judita Suarez are not buried in any marble mausoleum in La Paz, thank Goodness. Their bodies have gone to nourish the wilderness that they helped to tame—the wilderness from which they wrested a fabulous estate. In their simplicity, they lie in a tiny graveyard beside the white church at Cachuela. It has but three graves within its high iron fence. Nicolas and Judita lie side by side, and at their feet is the little girl who died at four years of age. She alone, never grew up to be educated in Europe and live in sophisticated splendor. No, she stays in the jungle with the proud old Empire Builder and his Rubber Queen, who "never knew how to take it easy."

✦ 7 ✦

AN ACHE IN THE HEART

Padre Eduardo, I would say, is a real missioner. His life revolves around river boats, altar boys and oatmeal-for-breakfast. His constant preoccupation is the thought of the black sheep of Puerto Rio.

I walked into the Padre's *sanctum sanctorum* at Puerto Rio and found him in a bowl of his own breakfast creation, oatmeal cooked to a soup in powdered milk. He did not need to be told that we had arrived in town minutes earlier on the river boat from Riberalta. There is no other way to get to Puerto Rio and, anyway, his Fifth Column of altar boys had spotted two Maryknoll Sisters as we stood on deck waiting for the boat to be tied to shore. Indeed, he had already arranged for us to stay with the Mayor's wife. Not much happens in town that Padre Eduardo doesn't know.

"Take them up to church," he told his cohorts. "I'll be there in a minute and give them Holy Communion." And out we marched under escort.

I tried to turn off at the road, but the guards objected.

"Padre Eduardo said to go to church."

"I know," I explained, "but I thought I should see if our baggage came all right. Padre Eduardo won't be at the church right now."

"Don't worry," they assured me. "Padre Eduardo sent two of us already to get your baggage and bring it to the Mayor's house. That's where you're going to stay tonight." So that was that. Outnumbered and out-maneuvered, we went meekly to church.

The church at Puerto Rio is all-time champ in the Midget Mission Church class. It seats, maybe, forty people in six little pews arranged three and three with an aisle between. There are no kneelers. Important folk and those with squeamish knees bring their

own prie-dieus with cushions, but most of us kneel on the bare wood
without any fuss.

Former pastors growled and continued for ten years to say
Sunday Mass to a congregation which so surrounded the little
white chapel that only the steeple and the roof could be seen above
their heads. Padre Eduardo growled for only two months. Then
he moved everybody to the local movie theater on Sunday mornings. It seated 200 and stood many more. Movies, by courtesy of
The Company, were shown on Wednesday and Saturday nights.
Padre Eduardo persuaded them to change to Sunday nights, as
he wanted to set up the altar on Saturday night.

We went to night prayers in the little white church. It sits on
top of a huge bare rock. In the moonlight, it looked just like a
white cap on a bald pate, perky, aloof and definitely jaunty. Padre
Eduardo stood at the bottom of the rise, surrounded by the pleading faces of his loyal altar boys. "My turn, tonight, Padre!" "Please,
Padre!" "Let me do it, Padre!" The Great Padre Eduardo nodded
his head almost imperceptibly toward one of the boys. Like a
shot, he sped off to ring the church bells.

We were eighty at night prayers. They tell me that in South
America, there are only women in church. That's true in Puerto
Rio; there are only women in church. But the men hang in at all the
doors and windows. I don't know whether it's gallantry or just a
prudent interest in the wide open spaces when the sermon begins
to hit home. We eighty inside were more than half children, who
come to night prayers as you and I used to go to the corner drug
store. They just love it. And not a peep out of them that shouldn't
be peeped, either! It's all serious business—and loud. The rosary,
hymn and Benediction were sforzando and allegro.

Afterwards, we had a wedding. No, not the white veil and
confetti type. But the man and woman stood before us all with their
four children ranged neatly behind them. The knot was tied, the
registry signed, and the whole family went home to celebrate.
Well, why not? A whole family reconciled to God is something
worth celebrating.

Padre Eduardo, too, went home to celebrate and with him went
his faithful hordes of altar boys. He was celebrating, not the wedding, but a victory over his icebox. The two of them had been at

swords' points for nearly a month. Only that afternoon the icebox had come out of its tantrum and decided to run.

Padre Eduardo got the boys all busy. He's a great one at finding work for willing hands. Hernando and Jorge were fixing up the missal stand; under the kerosene Aladdin lamp, Santiago was sorting out music for the choir; Benjamin bent his efforts to untangle the censer chains. Even little Pipsqueak (I never heard his Spanish name) was set to soaking off American stamps from old letters. Over all was Fernando, Altar Boy No. 1. Father most often called him "Ferdie the Birdie" both in private and to his face. Padre Eduardo often looked steadily from under his heavy brows at "Ferdie the Birdie." Twelve years old, bright, responsible, good humored, parents properly married. Yes, indeed, and Bolivia needs native priests.

Then Padre Eduardo sneaked off to the kitchen to luxuriate in a really cold drink of water. After all, ice-cold water can make you forget the jungle heat. The icebox had capitulated at last and should be on good behavior. He stepped into the kitchen and lit the kerosene lamp. He noted with practiced eye that Choco, his boy, had once more neglected to put water into the tin cans in which the table's four legs rested. Ants were demolishing the cake Mrs. Rojas had sent that afternoon. He brushed the ants off the cake in a matter-of-fact way, filled a pitcher at the pump just outside his door, and poured the water into the tin cans.

Then, with light step he advanced to the icebox. With his hand on the door-handle, he hesitated. Maybe, even, he would reach on to the top shelf of the cabinet he had made from a packing crate, and get himself one of those two cans of beer, the last remnants of the case his mother had sent him for Christmas. Ice cold beer! He owed it to himself, to make up for St. Patrick's day which had come and gone with no more notice than the ordo gave it. But grace prevailed—grace and prudence. "No, better not," he said to himself. "The Bishop will be coming along on visitation soon. It will look funny to bring out just one can of beer. On a hot night like this, water will taste plenty good."

He opened the door and luxuriated in the breath of cold air. "Good old icebox," he murmured. "We're friends from now on, no?" He reached for the water bottle. Hmmmm! Strangely light. Choco had forgotten to fill it! Ah well, poor boy, we all forget sometimes. He went to the kerosene stove to get water from the kettle for it wasn't safe to drink anything not boiled. But that too was strangely light.

Padre Eduardo sighed. He took the kettle and once more toddled out to the pump, holding his white cassock high so that the hem would not get muddy. He did not do his own washing now, but he had learned the hard way that mud around the hem of a cassock is not easy to get out. He filled the kettle, lit the stove and put it on, and resigned himself to waiting until the water had boiled, and then cooled, and been chilled in the icebox before he could enjoy his drink.

It was an hour later—maybe 8:30 P.M.—before he sat down to enjoy the evening. The boys had gone—commended, or encouraged, or firmly rebuked for their work as the case might require. The two best had the privilege of getting up at 5:30 to serve the 6 o'clock Mass. Miguel was awarded the bell-ringing for tomorrow. Pipsqueak and Simplicio would be permitted to sweep the church because they had done such a good job in polishing the candlesticks last Saturday.

With his court dispersed for the night, Padre Eduardo, the Altar Boys' Emperor, settled in the easy chair under the kerosene lamp, a sweating glass of ice-water and a piece of Mrs. Rojas' cake at his elbow. An ant or two still lingered on it and he broke it into several pieces just to make sure that the bulk of the invading army had retreated. He was satisfied that these were merely snipers left to cover the complete rout of their forces. He stretched out his legs, lit a cigarette and reached for a month-old *Time*. It had come that morning on the boat.

On the wall opposite was tacked the bright-striped *serape* he got in Mexico on the way down to Bolivia. Right in the center was a photograph—his mother and himself, taken a few days after Ordination. He was young Father Edward McWilliam then, and St. Sylvester's Parish in Watertown was mighty proud of its first Maryknoller. He smiled wryly, incredulous that he had ever been anybody else than Padre Eduardo of Puerto Rio. His eyes lingered on his mother's face. A simple woman, steady and sure, steering a straight course for herself through shoals and rapids to the heavenly shore.

"Well, she has landed there now," Padre Eduardo thought to himself as he glanced up from the magazine. He remembered briefly his brother's letter telling of her death, and the Mass he had said next morning in the white church at Puerto Rio. She had never been able to find the town on any map, much as she looked for it.

Padre Eduardo never allowed himself to luxuriate in sentiment. He said a Hail Mary for her and turned to practical matters—more specifically, to Mrs. Rojas' cake. It was good; as good as Mrs. Rojas was. She, too, was steady and sure. Wife of the Mayor of this town of 1,500, she led the women socially, politically and in religion.

"She can outbake them all, too," said the missioner appreciatively.

Then his thoughts turned to her husband. He wasn't so bad— married in the Church, came to Mass now and then, Communion once a year. But a hard nut to crack, nonetheless. He opposed every move to get better housing for workers; he let the red-light district run wide open; he kept a protecting hand over the anticlerical school principal who did all he could to keep religion from the public school children.

The Padre was back at his constant preoccupation—how to reach the stray sheep. All right, to think of the three hundred who came to Sunday Mass; all right, to luxuriate in the forty staunch Catholic ladies of the Sacred Heart Society; fine, to revel in the bright clean eyes of the altar boys, and wonderful to dream that at least one or two might succeed him as priest at Puerto Rio's altar. He smiled, remembering old Pablo who sweated and strained as, with three other reclaimed sinners, he carried the sepulchre in procession on Good Friday. "We've got to do penance, Padre," Pablo said wiping his brow. "S-s-sh! Don't tell the other men; I loaded it down with bricks."

But what of the others—the river boatmen who came in port late Saturday night and rioted until morning? At Mass time, they lay in sleep so sodden that even Miguel's heavy hand on the bells could not make them stir. What of the high school kids who ate up the anti-church books their principal lent them? Could he forget the girls who, even then, were patrolling the small streets? And the workmen, poor fellows, who never had a chance? They worked for The Company tapping rubber and smoking it from 4 A.M. to 10 P.M. for a mouthful of *cassava* and a swig of *chicha*. An empty sack cannot be expected to stand upright. The old question pounded hard. How can I reach them? What can I do to touch them?

Padre Eduardo groaned. "Dear Lord, I should be sitting here with a glass of super-duper ice water and a piece of the Mayoress' cake, while they don't even know You!" He groaned and turned practical again.

"Well, guess I'll turn in now. Better see what Choco has done about the oatmeal for breakfast first, though."

Yes, to my mind, Padre Eduardo is a real missioner. He has the missioner's ache in his heart.

•8•

OPERATION: FLAGELLATION

"Deathless Dan rode atop the lurching stagecoach. His steady grey eyes scanned the dusty horizon. Was that puff of smoke to the northwest a signal for marauding Indian tribes? He hugged his Winchester rifle,—that trusty firearm which had nicked off no less than twenty would-be robbers of the United States Mail. There was one fair lady and a valuable cargo of cloth aboard and the horses were far spent. But, please God, they would make Dodge City ere nightfall. Suddenly . . ."

Deathless Dan and his exploits leave me a trifle cold, now. For I, too, have ridden in a stagecoach carrying valuable cargo through pioneering country. Dan did his deeds in Nevada in the 1860's, but there is still virgin country to be opened up and fearless men are doing it. Our cargo was not cloth and fair ladies. No, in this day and age, pioneers need gasoline—and Sisters.

Our stagecoach went by the name of Ventura's truck. It was the only thing on four wheels in Guayaramerin. Ox carts have two wheels, airplanes have three. Guayaramerin, more often shortened to Guayara, is on the Mamore River. The Beni and Mamore Rivers meet in an acute angle like the letter A, and just before they meet, they are harassed by rapids, rocks, shoals and other things that river boatmen don't like. Therefore, when materials are floated down the Mamore, they are taken ashore at Guayara and transported to Cachuela on the Beni by truck over a road which is like the cross bar of the letter A.

When you read "road," don't have in mind anything concrete or asphalt, nor even red dog. Don't picture even the dusty country roads that joined town and village hamlet in the good old days when roadmakers had mercy on a horse's feet. No, the road from

74

Guayaramerin to Cachuela is merely two wheel ruts, so deep that
the axle flattens the grass between. They extend in parallel lines
through 25 miles of God's most primitive jungle.

Ventura's truck stood in the front yard one morning as we four
Madres locked the convent door and set out for Cachuela. It was a
3-ton truck which had been floated down the Mamore some ten
years ago. The back was piled high with 5-gallon tins of gasoline
crated in wood. Only a weak little fence-like thing kept them from
falling off the sides.

Our de-luxe seats were on top of the gasoline. Sister Victoria
Francis, who has spent most of her sixty-five years climbing no
higher than the steps of a Fifth Avenue bus, blanched when she
saw it. Her heart sank, I know. But she rose to the occasion. She
planted one determined foot on the wheel-hub and swung the
other up to the floor-boards. With some pushing from behind she
managed to mount to the top of the gasoline tins. So did we all.

Quite a little crowd of men had gathered round to see the fun, as
I thought. Now with one accord they leaped aboard. They were
the escort, and were we armed! Three men stood behind the cab
in the crevasse formed before the first row of gasoline tins. Two
carried long machetes (that big South American knife) ready to
lop off branches which might obstruct the way. The middle one
leaned a rifle over the cab roof. Besides jaguars and alligators whose
skins were valuable, there might be "other varmints" along the way
who would like to make off with a truckload of gasoline. Guarding
the rear were two other fellows with rifles, just in case . . .

Sitting eight feet or so above ground on a lurching truck is very
much like riding a colossal bronco. The main objective is to stay on.
We rolled out of the convent yard, and proceeded slowly down
the wide grassy street which runs through town. It was fully as
regal a procession as Queen Elizabeth's Coronation parade. Folks
came to the doors of their grass-thatched mud shacks and waved.
Even the cows and horses grazing placidly on the street looked up.
Then we passed the last straggling house and struck off into the
jungle.

The Sisters were scared. I know they were because I was, too.
Our speed was agonizingly slow, yet the truck bucked and heaved,
throwing those heavy tins of gasoline against the fragile sides with

wicked force. The wheels lurched into sudden ruts; they eased over half-exposed rocks. Each wheel had its own troubles and we felt them all. That was the most supple-bodied truck I ever rode in. Like a cat, it seemed to stretch and pull and squeeze in and out to suit the road bed. Lots of groaning, of course, went with it. Still and all, it did hump and hurdle and crawl over that fantastic road and remain intact despite it. It was like riding a rheumatic old dragon writhing off to die someplace.

We rolled cautiously over wooden bridges so rotted that nearly every floor log was gone—and us with 3-tons of truck, a heavy load and four husky Madres! As the truck tilted dangerously squooshing through a puddle, we hung on for dear life to the side-boards. It was all too easy to imagine the sides giving way under that weight of gasoline. We and the tins would cascade off the top into the jungle swamp that glistened wetly beside the road. By the time they pulled the tins off us, we'd be six feet deep in mud and worth no more than the simplest burial service.

In the meantime, we were going straight through heaven. High overhead, the great trees arched together making this a haven of coolness. On either side, the jungle grew thick, reaching out to pull us off the truck and hug us to itself, in a bear-hug of welcome.

We had to keep a wary eye out for branches. Among ourselves, we call this ride, "Operation: Flagellation." On the bare stretches of fair road, the truck speeds along at perhaps twenty miles an hour. Then we took a wicked beating from the branches. It seemed as though the jungle could hardly wait until we went by, before it closed over behind us.

It was a green, green, green world. But every now and then, we stirred up a perfect storm of yellow, white, light-blue and green butterflies. Some striped and spotted and vari-colored, too. Best of all were the big blue ones. Irridescent green and blue with black borders on their huge wings, they lazily wafted through the trees. Several fluttered within arm's reach and once we caught one. He was turquoise when you looked at him one way; and king blue when you shifted to see him in another light. We let him loose to flutter majestically away through the leafy green where nobody but jaguars and alligators could see his beauty.

After a while, we had recovered so much confidence in divine protection that we leaned back and marvelled at the pattern of leaves against the sky far, far above us. Several times I thought a sudden jolt would snap my head from its moorings and send it rolling over the side. The king of the jungle is the *almendra* tree which bears the famous Brazil nuts. Straight and dogmatic, it cleaves through the lesser trees to spread itself high, wide and handsome in the upper air. Other big trees like the *umbaibo* may twist and struggle to gain at last the heights, but the *almendra* pushes straight up, turning aside for nobody. Vines? Let them hang in festoons! The *almendra* stands waist-deep in greenery but it is never jostled by it.

There were big birds, too. Some white storks and long-tailed black birds. A red-headed bird and several things like quails. Once I saw a green *Paraba*, or buglet parrot.

Then we came into a large open space of maybe ten square miles. It was the epitome of desolation. Gaunt skeletons of trees stood here and there. On nearly every one an ant's nest like a huge tumor lodged in the crotch of a branch. Their black mud-tunnels streaked the dead trunk like the tendrils of an octopus. Such is the destruction of the ant in the jungle. It was a charnel house with the corpses of trees strangely bloated and ugly.

Then back to the jungle again with the green opening before you and closing behind. In a few minutes more we were at Santo Domingo, twelve miles and two hours from Guayara. This is just a clearing beside an overgrown stream. It was a sugar refinery for the House of Suarez and, as we have seen, old Judita Suarez used to come out to Santo Domingo every week to revel in the little old mud house where she lived when Nicolas was building his rubber kingdom. Judita's garden is overrun now and the sugar refinery machinery lies half buried in the jungle vegetation. But a caretaker lives on and runs a sort of half-way station for trucks shuttling between Guayaramerin and Cachuela. There are not many, but even two trucks a day here in this jungle means company.

The truck drew under a mango tree for shade and we all leaped off, climbing over the edge and dropping from the wheel hub. That is, all but the Madre Victoria. Having gained the heights once, she thought she ought to stay there until the end of the trip. She sat like a queen on the gasoline tins with her head high among the mango branches. But we three scouted here and there to see what we could see. Sister Angelica and Sister Elizabeth Ann spotted a grapefruit tree and set about picking fruit for tomorrow's breakfast.

We investigated the small cabin where the driver and men had disappeared. They were at a greasy table quaffing *chicha* and eating wild boar's meat. The woman serving them saw us and was all for giving us some too. It must have been good, for one of the young men bought the boar's hind leg to take home. He stuck it wrapped in banana leaves in the truck with us, the hoof and hairy lower leg sticking up grotesquely between two tins of gasoline.

Maybe it was the boar's meat; maybe it was the *chicha;* whatever it was, we were all a jolly crew as we climbed aboard our truck again and set off for Cachuela, now only twelve or thirteen miles away.

The men gallantly tried to hold the branches off from us. We, on our part, passed around a stick of Life-Savers—called here *Salvavidas*—and that cemented the friendship. These men are heroes to the small boys of Guayara and Cachuela. Like Deathless Dan of Wild West days, they swagger around town talking knowingly of far distant places (all of twenty-five miles away!). They spin tales of the valuable cargos they have carried through thick and thin.

Even so, they constitute the lowest choir of heroes, so to speak. Next are the river boatmen. Like the Mississippi pilots Mark Twain talks about, they can string tales for hours for any wide-eyed boy to marvel at. Quite out of this world, like the angels who merely touch the quiet pool of Guayara, are the airplane pilots who drop out of the skies once a week from such glamorous spots as Cochabamba and La Paz.

And so we whirled into Cachuela—we and the gasoline and our escorts armed with machetes and rifles. It was one o'clock. We had been going four and a quarter hours to cover twenty-five miles.

Terrible as the road is, it is an achievement that it even exists. In the old days when the House of Suarez was rolling in money, the road was excellent, they say, and the Suarez' Packard could cover the distance in less than an hour. Cutting that narrow passageway through the jungle without benefit of bulldozer, must have been a triumph of patience. Keeping it open is still no small job. Many times a great tree crashes across the road; the trunk must be hacked apart and a section removed just wide enough to permit a truck to pass. The mud holes—the worst of them, that is—must be lined with small tree trunks to keep the wheels from sinking straight out of sight. The bridges over a hundred small streams and swamps are rotting all the time.

A few days in Cachuela, and once more we found ourselves on top of Ventura's truck ready for the ride back to Guayara. This time it was loaded clear up to the top with corn in the husk. Together with eleven other de-luxe passengers, we rode in majesty on top of the corn. It was the closest to a hay ride I've had in many a year.

In four hours of lurching and swaying, I got the story of one of those people we refer to as DP's—Displaced Persons. It's the coldest term I know. As if you picked up a chess piece and set it down on another square. Or—and this is what has happened to the DP's— you put it off the board entirely as unwanted at the moment.

He was a Czechoslovak doctor. As a young man he lived through Hitler's take-over. In World War II, he saw his country pulled to pieces between opposing forces. In 1945, Russia came in and he fled. He and his family of three children tramped the crowded roads carrying what belongings they had salvaged, sleeping wherever night found them. Where to? England didn't want them. The United States was fussy, too. West Germany was jammed. Most of the world simply shut their doors. One DP camp after another closed down and shifted them someplace else. Eventually, they came to South America and drifted down to Bolivia. The doctor got a post at the Suarez hospital in Cachuela. But he was only a Company minion. He could not staff the hospital properly; he could not provide the care his patients needed; he dared not be liberal with medicines. Like the Spanish doctor in Cobija, his heart sank at the task to be done and the pitiful means at his disposal to do it.

He was worried, too, about his own family. There were five children now growing up in this Green Hell. They, too, were exposed to filth and disease. They would go to school no further than the sixth grade. Their cultural heritage was entirely denied them, except what he and his wife could tell them. Music, literature, art were away beyond reach.

But his big worry as we talked there on top of the corn cobs, was—the Future. Politics in Bolivia are always shaky, now the Communists were deliberately shaking the boat.

"I've seen too much of Communism not to know the signs," he said. "I'm going to Guayara now to catch a plane for Cochabamba. There, please God, I'll try to make contacts which will get me an opening in Argentina or Chile. It looks like another move for us. This time, I do hope to put down roots and stay for a while."

I thought of the political immigrants who once poured into our country from Europe. The Irish getting out from under England's yoke, the French escaping the Revolution, the Germans, Swedes, Poles, Italians, Croats, Hungarians, who came over here and set up life anew. They pushed West from the old settled places and gave their blood to Ohio and Kentucky, Wisconsin and Minnesota. They set up Little Italys and Little Hollands and Little Swedens, honing for the speech and customs of the old country. But their children quickly emerged as that anomalous creature, The American.

Perhaps it's too late to build new nations in this tired old world. Maybe Communism with its deadly poison against individual effort has eaten too far. Still, I could look at the Czechoslovak doctor speaking in his precise English and think, "You'll be dead and gone, my friend, but the new blood you are giving to South America may be the salvation of her. Mingling with the old Spanish and still older Indian, it will push up a vigorous growth in a dog-eared world, I hope. You are the grain of wheat, cast out of Europe and falling on this primeval soil. And you will never see the harvest God is sowing through you."

◆9◆

ONE WOMAN ARMY-FOR-GOOD

One of the nice things about Sister Elizabeth Ann's life is she never knows what she may be called upon to do. Each day, as she struggles up from her army cot at dawn, she can say, "Dear Lord, yesterday You got me to scrub the floor and meet the Archbishop and teach third grade geography and help old Mrs. Lopez die. I don't know exactly what You have in mind for me today but whatever it is, I'm ready to try."

Sister Elizabeth Ann is exactly half of the Maryknoll Community at Guayaramerin. She is the nursing half. The teaching half is Sister Kateri. Sister Kateri supervises a school for 222 children in six grades. She has seven lay teachers, only one of whom has gone beyond sixth grade himself. This exception is the male teacher who went to three years of a sort of Normal School in Sucre, after he finished sixth grade.

Even so, these teachers are the best educated people in town. Children in Guayara attend school usually from one to three years. Once they can read and write, no matter how poorly, their parents take them for work in the rubber *barracas*. Whenever a new teaching post is to be filled, Sister is swamped with applicants who, having passed third grade themselves, cannot see why they should not teach second grade at least. In pioneer towns, one cannot be a stickler for academic degrees. Even so, these good-hearted and willing teachers are getting a bit of normal training in after-school sessions with Sister Kateri.

The school situation in Guayara is picking up. When the Maryknoll Fathers came to town in 1942, no more than 100 children in this town of 1,700 people went to any school at all. Father Flynn started the parish school off in 1949. He had only the vaguest of hopes for Sisters to supervise it. He did the next best thing; he asked two Sisters to come and stay for ten days to give these untrained teachers some ideas. That was quite a session! Two Sisters came over from Riberalta and showed them everything from how to decorate a classroom to teaching songs and recitations. They ended up with a *"programa"* and a school picnic which showed everybody in town the advantages of an education.

Sister Kateri came to stay in December, 1951. There are 222 little ragamuffins in the parish school now, not to mention 140 in a public school which operates in a perfect wreck of a building, and 40 in a Protestant mission. Pretty good, when you consider that twelve years before, there were but 100 school children in the whole town.

But let's get back to Sister Elizabeth Ann. You will probably be exhausted just by reading what the One-Woman Army-for-Good gets accomplished in a single day. I tried to live through one of her days with her. It wouldn't do to let her know it, but between you and me, I rested for a week after.

The sky is greying around its edges as Sister Elizabeth Ann's faithful old Big Ben sets up his righteous clamor at 5:15. Sister comes from under her mosquito net and feels around for her clothes. Then, she lights her candle. Wordless and quiet in movement, she places her stiff little chair before Our Blessed Mother's statue in the middle room of the three-room convent. She sits down decorously with her office book on her knees and the candle beside her.

Soon another figure silently emerges from the heap of blackness into the small circle of candle glow. She, too, carries a chair and places it facing Sister Elizabeth Ann. The Maryknoll community of Guayaramerin, Bolivia, is about to recite Prime in choir.

The candle has paled in the dawn by the time the Sisters have recited office and made a meditation. They then gather their missals, straighten their beds and go off to church. Sister Elizabeth Ann notes with a practiced eye that the woodpile outside the kitchen outhouse is enough for cooking breakfast. As she goes by, Sister Kateri checks to see if the water buckets are filled. Then off they go across the grassy school yard to the whitewashed mud brick church to kneel in adoration before the Lord of Heaven and Earth Who comes to Guayaramerin just as readily as He comes to St. Peter's in Rome.

There are quite a few faithful ones there each morning kneeling on the red brick floor. It's wonderful to be one with them. Here alone, in all the world, is a man really and truly a man. Stripped of accidentals like money and position and education, he stands forth as a single unit of humanity—a man made to know, love and serve God in this world and to be happy with Him in the next. Go to any Catholic church at 6 A.M.; there you find this goodly company of men, each bringing his individual soul before God and saying, "Here is the soul you created and put inside of me. I bring it to You every day, just for a little look-see from You, so that I may hand it back to you someday, not too much soiled from this clinging world."

Between Mass time and breakfast, there's plenty to do. Sister Kateri is putting the house to rights. Sister Elizabeth Ann is struggling with the bread toasting on the red-hot top of the stove in the outside kitchen. She keeps a wary eye on the coffeepot lest it bubble itself dry. She has stopped in at the Fathers' house on the way home from Mass, to pick up a couple of eggs which they kindly keep in the refrigerator for her. These are boiling merrily now. The chickens insist on coming into the kitchen in spite of the screen door. Sometimes they are nice enough to lay their eggs right outside. Micheline, the cat, brings her kitties in to show them how they can rub up against Sister Elizabeth Ann's leg and get attention. Tinker the dog, condemned to stay outside, looks enviously in at the door.

Shoving a final piece of wood into the stove so that the coffee will keep hot for that precious second cup, Sister Elizabeth Ann balances toast, eggs, grapefruit and canned milk on a tray and takes it across the yard to the convent. Breakfast is served!

One reads aloud while the other eats. Then, turn-about, the second reads while the first has breakfast. By this time, Rosario has come. She is a neighbor's daughter who helps the Sisters in the kitchen. She clears the table and the Sisters prepare for the day's work.

Sister Kateri goes off across the grassy play yard to the thatched-roofed school. Several barefooted children stop their play and run up to carry her books, their brown eyes shining with excitement and their white teeth twinkling in the mile-a-minute Spanish.

Sister Elizabeth Ann waits to see if Melchior, the handy man, is going to come to work today or not. Quite often, it's not. Poor Melchior had a bad start in life and his addiction to *chicha* is not improving his chances to live long. He is, literally, a hewer of wood and carrier of water. Every day, he must fill two ex-oil drums placed on a platform ten feet above the well. He draws a bucket of water from the well; mounts a ladder to the platform; pulls up the water bucket and empties it into one of the drums. Then he dismounts the ladder and repeats the process. The Sisters have no pump. Efforts to get one have failed either because the pipes didn't fit, or nobody had equipment to make a proper thread, or the handle was stolen, or—something!

At 9:00, Sister Elizabeth Ann and I went to the clinic. It's a small place of only two rooms—one a waiting room and the other for treatments. As we slipped the key into the private entrance to the treatment room, it was obvious that the morning would be busy. The caterwauling from the waiting room spoke of a full assembly there.

They came in, one after another. Sister has nothing modern like a "Receptionist" but the people are quite honest in awaiting their turns. To most people in Guayara, Sister represents the medical profession. There is a hospital of sorts but the folks in town prefer to take their ills to Sister. The poor are quick to notice the kindly eye, the gentle hand, the quick sympathy of one who hopes to heal the soul as well as the body. They pay for their medicines as well as they can. Sister brings home at noon a goodly collection of eggs, ducks, chickens and rice. Some of the "medical fees" she has given away to even poorer patients who need a bit more food.

Our first patient was Orlando, a young man with malaria. Half an hour before, he had been sitting in the little waiting room burning up with fever. Now he staggered into the *consultorio* clammy cold, his teeth chattering and his whole body almost in convulsions.

Sister and I wrapped him up in a blanket and sat him in a chair.

She forced open his teeth and poured down a quinine mixture. The supply of more modern treatments was exhausted, and Sister had little hope of getting more quickly.

Orlando sat in a corner huddled in his blankets for an hour or more while we cared for other patients. Then with a grateful nod of his head, he slipped out the door and staggered down the street. He had an hour's walk ahead of him; he lived quite a distance in the *"monte,"* as they call the forests here.

Margarita was next. She had her three children with her. Simplicio, aged three, was infested by worms. Rosa, aged four, had a terrible sore in her ear. Little Jose's head was almost misshapen by two monstrous boils. Sister lanced them and, at every cut, Jose was comforted at his mother's breast. Both mother and baby were in need of a good cleaning-up, before the boils were emptied. But as they, too, went out the door into the street, they smiled their thanks and Margarita dropped a couple of eggs in the basket under the table.

We were just in the middle of treating a school child whose leg ulcer was oozing fetid matter in streams down her leg, when loud talking outside and the creaking wheels of an ox cart brought us to the street door. A woman was gasping in pain, laid out on the floor of the cart between the two big wheels.

"Magdalena!" Sister exclaimed. "What happened!"

The woman told her story quickly. She had been in a dug-out canoe on the river when a tree, its roots loosened by rains, fell from the bank. Magdalena's right shoulder, arm and ribs were crushed. Indeed she had almost been drowned, as well. The efforts to bring her out of the water had made a pretty mess of all the fractures. Nor had the jolting in an ox cart for a mile or more helped matters at all.

Sister sent to the hospital for the doctor. She sent to the rectory for Father; it looked like Magdalena might not pull out of this alive. In the meantime, she gave her an injection to quiet the pain. When the doctor came to take over, we went back to our patients in the dispensary.

In this little town of Guayara, Sister gives about 4,500 treatments a year. Of these, 1,200 are first visits. This is remarkable when you consider that there are only 1,700 people in town. But many of

Sister's patients come from the town of Guajara Merim across the river in Brazil, where they speak Portuguese. However, Sister's knowledge of Spanish helps her to make out what the Brazilians are saying.

In the afternoon, we went out for our visiting nurse work. First stop was at Lucita's place in town. It was more like apartment living than I ever expected to see in Guayara. A dark little passageway led from the street to a central court around which were gathered the various one-room habitations. The central place in the court was held by a large oven, a half-globe of baked mud resting on a shaky frame of bamboo. Here the various families did their baking, each one rushing to get it before the next could come. But, for all that, there was beautiful charity among them.

Lucita had a terrible foot. An ulcer of years' duration had eaten a deep hole right in front of the ankle bone. Like the other women, she was barefoot, but hobbled around using her heel only. Sister Elizabeth Ann came faithfully three times a week to change the dressing. Lucita was loud in her praises of the improvement.

While Sister bent over the loathsome foot, the other women gathered round for a chummy quarter-hour.

"And did you know that the Lopez boy is going back to Trinidad?"

"Yes, they say he has a job in the provincial government, no less! But he won't last long; none of the Lopez do."

A tall thin child brought in refreshments. She blushed furiously as she handed each of us a tumbler full of what I took to be iced tea. It was lemonade, I learned from the taste. But why that brown color? I set it down for a few minutes while helping Sister with the bandage, and learned the reason. For when I finished and went back to the drink, I saw that it was made of muddy river water. The sediment lay three-quarters of an inch deep in the bottom of the glass.

Sister must have seen my face.

"Drink it," she said in English. "River water looks awful but it's really cleaner than well water. Besides, they'll be offended if you don't." So down it went.

As we were leaving, one of the women said,

"Where are you going now?"

"Out to *Kilometro Uno*," Sister said with a twinkle. The women roared with laughter.

"We're all going there!" they called after us.

"What's *Kilometro Uno* (Kilometer One)?" I asked as we trudged along. "What's so funny about it?"

"That's the cemetery," Sister explained. "In the old days, the road to Cachuela used to be well marked with mile-stones or, in this case, with kilometer stones. One kilometer from town there was a neat marker, so that section is known as *Kilometro Uno*. The cemetery is out there. Now that the road has deteriorated so much, most of the people from *Kilometro Uno* have moved back to town leaving the dead practically alone to inhabit it. Only one family remains, the Rojas. We're going to visit them now. They're too poor to live anywhere else."

I should say they were! We walked right into the house, for there was no door to keep thieves out and no possessions to tempt them in. Nobody was around, either. Sister Elizabeth Ann poked a cautious head into the kitchen court and investigated what looked like a woodshed a few feet away. I was only too glad to sit down on a wood crate and wipe the perspiration off my face. A kilometer is five-eighths of a mile; that's a long way for an American to walk in the torrid jungle.

"Jorge at least ought to be home," Sister said returning from her exploration. "He's a boy about sixteen who, until we came last year, had never walked. He crawled on the ground or swung himself from hammock to doorpost on his pipestem legs. Poor thing! He was really only starved. I came out here every week and gave him liver injections. We give his little brother in school a weekly ration of food for the whole family, too. Jorge has improved immensely in the past year. The last time I was out here he was walking around almost normally. But that was a month ago."

"*Madrecita!*"

A thin tall woman, almost gaunt, stood in the doorway. She put down the basin of clothes she had been washing in the river and rushed forward to greet us. Her smile revealed no front teeth at all and only a few rotted stumps in back. It was Alejandra Rojas welcoming us to Rojas Manor in the most cordial way possible.

"Sit down!" Like Princess Margaret Rose graciously proffering

87

a gilt chair, she indicated the hammock. Sister Elizabeth Ann looked dubious. Those frayed strings might hold a Rojas but this Maryknoll Sister comes a bit heavier.

"Here!" cried Alejandra as she dashed outside the shack and came back with a bamboo stool. She seated herself on the hammock with a meaningful shove to her little girl Concha to rush out and get something for the Madres. I saw it and prayed, "Dear Lord, not more muddy water!"

"Where's Jorge?" asked Sister Elizabeth Ann.

"In the jungle cutting wood," said his mother.

"Jorge cutting wood?" queried Sister.

"Si, Madrecita," beamed the happy mother. "He cuts all the wood we burn. Ah Madre, it makes him so happy. You remember how he was when you came. His body was bad, but his soul was worse. He was so sad, so unhappy, so—bitter. Now he can help the family. Not much, but some. It means so much to us all. And all thanks to you, Madrecita."

"Not to me, Alejandra, but to the Good God and to the kind friends in America who give me the medicine for you. What use would I be to you without them?"

Concha came in now balancing two cups of—coffee, thank Goodness. It was the bitter black coffee South Americans like, but I was relieved to think that at least the water had been boiled. She brought in a tiny tin of evaporated milk, punched at the top. It was evidently very very extra special, saved only for guests of the highest rank. She proffered it to Sister Elizabeth Ann for her coffee.

"No, dear," Sister said. "I love it black. I wouldn't spoil this delicious cup of coffee by adding milk to it." The prevaricator! I know she hates black coffee. But I, too, passed it by and swallowed the bitter cup without a tremor. I could steal candy from a child—from some children, that is—but I could not have taken milk from Concha Rojas' skinny little hand.

We walked back to town. It wasn't so bad a jaunt for we had left a heavy-ish package at the Rojas'. Halfway to town we met a man and woman. The man strode ahead swinging his long *machete* sullenly. The woman trailed behind. She carried a baby on her back and a heavy bundle of sugarcane in her arms. The man stopped Sister Elizabeth Ann.

"Madrecita," he commenced without any further introduction, "something is wrong with her." He indicated the woman behind her. The poor soul put down her bundle, grateful for a little rest.

"I should say there is!" Sister Elizabeth Ann flashed. "She's over-worked and underfed. What's more, you beat her and kick her around, Jorge Aguirre." She laid a hand on the woman's forehead. "Right now, she has a fever as well. She ought to be in bed this very minute."

"Madrecita," Jorge placated her, "don't be angry with me. I'm a poor man and can't afford luxuries for my woman. As soon as we get home, she can rest."

Sister Elizabeth Ann pressed a bottle of vitamin pills into the woman's hand, saying nothing. The man and woman both thanked her briefly and passed on.

"What can you do with people like that?" Sister asked me as we proceeded on into town. "He's partly right. They have a clearing five miles into the jungle. The truth is, he has a wife who isn't strong enough for the life she must lead. He gets mad at her weakness and beats her. Why? Because he doesn't know any better and all the other men do it. He's as much a victim of his environment as she is."

But something brighter was coming down the road. It was a clump of children, running, dancing, laughing around a tall young man.

"Oh, it's Laughing Miguel!" Sister exclaimed. "I'm so glad you'll see him."

Laughing Miguel saw us and came over. He carried a basket of bread over his arm. He was selling it from one grass-thatched cottage to the next. But that was the least of his concerns. Merely his livelihood. Much more important to him were the stories he told the children, the dances he taught them, the silly little songs they sang with him. Laughing Miguel was maybe twenty-five years old but some stodgy old educator might tabulate his mental age around six or seven.

"Madrecita," he called out, "look at the dance we're doing!"

He put one hand flat on the top of his head and cocked the other on his hip; he turned and pirouetted a few steps forward, a few steps back. He burst into laughter. "Oh, how funny! We all like it!" The children imitated him, laughing and dancing.

"Poor Miguel!" Sister clucked as we went on.

"Why poor?" I asked. "He's about the only happy person in Guayara, it seems to me. He's the Pied Piper without any aldermen to worry him. I think he's the wisest man I've met here."

Walking in the heat, we started talking about the days thirty years before when Gertrude Altman and Ethel Danforth were high school girls at St. Joseph's Academy, Seton Hill, Greensburg, Pa. They weren't remarkable girls in any way but Sister Elizabeth Ann and I loved them. For she used to be Gertrude Altman and I was Ethel Danforth. Gertrude went on to be a nurse and Ethel ended up as a reporter on the Pittsburgh Press. Gertrude entered Maryknoll some years after me, when I was in the Philippines. She went off to Bolivia before I got back to the States. We had never met since those far-off high school days, until we found ourselves together tramping through the jungle town of Guayaramerin. There was lots to recall.

We were back in town now going down the wide grassy street. A woman came from a house and called us in. "I wonder if you will stop in to see my daughter," she asked in more cultured tones than one usually hears in Guayara.

It was a good home—for Guayara. There was a table, two chairs and a bit of faded linoleum in the front room. Grandpa and Grandma, complete with mustache on one and long flowing hair on the other, hung in heavy frames on the wall.

Beyond this room was a bedroom where a young girl sat on the hammock nursing her baby. She was nicely dressed and the baby was clean and healthy. But she looked at Sister with strangely resentful eyes.

The mother answered most of the questions; the young woman said practically nothing. A single "Yes" or "No" was the utmost she would give. Sister smiled kindly at her and gave her a few pills in an envelope, but the young woman was rigidly rude.

There was a dirty little child—two years old, I guess—who sat on the mud brick paving just outside the door. Senora Guttierrez, wishing to distract attention from her surly daughter, now picked up the child and brought her to Sister. The little thing screamed

Life is simple—and majestic—in Bolivia's jungleland. Hemmed by river and forest, a few families live miles from the next clearing.

Fiesta on the Altiplano is a wild medley of dancing and prayer. Dancers fill the plaza with color and sound.

Devout Indians mark the feast with Baptisms, special prayers for the dead and torches of incense.

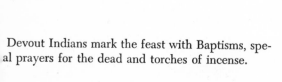

Left. Hats are a joy in the Altiplano!

Below. Me? Give me a hat that will last.

Above. Mine's an off-the-face model.

Above. If one is good, two are better!

Left. A dignified derby is "tops."

A mighty torrent flowing through untamed jungle—such is the Beni, broad highway of Bolivia's rubber country.

Above. A steady eye and good overshoes are musts for the missioner.

Below. River folk come to Mass in dug-out canoes.

After Mass, a neighborly chat.

Below. Conrado got this one by himself!

No cathedral too vast, no hut too humble, for the Holy Sacrifice of the Mass.

Palm Sunday and Good Friday in Bolivia.

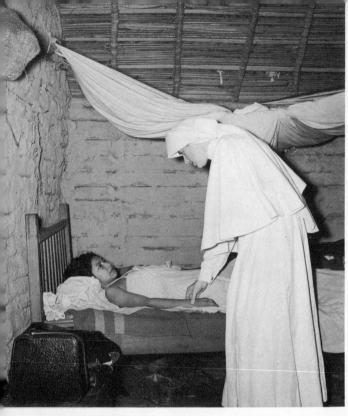

Left. The visiting nurse brings health and comfort into Riberalta's homes.

Below. Sister-doctor tries—and fails—to interest Carlito, swollen and listless from malnutrition.

Right. The old alligator-hunter submits at last to the doctor's care.

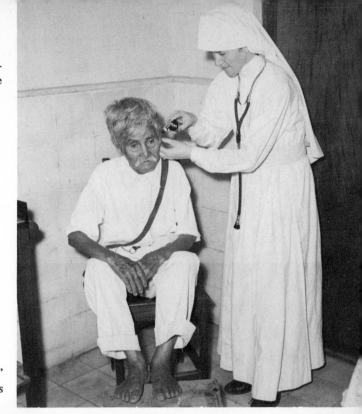

Below. "You're next, Rosa!" The waiting room is always full.

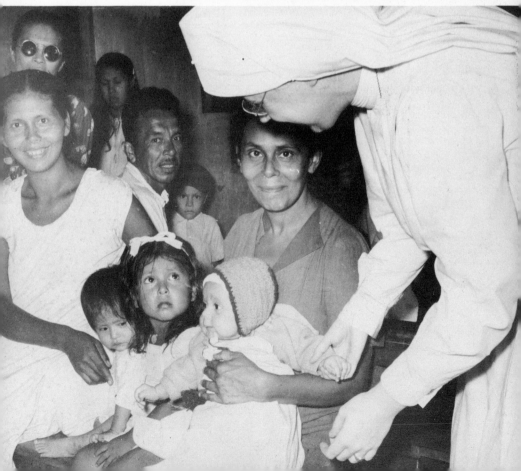

Right. Liquid rubber oozes from the tree into a small can.

Below. It must be smoked that very day.

Right. At 300 pounds, the ball is large enough at last.

Below. Off to Riberalta, first step to civilization.

Right. At the airport, latex waits for a plane.

Right. A heave and a ho, and off we go!

Below. He may be stubborn, but the mule gets you there.

Left. ABC's are tough, no matter where you learn them.

Right. The story book always draws a crowd.

Below. Ready? Sister James Elise starts the game off.

Right. A good cook makes a happy home.

Left. Patrick, the black monkey, shakes hands.

Below. Practice for The Big Day, First Holy Communion.

Above. Arriving in style in Cavinas.

Below. In Bolivia, Very Old and Very New are side by side.

and yelled although she had been very quiet while sitting outside.

"What's wrong with her, Madre?" the senora asked. "She has not walked for twenty days. She screams whenever we move her from the sitting position. It is our servant's child, but I am so concerned about her."

Sister's practiced hands were feeling along the little spine and down the legs. The child's yells were plainly of intense pain.

"What happened twenty days ago?" Sister asked.

"Nothing, Madrecita, nothing. It is all so sudden!"

The girl on the hammock spoke up. "Oh yes, something happened," she said with a sneer at her mother. "You were angry at the servant. You picked up the child and threw her against the wall."

Sister Elizabeth Ann set the baby down on the floor again, and she stopped shouting.

"There is nothing I can do for her, Senora," she said slowly. "She should go to a good hospital. Perhaps in Cochabamba? It will cost a pretty penny, I think, to help her. Are you willing to pay for it?"

Senora Guttierrez shrugged. She was embarrassed and angry.

"We will see, Madre; we will see. Thank you for coming," and she quickly showed us the door.

"Why was that girl so rude to you?" I asked once we were on the street.

"She has reason to be mad at me," Sister smiled grimly. "When she first became pregnant with that baby, she came asking me—of all people—to do something to prevent its being born. It was not that she felt ashamed at the illicit love affair. About 90% of our babies are illegitimate; it's quite common. But she was good-looking and having a good time. She simply did not want to be bothered with a baby. I told her then a few unpleasant truths and she still holds it against me."

Our last stop was at the Mendez home. What a change! This was one of the two families in town properly married. Alberto Mendez had had a heart attack a year before and since then his heart was no good at all. But what a happy house it was. Asuncion, his wife, Lourdes and Tomasa, the daughters, kept it spick and span. The dirt floor was clean, the rickety table dusted, the curtains faded and old but clean. We sat out in the court with Alberto in the hammock and his three sons around him. The eldest was cleaning his rifle, for he hunted alligators by night. One of the son's wives brought out the inevitable muddy water but it was a pleasure to drink it there. The youngest child, about six, sidled up to Sister Elizabeth Ann and stayed content by her side playing with her rosary. It was good to see a loving family spirit in this town of moral shipwreck.

Sister had taught Asuncion how to give injections to her husband when he had an attack. She gave her some ampules now asking, "How has he been lately?"

Alfredo heard her and called out, "I had a bad one last night, Madre, but Asuncion pulled me out of it. Sometime, though, it will be the last. Then surely, I'll be on my way to God in Heaven while this old body goes out to *Kilometro Uno.*"

We went out to the airport then—a wavy field of high grass which all but hid the shack which served as a waiting room, ticket office and restaurant. It was a long walk—for me—but Sister Elizabeth Ann seemed to enjoy striding down the dusty path. The weekly plane had come and gone that day. Sister went quickly over to the small pile of packages, crates, and loaded baskets it had left on the field.

"Anything for us?" she asked the man.

"Nothing for you!" he answered.

We trudged back to town. "I wonder if he forgot," Sister said biting her lip.

"Who forgot what?" I asked.

"There was an American priest who came down here about six months ago," she explained. "He was so enthusiastic about my work and promised to send me some medicine as soon as he went back to the States. It never came. I'm wondering now if he forgot —or whether he sent it and it never reached me. Oh dear, that's the worst of our difficulties. So much disappears in the mails and in the customs.

"One day, not so long ago, Pedrito in the third grade came to school with a scrap pad made of very familiar pictures. They were the Christmas cards we had sent out to friends and benefactors two months before.

"'Where did you get those?' Sister Kateri asked him.

"'Behind the postoffice,' he said innocently. 'There's a big pile of paper there!'

"We investigated ourselves. Sure enough, there were letters we had written home, business notes, orders for school equipment and even two checks we had sent paying for materials, all half-torn and dirty. The postmistress had not even troubled to burn the evidence.

"Others were annoyed, too. They complained to La Paz. The postmistress wasn't exactly fired; she was merely transferred to another town here in the jungle. It's hard to find people to take posts in a place like this, when the political plums are so much juicier in La Paz and Cochabamba."

We went home then. The day was far spent. So was I. But Sister Elizabeth Ann was good for several busy hours yet. As we came in, Rosario told us that the woman next door was ready to have her baby and was calling for her. She rushed over there.

She was back in an hour or so and we sat down to dinner just as the electric lights went on all over town. This is quite a thing. At seven o'clock, the town engineer turns on the lights. He cranks up one of those mobile generators mounted on caterpillar treads which are used to supply power for temporary Army installations. With a roar, the motor turns over. It is housed in a shed next to the convent. The engineer throws a switch and Guayaramerin's 125 electric bulbs glimmer and glow. We Sisters have one of the bulbs; two more hang from wires in the church; the Maryknoll Fathers have two, and various people in town have the rest. To get an extra bulb installed in your house takes more civic red tape than it's worth.

There are evening devotions in church at which Sister Elizabeth Ann plays the decrepit organ. After that, she and Sister Kateri sit under their lone electric bulb talking, reading and sewing for a blissful hour. That is, if a sudden call does not interrupt it.

Usually the Maryknoll Sisters' light bulb has been off for an hour or more by the time the city engineer gives a warning blink all over town at 10:55 and finally shuts off his motor at 11:00. Guayaramerin is left to slumber in the silver of the tropic moon, lulled by the rush of a great river pouring by to meet the Amazon.

◆ 10 ◆

ON THE TONGUE OF AN ALLIGATOR HUNTER

Down in Riberalta, they don't have VIP's. They have Top Shelf People. Fortunately for me, Sister Victoria Francis was Very Top Shelf. Furthermore, she brought stuff for the Top Shelf with her, and that made her rating even higher.

You see, in these hinterlands, the Sisters stock their larders with class distinctions in mind. The humble stuff—rice, yucca, bananas and so forth—goes on the floor. Ordinary stuff goes on the middle shelves. But high up—out of reach of the uninitiated in the house —go any cans of meat or fruit and, if they have it, a box of American chocolates. Those are definitely Top Shelf items reserved for great feasts and for times when Top Shelf people come to visit. Then, *La Superiora* gets such a rush of generosity to the heart that even the no-'count *periodista* shares in a wholesale devastation of that sacrosanct Top Shelf. Suffice to say, we blitzed Riberalta's top shelves.

Riberalta is the big city of the whole Pando-Beni area. And yet, it is such a dinky town. That's what amazes one here—even the centers of population are so small. They don't even have electric lights in town. They used to, but folks wouldn't pay their bills so the company that supplies the power got mad and took down all the wires and poles. So we use kerosene lamps and candles.

In this jungle land you have to keep your mind pretty spry, for you are hopping from one century to another all the time. You come in an airplane and, as you get off, you see several bull carts on the grassy field ready to load up the plane. You have ice cubes in your water at dinner but the cake comes out of a wood-burning stove that would have insulted your grandmother. You read in the evening by the light of the kerosene lamps and take your

94

shower in the flickering light of a candle. The city streets are as wide as an 8-lane divided highway but they are high with grass and serve as pasturage for sheep and cows at night. You can talk by radio-telephone with Cochabamba, if you go into a little grass-thatched hut on main street where the radio station is.

Riberaltenos tell *con mucho gusto*, the story of a big B-27 which owes its life to primitive transportation. The heavy plane, loaded with cargo, bogged down on our soft landing field and sank to the hubs in mud. The forces of modern civilization were mustered to aid their fellow monster—the town produced a tractor, a number of jeeps, even a bulldozer. Using a thick Manila rope they sweated and strained but either the wheels spun around in the mud or the rope broke. The B-27 stayed where it was. Finally they were all sent home in disgrace. A team of oxen and a length of raw hide were brought on the scene. In no time, the plane was free. The ox uses just dead weight; no tremor of a motor weakens the tow-line.

Another time, when a plane was stuck in the mud of the landing field, the twenty-five passengers got out, put their shoulders to the task and, heave-ho, freed the plane. This is one of the few cases in history when airplane passengers could "get out and push."

The longer I lived in Riberalta, the more it seemed like a frontier town of the old Wild West days. Some of the business houses have a hitching rail outside with one or two horses and oxen attached thereto. Now and then a horse and bareback rider thunders past the house. When the twice-weekly plane buzzes overhead, lots of people sally out to the airport just to see what's happening in Cochabamba or Trinidad or other stops on the route. That's how we find out which of the Maryknollers has gone where.

Down there, too, distance means nothing—or distance means so much. The plumber who put in the faucets and pipes in Guayara-merin had to be imported five hundred miles from Cochabamba. Wouldn't it be too bad if that plumber forgot his tools as they do in the States! But there was nobody more convenient for the plumbing job. On the other hand, for a trip of twenty-five miles or so, you must take seven hours in a little boat with an outboard motor, stay overnight at your destination and return the next day.

Bolivia needs missioners with long arms and legs. The long arms can wrap around suitcases, boxes, and gunny sacks and claim they

95

are "hand luggage," while the long legs can get quickly to the plane before the officials see just what you *are* carrying. Sister Ann Catherine's proportions are beautiful for this work. She has brought pottery, statuary and dogs down to the Beni as hand luggage. Last time, she got four sacks of potatoes in that classification. But her greatest feat was a year ago. "The officials would not let me ship a Christmas tree and a live turkey as baggage," she said. "I walked on the plane with a Christmas tree under one arm and the live turkey under the other gobbling his head off. The government is fussy about spreading poultry diseases, so I had taken my beastie to a veterinarian. He took his little head in his hand and glanced deep into his shining eye. Then the vet signed a medical certificate for my turkey and I knew I could not be stopped on that score. Nobody was expecting me on that plane and when we landed, I had to walk through the streets carrying my Christmas tree and my turkey to our convent."

In Riberalta they have the only honest and frank music critic along the river—and that is Father Collins' dog. The dog attends every Mass, often crouched just under the altar. When the Sisters start singing, he sits up and listens. Then he gives his opinion of it in long, sustained howls of anguish. The only singing he doesn't mind is Father Collins'. So when somebody else is saying the Mass, Father Collins often sits in a front pew and sings the common, with the dog curled at his feet drinking in the music.

Sometimes Father has someone for confession and he advances to the confessional singing all the while. The responses come at just the right time from Father hidden in the box. Toward the end of Mass, he might go to the sacristy to vest for the next Mass but the "Et Cum Spiritu Tuo" and the "Amen's" float out from the sacristy faithfully. The dog just loves it, no matter where it comes from.

Riberalta is the center for our work in this area. We staff three schools and a hospital and do extensive catechetical and medical work in the town and surroundings.

The school Sisters have San Jose Convent right on main street. Across the wide grassy street is a musical family which delights in singing. Gathered round Papa and his guitar are the sons, daughters and neighbors. They usually start up as the sun goes down and keep it going far, far into the night. But they are very friendly to us. Very. On special nights, such as big fiestas of the Church, or on somebody's feastday, they move across the street and perform just outside the dormitory window.

With the copious aid of lay teachers, we staff three schools. One is the parochial school of Our Lady of Mount Carmel. Another is out in the San Jose district, about a mile from the center of town. Together they give a Catholic education to about 600 children. The tuition rates will make you smile. They range from 10 cents a month down to 4 cents if there are several children from the same family swinging their bare brown legs from our benches. At that, most of the little ones are "special cases" and come in for drastic reductions.

The problem has always been with the adolescent group. The children graduate from sixth grade and there is no place short of 500 miles where they can continue their schooling. In a country where 85% of the people cannot read or write, there is not much call for higher education. Indeed, few continue beyond the third grade, if that. In an effort to light up this jungle of ignorance, we Maryknoll Sisters started what we euphemistically call, a Professional School. Here the boys and girls spend the morning at academic subjects—language, math, etc.—and the afternoons at what they really need. That is, a good session of hygiene, home-nursing, dressmaking and cooking for the girls, and agriculture and carpentry for the boys. The idea is, that if the young people can be induced to take an intelligent interest in making a home attractive and in feeding children the right foods, then family life in Riberalta will be on the upgrade. Let's hope so.

The other convent (Annunciation) houses the Sisters who staff the Riberalta Hospital, and those who do the catechetical work in town, teaching religion twice a week in the public schools, taking the parish census every so often and going up and down the river to teach a whole village for two to four weeks at a time.

I went with Sister Patrick Joseph on the census. It was the Chonta district, a collection of huts. We crossed a wooden bridge while an ox cart splashed alongside fording the small stream.

We approached the first house. A woman was cooking at the dried mud oven *(horno)* outside. A black monkey, in a dither of

97

expectation, swung from the grass-thatched roof. He couldn't keep still. Now he was hanging by his tail, now scrambling up a pole, now leaning over where he could get the best smell of food. As a last resort, to let his mistress know how much he wanted something, he would leap to the ground and climb up her leg to her shoulder in a flash of long skinny black arms and legs, flying in all directions.

But she paid no heed to him. She was watching us advancing toward her. When it was obvious that we were headed to visit her, she threw the monkey off and came forward with a broad smile. Not a tooth in her head, although she must have been less than thirty-five.

"Madrecita, Madrecita!" she welcomed us, leading the way to her thatched mud house and setting out two plain wooden chairs. She herself sat on the hammock which was strung catty-cornered across the single room.

It was a clean room. The mud floor had been swept; a once-white cloth was stretched on the small table where two baby parrots strutted and flipped out their wings. The woman put her finger in front of one and he hopped on it. He had a bad sore on the back of his head; the woman stroked his green feathers. Her horny fingers went gently around the sore spot.

"A hen pecked him," she explained. "That hen." And she pointed to a hen and brood of chicks who were scratching in the corner. With that, a pig came in the door, advanced across the mud floor and stretched out in quiet peace at her feet. She picked up a towel and leisurely swung it around her legs, face and arms to keep off the *marigues,* a tiny pest which comes in clusters around any man or animal who happens to stand still in the Beni. We were ready for the interview.

"What is your name, Senora?" Sister began.

"Maria Magdalena Policarpia Guttierrez y Perez." All of that went down on Sister's paper.

"Are you married, Senora?"

"Ah, no," she said. "I am single."

"Then you live here alone?"

"Yes, Madrecita. I and my children live here alone." This is no shock to Sister Patrick Joseph.

"Where is the father of your children?"

"Oh, he's someplace. Out gathering rubber, I think. That is where he went last time." She shrugs a bit diffidently. You can't expect one to keep tabs on people.

Sister tried another tack.

"What is your birth-date, Senora, please?"

This is really a tough one. Poor Maria Magdalena Policarpia twists her toothless lips and rolls her eyes and knits her brows. She really does not know. So Sister tries to be helpful.

"Do you know what year you were born in?"

The face brightens. "Yes, Madrecita. I know it very well. I was born the same year as the flood. Not when the water came up to the palm tree near the barracks, but the time when it covered all the island. Many old people can tell you about that flood. My man, too; he remembers it very well."

"Would they know the date of that flood?" Sister persists.

"Date? Well Madrecita, it was a very, very long time ago, you know." The woman leaned forward. "This will help you, though; it was the year I was born." She sat back with a smile and renewed her swishing of the towel.

Sister skipped the point. Perhaps the children's ages would give an approximation of hers.

"Your children, Senora. How many have you?"

"Eight," came promptly. "Five boys, three girls."

"Names?"

"Eriberto, Antonio, Magdalena, Jesus, Mario, Elba."

"But that is only six. What are the names of the other two?"

"Other two? Did I say eight?"

"I thought you did, Senora."

"Ay, Madrecita, let me think." She sank her chin in her hand and laid the towel aside to concentrate better. The little parrot, as if to help the process, hopped to her head and scratched a bit. The hammock swung back and forth a few minutes while she stayed in deep thought.

"Never mind, Senora. Maybe we can straighten it out when we get the children's ages. When was Eriberto born?"

"Oh, he's a big boy. He's out with my man right now. Old enough to earn $3.00 a month. He's a good lad, Eriberto."

"When was he born? Do you remember?"

"Ay, Madrecita! How could I ever forget? He was born on a Thursday."

"How do you know it was a Thursday?"

"Well, very simple. My man was working on the Triunfo, and that river launch sails on Saturday every week and comes back on Wednesday. My man came home the day before I was delivered of Eriberto. He was my first baby and I wanted my *señor* home to see him right away."

Sister is just about to say, "You wouldn't know the year, by any chance, would you?" but thinks better of it.

"How about Antonio. When was he born?"

"St. John's Day, Madrecita."

This is hopeful. Sister pursues the cue.

"St. John the Baptist? St. John of God? St. John the Apostle? St. John Capistrano?" But the victim is only confused.

"Just St. John, Madrecita. I don't know all those other people. My mother told me it was San Juan; she said we should call the child Juan. But me, I like Antonio."

"How big is Antonio?" Sister asked. The woman looked around the room. A holy picture was hanging about five feet from the floor. "Antonio when he stands comes just to the bottom of that picture," his mother said.

Sister wrote down, after Antonio's name—five feet high.

"And now, Magdalena, how old is she?"

"Twelve," came the answer, sharp and decisive. A sudden light struck Sister. This woman knew nothing about dates but she did know ages. From then on, the questions got someplace. We even went back over Eriberto and Antonio. They were fourteen and fifteen respectively. Jesus was eight, Mario five and Elba four.

Still on the trail of the two missing children, Sister scanned the list. "Magdalena is twelve and Jesus is eight," she said. "Did you have another child between them who died?"

"Yes, Madrecita, my poor little Crisostomo died at two months. And Roberto was born in there, too."

"Roberto? Where is he?"

"With his god-mother in Trinidad, Madrecita. Her children were all grown up and she asked me for Roberto. So I gave him to her.

Ay!" her eyes flashed as she understood that one of the missing children had been found. "I was right! I do have eight children. The other is Josefa. I was sick and gave her to my cousins. They have moved away now; I don't know where." She was elated with herself.

A younger woman had come into the hut during the interview. She was puttering around in a dark corner. Only when she un-draped it, did I see that there was actually a sewing machine over there. The young woman sat herself down at it and began a long seam. The black monkey perched on the side watching the flash-ing needle with fascination.

"Who is that woman?" Sister asked Maria Magdalena Policarpia.

"She is my guest, Madrecita. I do not know her name. She came here when her baby was born; she was very poor with nobody to care for her."

"And you took her in, Senora? That was very kind of you."

"Ay, Madrecita. She had nobody. She has been here a year now. I call her Teresa."

"How long is she going to stay?"

"I do not know the answer to that. You had better ask her, Madre."

"But you said you lived here alone, Senora."

"I do. I am single. I live here all alone with my children and my guest."

"Does your man come home often?"

"Sometimes yes, sometimes no."

"When he comes home next time why don't you ask him if he wants to be married in the Church?"

Evidently there were two sides to that question. The woman stood up from the hammock.

"No, no! I will not ask him that! I do not want to be married to that man, Madrecita. I have lived with him eighteen years and I know how pig-headed he is. He is not the husband for me. No, no, not for me. I will stay single; I want my freedom."

Well—you can lead a horse to water but you cannot make him drink. "Let her stay in the state of single blessedness." Sister thought.

"Very well, Senora," she said smiling. "You have been very kind to answer all my questions. I will come to visit you again, if you don't mind." And we started to gather our things. Teresa slipped out of the room and soon came back with the inevitable two glasses of lemonade made of muddy river water. But we drank it eagerly; long walks in hot sun do things to a squeamish stomach.

Both women smiled happily. They felt themselves honored by our visit; their innate hospitality warmed us. I looked with holy envy on Maria Magdalena Policarpia. Here she was—with little idea of dates, let alone of the Sixth Commandment—yet practicing what Our Lord has said we will be judged by. This woman, her "guest," had shared her table for a year, simply because "she had no place to go." It seemed to me I heard the words echo in that little hut. "I had no place to go and you took Me in."

The black monkey deserted the sewing machine and climbed on her shoulder. The woman's rough fingers smoothed his small black head affectionately.

"What do you call your monkey?" Sister Patrick Joseph said, just to make conversation.

"He is Patrick, Madrecita, because he is so black."

Sister Patrick Joseph swallowed her lemonade fast and we left. When we stood on the grassy street outside, I said,

"You forgot to get the address of that house."

"Oh, no, I didn't," she said. "There are no addresses. I'll call that house, Catty-Cornered from the Palm Tree. If that palm tree ever falls down or if somebody plants another one in Chonta district— well, heaven help the poor census-taker!"

The Sister-catechists often go on week-end trips to nearby hamlets on the river. You see, in an ecclesiastical set-up such as this type of country demands, each river is a parish in itself. In the larger *barracas*, or rubber centers, it is possible to have a resident priest, but many rivers have no large *barracas*. The Madre de Dios and the Orton are two of these. A priest will start up the Madre de Dios in September, let us say. He stops at each hamlet along the way for a day or two, saying Mass, hearing confessions and baptizing the babies. On leaving he will say, "I'll be coming back here in February. Have all the people near and far informed of this." In this way he covers all the towns clear up to the source of the stream, sometimes away in Peru. This may take two months or so. Then, he starts back downstream. At the appointed places, he may stay for two or three weeks, giving instructions, preparing children for First Holy Communion, taking a census and anointing those who may die before they see a priest again. The trip down may take nine months or more. Father will stay at Riberalta a few weeks, resting and fiddling with his outboard motor to get it to work better. Then he's off again chugging upstream once more.

This takes care of the far-away places. Father Jakowski takes care of nearby spots. One week-end he says Mass in several places upstream on the Beni; the next Sunday, he goes to a town on the Madre de Dios which flows into the Beni right at Riberalta; on the third, he works downstream on the Beni, etc. Often, a nurse and a catechist go along with him to do what they can for the people.

I went with Sister Albert and Sister Louis Marie. Sister Albert is a veteran of nineteen years in China. She is more familiar with sampans and pagodas than she is with dug-out canoes and thatched grass roofs. But souls are souls anywhere, so Sister Albert tucks her catechetical chart underarm and tries to curl her tongue around Spanish verbs. But she does manage to get a touch of Chinese accent on it all.

I never think of Sister Albert but I remember a time when we had a women's religion class in one of the bamboo huts of Riberalta. The women—poor things!—had been deadened by hard work, no education and poor food. Yet they were eager to learn, and dropped their housework for an hour on Tuesday mornings to gather in one of the houses for a lesson.

Sister Albert explained in simplest terms the nature of God— how He is pure spirit, has no body, and is not affected by this material world in any way. When she finished, she asked the rhetorical question, "Can we, then, see God?"

With one accord, they nodded a vigorous "Yes." And one woman called out, "Como no!" This in Spanish has the same force as "Sure! Why not?"

Sister Albert swallowed hard and began at the beginning again.

Sister Louis Marie is a nurse from Berkeley, California. We were going to Agua Dulce, about 25 miles upstream, a sort of leper colony. At least, it is so called although only nine of the sixty inhabitants have the disease. It is the official place for lepers in the district. Sister Vivian, the doctor, had been there a few weeks before, taking tests of all sixty inhabitants. Sister Louis Marie was to check up on the bad cases and give hope to those who were responding to treatment.

We set out on a Saturday morning. Blankets, food, thermos jug, mosquito nets, hammocks, a cooking stove (one burner), a small bottle of water purifier, plus three sturdy Madres. All of these descended upon Father Jakowski's boat, and all of them were stowed away neatly. The boat is like an overgrown rowboat with an outboard motor. A wooden roof adds a touch of elegance. Father himself with dark green glasses and a classic profile looks like a yachtsman. What they call "the port" in Riberalta is only a flat place in the river bank. We had to wallow through mud to get out to the boat but, once there, we could turn and wave to Sisters Angelica and Marquette on the bank.

It was a quiet, restful seven hours upriver, except for an hour or so when the motor died and had to be taken apart and cleaned. River water is muddy and the cooling system clogs in a few hours. Then we stopped at San Jose where a single family lives. Father says Mass in their house once a month. You should see the respect they have for the altar. It was in their best room and covered with a clean sheet—I mean, as clean as anybody could get it, using muddy river water the color of iced tea. I can't begin to describe the bamboo walls which let light through every crevice, and the mud floor, and poor benches.

It was almost dark as we nosed under the trees on the river bank at Agua Dulce. In the gathering gloom we could see many willing hands reaching out to tie the boat, to take our things, to help us ashore. The whole settlement was on the bank eager to escort us to the big bamboo hut that served as a chapel. It was quite a way up the bank, through the town and beyond, to this small church. Sister Albert was surrounded by the children holding to her hand. Sister Louis Marie was talking earnestly to two or three grown-ups as we walked along the dark path in the jungle.

We set up our quarters in the sacristy. It was tiny—no more than 10 x 6 feet. But we got an army cot sidewise and one lengthwise and strung up the hammock kitty-cornered. We got out the burner from the baggage and boiled some of the muddy water for coffee. This, with the rest of our sandwiches, made a good supper. Father had retired to sleep on his boat. He stretched out on top of the locker there.

The people came for night prayers. They do this every night in the village. I could see them coming through the trees with small kerosene flares. They knelt on the bare wood floor, and prayed aloud before the empty altar. Afterwards, all the old friends came up to talk, to get the latest news from Riberalta, to ask about this Sister, or that, to tell of some trouble and to ask for prayers. The children were off to one side with Sister Albert.

After they had all gone, we three set to work. Father had asked for a High Mass in the morning. So, Sister Louis Marie (coloratura soprano), Sister Albert (tenor robusto when you can hear her), and I (basso profundo, weak on pitch, but strong on volume), held a choir rehearsal.

It really wasn't so good. But we agreed that I should start things off because I could at least be heard. The next morning at Mass, I started off with the Kyrie, but soon lost count. After only two of them, I swung into the Christe—fortissimo. The other two came along with me, but at the end of that Christe, Sister Louis Marie was all for going back and picking up the Kyrie we had skipped. We fought it out for a couple of notes. Then she succumbed to superior volume and came along with us. From that time on, we had her tamed. Toward the end of the Credo, my voice cracked and went dead. Sister Louis Marie laughed outright. Sister Albert carried on with a brave quaver but Father picked it up and finished the Credo from the altar.

We left Agua Dulce immediately after the early Mass and slipped down river for an hour or more to San Jose. The shore was lined with dug-out canoes; folks from across the river, up and down for several miles, had piled the children into the family canoe and come to Mass. As I looked at the boats bobbing in the water, I thought of the parking lot in front of churches in the States, filled with automobiles on a Sunday morning.

The Mendez family who live in the only house at San Jose played host. The altar was set up for Mass in their hut. Sheets curtained off the bed in the corner. The mud floor had been swept and crude benches arranged in rows. The sun streamed through open slits in the bamboo walls; the flies buzzed lazily. Father vested reverently and advanced to the altar as if he were in a cathedral. The people knelt. The ancient ceremony of the Mass which fits itself to every circumstance men find themselves in was about to begin.

We had a hard time getting away after Mass. So many people had brought us bananas and grapefruit. There were several baptisms. Mr. Mendez, learning that I was a greenhorn in the Beni, took me off to show me the alligator skins he had soaking in brine. Mrs. Mendez insisted we have a cup of coffee. In the end, it was 11:30 before we pushed off for our third stop, Valparaiso.

Most of the people had dispersed by the time we tied up to a tree on the river bank at Valparaiso. We sent messengers around, however, and many returned for Mass at about 12:30. We made breakfast after Mass, boiling the water in a clay pot one of the women lent us. This rested on stones over a fire of brushwood. I was elected chief fire-tender; my years in Japanese internment camps in the Philippines during World War II stood me in good stead. In those days we used to cook our rice on just such makeshift stoves.

Once more we boarded our little boat and slid downstream to Riberalta. We were all deep in our office books, or quietly saying the Rosary. It was a time to think of big things—the wide river, the vast dome of blue sky, the great trees on the river bank, and God who made them all and yet is not ashamed to come into a hut and rest on the tongue of an alligator hunter. Indeed, He loves to do it.

A jaunt such as this teaches you one great thing—the essential role of the priest. His work is to say Mass for people, to give them the chance to offer sacrifice to God and to direct toward God the loving devotion of the people. This was why Father Jakowski was educated, was ordained and sent down here. This is why the boat was built and why the outboard motor was purchased and sent down here. This is why the promoters at Maryknoll speak in schools and churches and stand at the doors and pass the basket. So that the Mass can reach the people who would otherwise live and die without it. I had never seen it so stark before.

◆ 11 ◆

RIVERS, ALLIGATORS AND SOULS

Do you like Brazil nuts? So do I!

You will feel for me, then, when I tell you that for a week, I had to eat, sleep and work on a boat loaded with Brazil nuts without a nutcracker in sight. The temptation to uncover the hold and wipe out the cargo some dark night, was almost beyond my moral strength.

But there were other Sisters sleeping on the hatch cover and they might not have been so fond of Brazil nuts as I. With this salutary thought in mind, grace won the day.

We were on a luxury cruise up 250 miles of the Beni River to the old mission of Cavinas. Most of the day, I sat on a rough stool on some boards over the cargo of nuts, with a rifle stuck in the rafters above to shoot any alligator we might see. Alligator skins bring good money down here—but not nearly so good as they bring in New York.

Schedules on the Beni are always on the nebulous side. Nobody makes connections. Nobody. The boat gets stuck on a mud bank, or the channel changes overnight, or a jungle tree falls athwart the channel. That's how Brother Gonzaga was killed a few years back. In the early evening, he was sitting on the small hatch by his engine, chugging along near the shore. Bishop Lane, Superior General of Maryknoll, and some priests were up front talking mission problems. Brother was quietly saying his rosary and thinking the nice thoughts he always thought when—crash!—a great tree, loosed from the shore by the swift flowing river, fell right over them all. The bishop and priests were scratched by the branches, but poor Brother was crushed to death by the trunk.

First the boat we hoped to have was coming in tomorrow, and

then next week. First we could have one boat and then we would have to take another. It got to the stage where we told the man—"Anything that floats, and the sooner the better." Then it was that the final deal was made, "Take Carmen. She's in now and can leave tomorrow."

Bedding, curtains, toothbrushes, food, towels, dishes, camera, pots and pans, folding tables, binoculars, army cots and hammocks, folding chairs, my typewriter, holy cards and medals, laundry soap, basins, spiritual and other books, clothesline and clothespins, as well as our personal effects, were brought to the good ship Carmen and its "*alberinga*," the Tunari. Oh yes, and Sister Marquette brought a concertina although nobody could play it. We missioners think of everything!

The heavens opened for the occasion. It was a rain spectacle such as Riberalta alone can stage. The thatched roofs dripped; the ox carts wallowed; even the horses, cows and pigs who usually crop the grass in our streets no matter what the weather is, stood under the eaves and looked bleakly at the wet, wet world. It must have been a bit of entertainment in their humdrum lives to see us careening through the mud splashing into the jeep. Sister Albert had her fingers plugging several holes in the canvas cover, but ignored the whole open side. Sister Victoria Francis had one of those fancy fold-up umbrellas opened at the side. I was sitting in two inches of water but shielded the camera bag with the rest of me. Sister Genevieve Teresa plunged the jeep gayly into each mudhole as it came, swam with it to the other side and emerged shaking the drops off like a dog. Several times I thought she would shake one of us off, too. But every time she called over her shoulder, "Still with us?," we could say, "Still with you!"

The port in Riberalta—I mean the big port where the major shipping interests are concentrated—is variable. In high water, it's the grassy bank; in medium water, like now, it's down a steep slippery mud cliff; in low water, it's quite a walk out to the shrunken stream. We slipped down the mud cliff; somebody had cut crude stairs in it but rain and passing footsteps had worn them smooth. Then we teetered up the wet plank and landed in a welter of baggage on the deck.

Some eight or ten of the Sisters we left behind stood up on the

bank in dripping habits and waved us off with all the éclat due
a Queen Elizabeth sailing.

The good ship Carmen, like many a lady down here, is not much
on looks but good for hard work. She's made of iron, once painted
a dull grey. About 35 feet long, she carries a big Diesel engine and
not much else beside. That's her function—to provide power. We
set up housekeeping on the *alberinga* which is built exactly like
the Carmen but without a motor.

The system is something like China's where a single motorized
boat will pull three, five or seven sampans or junks behind it in a
long string. But in Bolivia's jungle, the rivers twist so much that
it wouldn't do to be so strung out. The motor boat has several others
lashed tight beside it, so that the whole outfit looks like a phalanx
of boats moving broadside down the wide river.

It was the bottom of our *alberinga* that was filled with Brazil nuts.
Following the advice of most masters of the spiritual life, I firmly
turned my mind from the thought. But I wondered how many of
those masters ever slept on a hatch cover over Brazil nuts. Precious
few of them, I suspect.

We had the whole *alberinga* to ourselves. The captain and his
crew kept to the other boat more or less, but they had the kitchen
at the end of their boat and we had the lavatory at the end of ours.
So there was more or less constant hopping back and forth.

I couldn't keep track of the crew very well. Sometimes there
seemed to be twenty men swarming over the deck and at other
times only five or six. The others had gone off for a snooze someplace. What might look like an old torn blanket thrown into a
corner, or tossed up on the roof, or rumpled beside the Diesel
motor, was probably a crewman getting in a little extra Forty
Winks for himself.

The Carmen was made 34 years ago in Germany, brought in
pieces up the Amazon tributaries to Riberalta and assembled there.
With a fairly new American Diesel motor, it's the fastest thing afloat
in these parts. As I say, not much on looks but everything had a
place and everything was in its place. The rifle belonged up under
the roof, the long pushing poles went in slots alongside, the captain's
hammock was tucked up neatly and the bucket of muddy river water stood in a corner with a drinking dipper beside it. *Esta es la vida,*

no? I think we Maryknoll Sisters are all Tugboat Annies at heart. What if there *is* mud on the floor and the anchor is rusted!

Although we kept pretty much to our respective boats, the crew and we had the grandest relationship. If you began to lower a bucket over the side to get some river water for your ablutions, somebody was quick to do it for you. When you got up in the morning, your feet were hardly out of the mosquito net before two or three are there to fold up your blankets, take down the net and wrestle with that invention of the devil, a folding army cot. You see, on an ordinary trip, they would have been putting cargo on and off, getting passengers here and there, stopping at every back yard for wood. But, as I said, this was a luxury cruise. We had chartered the boat; all they had to do was to get us over 250 miles of river to Cavinas and back again.

The pilot steered and the cookie cooked. One man kept busy constantly, dipping a pole over the side to sound the river's depth. The channel changes overnight in the rainy season. But the rest of the crew hadn't much to do on a non-stop flight like this.

It's a beautiful river, majestic. Anyone who thinks that the Beni is a tangled creek pushing its way through impenetrable forests, should revise his picture. This thing looks like the Delaware in Philadelphia, or the Ohio near Cincinnati, or the Missouri, or even the upper Mississippi. Or like the Hudson around Albany. It's more than a thousand feet wide at its widest and right here it's a good eight hundred and fifty feet.

What a river! What a chance for pioneering! The Jesuits in New York State tramping from one Indian village to another, Père Marquette sailing up the wide Missouri, Charles Nerincx plunging into the Kentucky wilderness—the grand old missioners who carried the Faith throughout this country of ours, all came to mind. We would swing around a river bend and see ahead something exactly like old prints of Detroit in 1701, or Cincinnati in 1790. Just four or five huts on a river bank and a few canoes hurrying toward it.

Things are so spread out in a frontier country. So few people. So much scenery unrelieved by anything man has made. There are sixty-seven hamlets along the 250 miles of Beni River we covered. The population figures read something like this:

Las Piedras	10 families
San Jose	2 families
Exaltacion	4 families
San Pedro	8 families
Concepcion	1 family and so on.

Thirty families constitute a big center and the metropolis of them all is Ethea with 103 families. That is way ahead of any place else. There are only fifteen towns with thirty families or more. Twenty-six of them have less than five families.

In all the 250 miles of river travel, we passed only one other motor boat, piled high with wood for fuel and the top decorated with tables and a dresser, somebody's household goods. We passed also a small boat filled with bananas, and two canoes-full of Chacoba Indians. These people, the aborigines of the area, wear rings in their noses, don't speak Spanish and have not yet devised a monetary system.

When we got abreast of the clearing, everybody there would be on the river bank waving. Usually the people had heard our boat for some hours ahead. They were lined up on the bank for the big event of the day, just as in the old days people would watch for the stagecoach to pass through town. We waved and they waved back. IYAN! What a thrill!

It really *is* a thrill for them. Launches come along about once in two weeks and not all of them stop everywhere. Often more than a month goes by with no contact between these *barracas* and the outside world, other than this wave as the launch goes by. I used to wonder how they knew we were coming, but the Maryknoll Fathers tell me that village folk can hear a motor launch coming for five and six hours ahead of time. Sometimes for a whole day ahead. The river winds so much that the sound has not far to travel in the straight line. Indeed, from the air, it looks as though every river in the Beni does a most exaggerated snake-dance through the jungle.

We travelled mostly by day. At night the dank mist rises from the river, rolling up like a deep fog. We then turned to the shore and tied up to a tree. It was as simple as that. The boat boasted a heavy anchor but it was never thrown overboard. My own private suspicion is that it would sink 60 fathoms deep in the soft mud and drag poor old Carmen after it.

And in the morning—ah, here is a chance for sheer poetry! Let me wake you up on the Good Ship Carmen! Imagine the cold grey dawn stealing o'er the deck. The Carmen and her *alberinga* are tied up close to shore. The mosquitoes are singing like mad in the dewy jungle dawn. On the roofs of our boats are shapeless forms —quiet. The captain is strung up with a mosquito net over him in a hammock over the engine. We Madres are stretched on army cots. The mosquito nets are strung like a hit-and-miss washday line here, there and everywhere. No one stirs.

Something splashes in the water. Was it a water snake? Or a white crane out early for a fish breakfast? Or a sleepy alligator flopping off a dead log into the water? Nobody bothers to find out. But the noise begins the day. Cookie, who had bedded down by his faithful old wood-burning stove, throws off his blanket and stumbles wearily to his feet. He wastes little time in either morning prayers, ablutions or dressing for he is as fully clothed as he ever is. He pads over to the hatch where his cooking wood is stored, lifting his bare feet considerately over the muffled forms on the deck. Then with his arms laden with split logs, he starts back to the galley. He doesn't navigate so accurately now for he can't see over his armload of wood. He kicks one, stumbles over another, pokes his wood into the sleepy bulge in a hammock and drops a log or two on somebody else.

Everybody gets up now. Life fits into well-rutted routine. The engine men start up the roaring Diesel engine; the pilot boy sits on his stool behind the wheel; the lad who dips the pole to see how far away the river bottom is takes his post on the gunwale. The captain drops lightly from his hammock to the floor, gives the signal and two of the common "*mozos*" run to untie the launch from the tree on the bank. They shove it off the bank and leap aboard. Hurrah! We're off for the day!

Cookie, who started all this, is happy in his galley. Really it's quite shipshape. His pots and pans hang on the wall; his bunch of bananas stands in the corner. A string across a sort of window at the end of the boat is strung with *charqui*, a dried meat that smells awful. A kettle spouts clouds on the stove and the smoke goes out a hole in the roof. Up there, in a box, are two chickens and a few ducks waiting for "that fateful moment." But, while they live, they miss nothing of the passing scene; their heads and long necks are enjoying every bit of scenery.

Cookie serves breakfast. One by one the men come in line while he loads their plates with rice and meat and mashed bananas. Then he sets the table for the captain. A white—or rather, once-white—tablecloth, knife, fork and spoon, plate and glass. A glass pitcher no less. Cookie dips the glass pitcher overboard and gets a quantity of brown river water. This is for Captain to drink.

By this time, we too are up and about. Mosquito nets are folded; army cots disjointed down to a bundle of sticks; hammocks stowed away. Whoever is Officer of the Day (we each took a day at it) connives with Adelina who was brought along for the purpose, and the two conspire to put together a breakfast. Every meal is buffet style. The cooking pots are set on two card tables. You pick up a plastic plate and help yourself. Then you sit down anywhere —on a hatch or a pile of boards or even, if you are conventional, on a chair. It was more like Internment Camp living than anything I have had since World War II.

The first stop was San Pedro. Everybody was out to watch us go by—they thought. Imagine the delight when we drew into shore and got off! There is a *"sanatario"* here who had once worked at our Riberalta Hospital. He is a quasi-nurse, laboratory technician and elementary pharmacist. He proudly showed Sister Marquette his little cabinet of medicines. He is the only person with any medical knowledge whatever between Riberalta and Blanca Flor, a distance of at least 150 miles. His wife is the school teacher so we went over to see the school. It is a large, thatched hut with walls up to about six feet. A portable blackboard stands in the middle facing both ways. This divides the school. There is absolutely no other partition. As soon as we came, a school holiday was declared and the children trouped around with us.

This is the Brazil nut center. Here women sit at long tables and crush Brazil nuts endlessly. The shells were used to keep the muddy river bank dry for San Pedro is a progressive little town.

113

We pulled into Blanca Flor at nine o'clock in the evening of the third day of travel. The shore was filled with people to meet us. It is easy to distinguish the white cassock of Father McGowan. Right behind him was a pet pig, a sort of wild pig which has been tamed and now runs around the town like a dog. With flashlights and torches, we climbed the slippery banks and had a town séance in the parlor of Don Juan's house where the administrator and his wife live. It was clean and neat, but had only a rough mud floor, a big table, a few chairs, and several framed snapshots on the walls. Everybody was bubbling over with excitement from Don Juan's wife down to the poor souls who crowded at the windows to watch us drink *"Agua gaseosa"* or the local soda pop.

Since we were going to stop again at Blanca Flor on the way back, we stayed overnight here (sleeping amid a billion mosquitoes on our boat). In the morning we heard Mass celebrated in the same parlor, and left right afterwards.

That was at 9 A.M. Again the whole day passed watching the strange birds, the big fish who flopped out of the water and back again, the trees strangled and dripping with vines, the river wide and deep flowing like a 20-lane highway through this primeval land. Sunset came and night. Still we chugged along the overgrown banks, skirting the rapids and the strong current in the middle of the river.

We chugged through most of the night, but by 4 A.M. the river mist was so thick that the headlight just bounced back again from the billowy steam that rose from the water. We pulled over to the shore, drove a stake into the mud bank, tied a rope around it and the crew bedded down for a few hours' rest.

Up and off again at six o'clock. There were only two hours more to Cavinas. Almost as soon as we docked—I mean, as soon as the board was placed from the boat to the mud bank—we had Mass in one of the huts there on the river bank. Father Maskell had attached himself to our party at Blanca Flor the night before. We had him all the way back to Riberalta.

Cavinas you will find marked on most maps. You'd think it would be quite a town. But Cavinas is really in two parts. On the river bank are a few huts—ten or fifteen maybe. Then about four miles inland is an Indian settlement where the rest of the 85 families live. There was some delay about getting news to Father Laszewski that we had arrived, so Sisters Marquette, Anne Marion, James Elise and I started to walk the four miles inland. What a jaunt! Through beautiful jungle woodland we followed a trail rutted by ox carts. Just before we came to the town, we went through a huge field humped here and there with high ant hills of red clay. It was weird to see this city of ants, so to speak, on the flat field. The hills were almost as regular as the shocks of wheat on a harvested field.

Then, passing through a gate, we came into the city of Cavinas, a number of thatched huts set in neat rows and dominated by the beautiful church which Father Fritz built some years ago. You gasp to see such a church here. Almost as soon as we arrived, Sisters Angelica and Victoria Francis rolled into town on an ox cart. It was a stylish turn-out with four oxen and a couple of footmen running alongside to whip them up while our two sat on a wooden box covered with one of our thin mattresses.

The interesting thing about Cavinas is its history. It was given to the early missioners to hold in trust for the Indians. The missioners were to civilize them, teach them useful things, and Christianize them. Hence this settlement which works a rubber *central*. Maryknoll holds it in trust for the present settlers. Father Laszewski is the be-all-and-end-all in the whole place. He is priest, mayor, judge and father to everybody there. He decides where and when they work; he decides how much *chicha* they can have for a fiesta; he regulates their goings and comings. He runs the store, too. We were surprised to see some table-model sewing machines on the shelves. Father is eager to get the women interested in beautifying their homes.

The Indians were not at all friendly. About a year ago, four of our Sisters went to Cavinas, the first Sisters who had ever come there. The Indians went into their houses and hid. The Sisters were unable to get even a glimpse of the people. We fared a little better. Two or three children stood in a doorway and we went over to talk to them. Their mothers came out of hiding and we had a pleasant chat. Later we went around to the back door of a hut and found another family. But several times, the women and children

115

ducked down below the window sill when we turned quickly and caught them peeking out at us. It will take years to break down their distrust of the white man.

Father had a super-meal for us. It is quite a day in his life when six Maryknoll Sisters drop in. Then, soon after, we all got on to the ox cart and went off for the port. Riding an ox cart looks very unthrilling. But let me tell you, when one of those big wheels jolts suddenly into a two-foot deep hole you feel that your head will snap right off your shoulders. How the wooden wheels stood it I don't know. But those wheels and the axle, too, are made of solid mahogany, strong as steel and maybe stronger.

The trip downstream back to Riberalta was fast, very fast. It had taken us sixty strenuous hours chugging up the river, not counting the six hours each night we slept by the river bank. We came down in twenty-four, almost one-third the time. And, whereas we had sneaked upriver close to shore, we came down triumphant midstream on the way back, like the Queen Elizabeth sailing down Fifth Avenue.

So when we left Cavinas at around three in the afternoon we zipped down to Fortaleza by 6:45. Here was Father Flynn in the welcoming crowd. He took us up to Don Jose's house, the administrator for the owner, Seiler and Co. Don Jose was awfully nice, gave us a supper and insisted we stay to eat it.

In the late evening, once more we walked the single plank which connected the Carmen to the shore and set off for Blanca Flor. This time we had Father Flynn as passenger. At Cavinas, we had taken on a man who was very ill; he was bound for our hospital at Riberalta. In this kind of pioneer country, you develop pioneer charity. It is nothing at all for somebody to hitch a ride on any conveyance on the river. We had brought mail for "the priests up the river," as they call these missioners isolated in small *barracas* on the Beni. There is no regular mail service to them. Mail comes only by courtesy of "somebody going up the river."

Father Flynn is a young priest from Cleveland, Ohio, perhaps in his early thirties. His boyish face was sensitive and alert as he played the host at Fortaleza. I thought then of how proud his mother would be if she could see him here in this jungle giving his talents to God.

Once the Carmen had cast adrift from the shore and was chugging downstream, Father Flynn started to read the mail we had brought for him—the first in six weeks. It was an unforgettable picture to see him beside the small kerosene lamp, in his white cassock, tilting the letter to bring the dear handwriting into a readable position. His earnest young face was absorbed in the news from home.

Later he told us, "There was a telegram in that packet of mail. At first I was almost afraid to open it. It was from my father. He sent the telegram two weeks ago saying that he is coming to Bolivia in July." Father Flynn smiled. "Dad said at the end, 'Reply by wire.' He doesn't understand how impossible that is. But he will, after July."

While we moved swiftly downriver, the mosquitoes couldn't keep up with us, thanks be to God. But when we pulled into the shore at Blanca Flor at midnight, they came to the banquet in clouds. The triumphant singing of those smart enough to find a hole in your mosquito net and the growls of the frustrated ones outside were enough to keep you awake all night. Mosquitoes in The Beni, the missioners say, are the brainiest of their whole tribe. They're the only creatures in the district who eat enough to be smart.

We spent Pentecost at Blanca Flor. Mass was celebrated in the school building which is a thatched mud brick place with walls about five feet high. We sat on the children's benches. The women filled the other seats and the men stood outside resting their elbows on the 5-foot wall. It was a Missa Cantata with three girls singing the Gregorian Mass—fruit of Father McCloskey's efforts when he was up in these parts.

It was my turn to be Officer of the Day. I was to produce the breakfast. I felt like the old Irishwoman who used to say, "If we had some ham, we could have ham and eggs, if we had the eggs." Our ship's commissary was certainly bare; nothing at all for a Pentecost breakfast. Only two eggs for ten people!

But leaning against the rail of our *alberinga* was a stem of bananas. Well, bananas are nourishing, the United Fruit Company ads tell us. So I served a breakfast that would delight their Home Ec ladies. This is the menu:

> Fresh bananas
> Fried bananas
> Banana Fritters (with my 2 eggs)
> Coffee

I hope your family likes it better than mine did!

Blanca Flor is notable for us because it is the site of a sociological experiment of the Maryknoll Fathers.

The site of the plantation is four miles inland. We walked there in the afternoon, accompanied by three-quarters of the village of Blanca Flor. Most of the time we had to string out single file treading the narrow jungle path beneath the great giants of the forests. There was nothing on the plantation site then. It had been cleared of big trees, however, no small job. It looked like a big field of high grass. It was here that 10,000 rubber trees would be planted.

Here, too, would be a quasi-boarding school for children from the hamlets all up and down the river. At the present population figures, it is impossible to provide each village with a school. The Maryknoll idea is to have the children come to Blanca Flor on Mondays and go home on Fridays. This will mean that they keep up their home ties and yet have a decent education. This is where we Sisters come in.

It will take years to get the project underway of course, but Father McGowan is young and enthusiastic. More power to him!

The next day, slipping fast with the current, was uneventful until late afternoon. Then—we passed a two-story house. You are not amazed? It was "a house upon a house," as the boatmen said. For years, this was the only two-story house in the entire Beni district, a territory, as I told you, as big as New York, Pennsylvania and New Jersey combined—110,000 square miles. It stands in majesty on the river bank, rearing its height about the foliage around.

The house has now lost its unique position. The Maryknoll Fathers put two stories on their Vicariate House in Riberalta and the new school convent there will also have two stories. These Americans! They build their skyscrapers wherever they go! Just to show you how unusual a two-story house is in The Beni—when plans were drawn for the Fathers' house, the architect forgot to put in any stairs. A year later, in designing the convent, he forgot again. As a result, the Fathers had to put in a sort of ladder from their recreation room downstairs to one of the bedrooms above. We Sisters are less agile and more artistic. We have a stairway built on the outside. It looks nice, but you get a trifle wet in bad weather.

CHILE

Antofagasta

Santiago
Curepto
Galverino
Chillan
Temuco

KEY

◆ 12 ◆

LLAMA MILK AND COCA-COLA

I looked at Sister Victoria Francis. Sister Victoria Francis looked at me. We both looked at the breakfast before us—and shivered.

We were in La Paz, only 16 degrees South, but 13,000 feet up in the air, very close to where Jack Frost cooks up his glaciers and icebergs and snowflakes. We saw evidences of his work sprinkled on top of the snow-clad peaks of the Andes seen through our window.

But I was not on speaking terms with Jack, just then. We had just heard Mass in a freezing chapel and lived through a half-hour's meditation there. My mind kept reverting to the thought that there might be some advantage in a good long stay in Purgatory. I think I'd like to get warmed up before I start an eternity in Heaven. Only the thought of hot coffee sustained life.

And now here was the breakfast. A plate of llama-milk cheese, two cupcakes and three bottles of Coca-Cola. Then, the Indian girl server brought steak and french fries. Goody! But one look at them showed that she must have started off at an early hour and gone down a few ski-jumps enroute from the kitchen, before she showed up at our door. Ah well, should missioners, at any time, shy away from steak and french fries for breakfast? And are Americans to condemn Coca-Cola? After all, we wished it on an unsuspecting world. That—and Bubble-gum.

Just how hard we wished it, is a good subject for meditation. Truly, it can be said "The children of Coca-Cola are wiser in their generation than the children of light." For, in the conquest of South America, Coca-Cola took over where Pizarro left off. It has finished the subjugation of the continent. Of the 23,000 miles I travelled, up, down, and over South America, there was hardly one which did not urge me at some time to "Drink Coca-Cola." "TOME COCA-COLA" say the signs. The school children carry notebooks with TOME COCA-COLA; the traffic police perform under umbrellas blazoned with TOME COCA-COLA; the electric signs in big cities cry out for all to TOME COCA-COLA; Indian women in the markets sit under sunshades which urge one to TOME COCA-COLA; even the pious ladies in church draw their mantillas over their heads and kneel in quiet prayer softly wafting a breeze generated by a COCA-COLA fan. Many and many a small town has saved a pretty penny by permitting the kind Coca-Cola people to print their street signs. As a result, one reads, "Avenida de Los Liberadores Tome Coca-Cola," "Calle San Martin Tome Coca-Cola," "Plaza de La Revolution Tome Coca-Cola." The Coca-Cola company performs the same kind office to mark One-Way streets in cities big enough to have a traffic problem. This is even more pointed. The signs read, "Una Via—Tome Coca-Cola." Small wonder that a shivering Indian high in the roof of the world, will spend his last Boliviano for the privilege of TOME-ing COCA-COLA! If Americans only had as much energy—and money—to spread the knowledge of God!

The little Indian server—Rosita was her name—was cute, in the old sense of the word. She spoke no Spanish, only her Indian dialect; so communication between us was practically nil. But she knew her instructions. "Never give a guest any coffee until he has eaten the last thing on the table." Furthermore, she was a woman of principle; she would not budge. Every time she looked around the screen, we went through contortions asking for coffee. But she noted with a keen eye that some of the llama-milk cheese was left, and half a glass of Coca-Cola remained. I tried slipping the cupcakes into my lap but she caught me at it. I had to pretend that they fell there by accident. Finally, the last crumb was gone. Still the coffee did not come. I was ready by then to finish up the plates and silverware, if that would earn a cup of coffee as well as a stomach-ache. Then she came, smiling shyly, with a silver pot of hot water and a small pitcher of *concentrada*. This is coffee brewed to a wicked strength and allowed to sit around for a few days to become confirmed in crime.

We were ready for her. We leaped upon the silver pot and wrapped it in as many sweaters, shawls and blankets as we had on hand. This was to conserve what warmth was left. At 13,000 feet altitude, water boils at a very low temperature. Furthermore, Rosita had walked leisurely from the kitchen at the other end of the building with the bare-naked pot exposed to a frosty breeze. Mingled with cream and cold *concentrada,* we feared that even the hot cup of coffee would have a rim of ice.

There is an old rule which Adam learned in the Garden of Eden: "Nothing worth while comes free." Cold coffee is a pittance to pay for La Paz. For sheer grandeur of setting, there is nothing like it. Hong Kong has a beautiful harbor; Manila's sunset over the Bay is stunning; Hawaii is unrivaled for sea, sky and green mountains. New York's skyline is a monument to man's ingenuity. But God Himself gave La Paz a skyline no man can hope to build,—a solid phalanx of snowy Andes.

The city cuddles at the bottom of a canyon 1,500 feet deep. It's a sudden cleft in that Altiplano which stretches 500 miles north and south through Peru and Bolivia. A cleft three miles wide and ten miles long. Cliffs rise from the city to the Altiplano. A modern automobile road wriggles up the cliff to reach the airport, the highest commercial airport in the world—some 14,500 feet above sea level. At such an altitude, the air is very thin. Planes must taxi two miles and more before they can lift off the ground. Then, they skim off the cliff and over the city, just as fighter planes take off from an aircraft carrier's deck. To the passenger, it seems like zipping right off the edge of the world. It's even worse when you are landing. You feel the plane losing speed and falling gently and yet there's absolutely nothing to land on. Then all of a sudden the cliff slides underneath you and you land like a bug alighting on the kitchen shelf.

We tramped around La Paz going from one education office to the next on business. But I'm afraid my business head was not in working order. For I had fallen in love. Yes, fallen in love with a hard, cold chunk of solid stone known as Illimani. A big thing, 21,000 feet high. A proud thing, rearing its snow-covered crown up to heaven itself. And yet, rather coy. You look up while trudging up a steep hill, and there is Illimani over the crest of the hill. You come around a dingy block of buildings and catch your breath; there is Illimani filling the end of the street. You walk the halls of a shabby building and find Illimani framed in the window of the first office you enter. You come out from church where you have had the grace to see a lot of fly-specks on your shop-worn soul. But there is Illimani radiant in his white mantle.

Even Illimani could not divert my attention from the Indians. These are the Aymará tribe. The women, as we've seen, wear derbies. The story is that, about a hundred years ago, a London manufacturer brought his overstock of derbies to South America. The Aymarás were fascinated with what a derby could do for a face. Horse-riding British women have known this for years. The Englishman sold out on derbies and went home to make more. There isn't an Indian in La Paz now who would be seen without her derby—indoors or out. In the Indian markets, derbies are stacked up high on tables, on the ground, on the saleswoman's head. Pink, purple, green, red, grey, or an ultra-conservative black. They perch over one eye, or tilt over the forehead, or loll toward the back. When you see one resting solidly between the ears, you know that it is probably serving as a hot-dish cover. Milady is carrying a piece of cheese, or her bagful of money, or even a dish of hot stew on her head and wants it protected by the derby.

La Paz is where you see the rich Indians—and haughty! I asked several to pose. They were glorious in shawls of delicate pink and green with long tassels of silk. Earrings encrusted with gems and filigree work gleamed against their dark skins. The derbies were glorious, sleekly brushed, and set just right to bring out the thickness of the two black braids of hair. They looked at me first with annoyance, and then with genuine aversion as they saw the camera. They walked away. Surprising, because nobody had turned me down before. But these Indians have a superstition that if a photograph of a person is destroyed, that person dies. They get around it by not having any photographs. In the market, I got one to pose only by promising to buy something.

La Paz was, for us, a jumping off place for Chile. We got on the train in the city itself. The hour or so of climbing up the cliffs to the Altiplano was torture for any kind-hearted person. Our poor little old engine, I thought, would have a stroke any minute. It wheezed and puffed and groaned and gurgled. Each chug might

be its last. We twisted and turned. We backtracked on our trail
again and again, getting ever higher. Finally, we emerged on the
high shelf overlooking La Paz. I got out and went up front to thank
the little engine. It was puffing easily now, but the fireman who
had stoked wood into its flaming mouth like mad all the way up,
was wiping his brow with relief. We gave the engine—such a
sweet little engine, nothing like our burly big Diesels,—an appre-
ciative pat and climbed aboard once more.

What a ride! All afternoon we zipped over flat land. This is
the southern end of the Altiplano. It was like being caught in the
middle of a giant mah-jong set where the snow-topped Andes form
the Wall of China. We were nearly three miles straight up from
sea level. Nothing but scrubby bushes showed above ground;
the eye travelled unhampered straight over to the mountain rim.
Llamas galloped away as the train whizzed by. The Indians were
muffled in woolen scarves up to their noses as they plodded after
their flocks. It was cold and got colder still as night fell.

At nine o'clock at night we had to change cars at Oruro, to get
into a *dormitorio,* or sleeping car. An awful scramble. We pushed
the baggage out the window into the arms of a couple of porters
while hundreds of Indians and Bolivians fought for a chance to
come into or get out of the doorway. For a while, I thought we
would have to follow the baggage out the window. But after some
forceful language and generous use of elbows, we got through the
door and found ourselves outside the car, sitting on our baggage.
You don't need Castilian Spanish in such a situation.

When *el dormitorio* was hitched to the train, we climbed
aboard and found our bunks. It was a cabin for four, two uppers
and two lowers. The other occupants were two women with
babies. There were no curtains on the bunks, so we had to be quite
simple. So were they and so were the babies. The only water was
a bottle-full on a metal washstand. It was so cold that we used
it sparingly and the other women, not at all.

During the night, I found our conductor stretched out on the
floor, in the corridor outside our cabin. He blocked it completely.
It was only about twenty inches wide. I stepped on what I hoped
was only a lump of blanket and proceeded on. Cold? It was freezing, bitter, biting, shriveling cold. It pierced you like an icicle

going straight through your ribs. I raced back to bed, taking a running leap over the prone conductor, and popped back under those covers like a jack rabbit into his burrow. I stopped just long enough to peek out the window. We were riding through white snow!

And we were no further south of the equator than Guatemala is north of it. Much closer to it, indeed, than Miami and southernmost Florida.

Seven o'clock found us still huddled in bed. So did eight A.M. And so did 8:30. But the baby started to cry on the next bunk and the women were stirring, so we gritted our teeth and heroically clambered out. Breakfast in the diner was served to people in fur coats by waiters muffled to the ears. The coffee steamed, the eggs steamed, our breath steamed. We took off our gloves only long enough to handle the forks and put them on again between courses.

We went back to the cabin and did a mummy act with every blanket on the bunks. I wrapped up Sister and she wrapped up me. The two young women in the cabin put on fur coats and snuggled the babies in under them. Sister Victoria Francis looked like a crustacean from the geologic ages. Only her eyes moved from a little peep hole in the blankets as she tried desperately to say some prayers. Some time, just for fun, try to turn a prayerbook page wearing two sets of gloves. Not so soothing to the disposition.

In mid-morning we realized that we weren't going through snow at all. The white stuff on the ground was nitrate salt. The scenery was magnificent. Those glorious Andes without a tree or a bush or a building to stop the view. It was so barren, so flat. We saw no animals and no men, for hours and hours. Often we skirted the shores of what must have been a lake in geologic ages but the whole surface was covered with a white crust of borax. You might think it a frozen lake, because sometimes there would be a small patch of water near the edge.

By this time, we were getting fussy about our mountains. In the beginning we would call excitedly, "Oh, look at that snow-capped beauty!" But a plethora of gorgeousness dulls the appetite. We merely remarked, "If you care to look, there's a rather nice one over there."

128

We went across the northern end of Chile all that day, although it's only 250 miles wide. At 10 P.M. we pulled into Antofagasta. For hours we had talked about the glorious hot bath we were going to get in the hotel. As I wrote before, the water in La Paz is just one degree up from an ice cream soda; the train was full of cinders with only a small bottle of water to wash in and to drink. Furthermore, the plumbing at Cochabamba had not been at its best before we left. We had plenty of reason to yearn for a hot bath.

So we ordered a room with a bath at the Plaza Hotel and happily followed the *mozo* to room #1, The Bridal Suite. An all too familiar sight greeted us in the bathroom. The tub was filled with water and a pitcher stood alongside so that you could dip out water for the toilet and washbasins. It was ice cold, of course. Well, the room clerk had said that for hot water, we should ring for a boy and tell him what we wanted. So we rang. A Dickens character answered.

"A pitcher of hot water, please."

"Huh?"

"A pitcher of hot water. Better make it two pitchers."

His eyes all but popped.

"Water?" he said. "There!" and he pointed to the tub full.

"Yes, but we want it hot."

This time his jaw dropped as well. "There is no water at all," he said. "Maybe tomorrow!" and he vanished.

The next day, we could understand his consternation. Antofagasta is perpetually on a water shortage. It's in the middle of the driest area in all Chile. The papers talk of nothing else; the people speak of it all the time. Somebody wrote into the papers about a group of Americans in a barracks of the Anaconda Copper Company at Antofagasta who had the initiative to drill a well on their property and thus secure adequate water. Why can't we all be like those *sobrinos de Tio Sam?* (nephews of Uncle Sam) the writer asked.

We had no bath that night, nor the next, nor the next. We had to stay three days at Antofagasta before we could get passage on a plane to Santiago. We were lucky. The Maryknoll Fathers tell of a group of new missioners who spent two weeks in Antofagasta and finally had to charter a plane to get them to Santiago.

Antofagasta is built on desert sand in more ways than one. The great Atacama desert which takes up the northern third of Chile lies in, around and under the city, and is sprinkled generously on the floors, chairs and tables of its houses. The greenery on the plaza and potted plants here and there put up a brave front, but everybody knows that Antofagasta is a desert town.

Wives and children of American engineers come here for shopping. Their skins are leathered by the unending sun and sand of the mining plants out in the desert. Derricks, tractors and trucks are unloaded from the ships. They stay a few days in Antofagasta. Then they, too, travel out to those camps to work until the bright red paint cracks and peels under the sun and the motor is clogged with desert sand. Grizzled prospectors come to town sure that they have found new deposits of copper, or zinc or nitrates which will make them fabulously rich. In their exhilaration, they often go for a ride.

We went for a ride, too. We hired a talkative taxi-man named Eugenio to take us around town. He showed us north, south, east and west in the city. Then just as the allotted hour was about to run out, he exclaimed, "I know what you ought to see!" With enthusiasm, he pressed the accelerator and zipped out of the city. It was an excellent road through desert sand. I was used to the hard baked clay of Peru's shoreline but this was real sand. It was like a beach, but so vast that eye could not see any end to it. The tawny hillocks were ribbed by the scorching wind.

Eugenio could drive as fast as he could talk. I peeked over his shoulder at the speedometer. 100, 110, 120 Kilometers—we were doing 60 to 75 m.p.h. The breeze tore through the window in front; our veils whipped out the back. Five, ten, fifteen minutes of this without meeting another car, nor seeing a single human being. I had visions of Mother Mary Columba back at Maryknoll getting a ransom note. "If you want your two footloose religious back, you will have to pay for them." And, possibly, she wouldn't be able to squeeze the item into this year's budget. Or the next. Years later, a prospector's donkey would stumble over two mummified corpses half buried in desert sand. . . .

Before I had given us a decent burial, Eugenio swung to the left. He left the concrete road and picked his way along a path of

sand a little harder than the surrounding drifts. After two miles
of this he stopped suddenly. A good thing he did, for we were on
the brow of a cliff overlooking the Pacific Ocean. Below us and
some little distance out was La Portada, an arched gateway worn
by the ocean in the soft rock. We feasted our eyes on the water,
blue, white and—wet! The pelicans wheeled and twirled above
and below us. How graceful they are in flight! Then of a sudden
one would flop down to the water in a queer disjointed fashion to
dive after fish, like a bag of bones thrown into the sea.

Eugenio was doing his duty by the scenery. But my mind was
too weary to follow his machine-gun Spanish. I'd much rather
watch the pelicans. We left the spot reluctantly and once more
zipped back to town. Eugenio stopped, opened the door and held
out his hand.

"450 pesos, please!"

I was amazed. "Why, Eugenio, the official rates are 150 per hour
and we were gone less than two hours. How come, 450 pesos?"

"Ay, madre," said the wretch with a gleam in his eye, "that is
for others. I drive fast. If I drove like them, it would take me three
hours. 450 pesos, please."

"You're a fast talker, too," I thought. "I can't think up Spanish
fast enough to outwit you." So we paid.

Eugenio could have used another point. His car, though of a
respectable age, was many years younger than other taxis which
line the plaza.

Besides, except for skirmishes here and there such as the one
with Eugenio, we had little to do, once the airlines office had said,
"No, there's no room for you on today's plane." There was a lovely
church on the plaza where we prayed. At other times, we took to
sitting on the little balcony outside our Bridal Suite and guessing
the vintage of the cars rolling by. We're old-timers ourselves. I can
remember when wire wheels and balloon tires were the latest
thing out. Before them, was the Wooden Wheel Era. There were
plenty of wooden wheels rolling past the Plaza Hotel.

Dictionary in hand, we read the daily newspaper. Sister Victoria
Francis says you can judge a city by its want-ads. She found somebody who was willing to give a 1925 Oldsmobile in exchange for
a hand sewing machine. That seemed to me a fair trade.

That there was a newspaper at all, intrigued me. Coming directly from Bolivia, where 85% of the people cannot read or write, I luxuriated in the sight of newsstands. What a joy to see bundles of newspapers put on and taken off trains! How thrilling to see people turn a page, poke it to get it straight, fold it over and settle down to read, just as they do at home! Newsprint is one of Chile's major imports; everybody reads in Chile.

On the train to Antofagasta as we sat in the day-coach waiting for our bunks to be made up, a young workman in overalls took the seat opposite. His guitar was slung across his shoulder and his fingers strayed stealthily over the strings—not actually playing but just fondling them. After a while, however, he settled down to serious business. He placed the guitar carefully on the rack overhead and took a paper-back book from his hip pocket. In no time at all, he was deep in *Los Ultimos Episodos de Nick Carter* (The Last Adventures of Nick Carter.)

Small wonder the Chileans read their newspapers! It's a pleasure to do so. The Age of Chivalry lives on in Chile's journalism. Newspapermen take time to say "Thank you" and to lay a few bouquets at each others' doors. Take, for instance, this version of a plane accident near Copiapo:

A PLANE BURNS IN THE AIR: 7 DEAD

THE ACCIDENT OCCURRED YESTERDAY,
AFTER 3:30, IN THE AIRPORT
OF COPIAPO

TODAY THEY BRING TO SANTIAGO THE
REMAINS OF THE 7 VICTIMS

A version of the Tragic Accident
Which was Given to Us by a
Colleague of the Periodical
"The Country's Friend"
of Copiapo.

[A regular news story follows; then,—]

Moments after having known the news of the tragic airplane accident of yesterday, we called on the telephone to the newspaper, "The Country's Friend" of Copiapo, in order to solicit greater details of the tragedy.

Our colleague, Senor Sepulveda, listened graciously to the request which we formulated to him, and gave out to us a complete version of what occurred, which we insert in this continuation, omitting, naturally, the data contained in other information which we give in these same columns:

[Senor Sepulveda's story follows]

In the end, our kind informant told us, a plane was expected in Copiapo to take on the bodies and to bring them to Santiago today.

Now, I ask you, who would not be a better man for reading this courteous exchange between two gentlemen of The Fourth Estate?

It was wonderful, too, to catch up on the baseball news—excuse me, the "beisbol" news, as they spell it in Spanish. Every major league game was faithfully reported in the daily papers. It is even harder to translate than the ordinary Spanish, because it is really English in disguise. H's are written as j's and the long i's become ai. It took some puzzling before I made out that Spahn of *Los Bravos* made a *jonron* against *Los Gigantes* before *an assistencia* of 21,539 *fanaticos*. Also I read that Harvey Haddix scored 5 *jits* against *Los Filis* and gave *Los Cardenales* a *triunfo* of 17–3. In Cincinnati, *Los Rojos* lost to Pittsburgh's *Los Bucaneros* who won the first game against *el pitcheo* of Paul La Palme.

Came the day! "Yes, you can take today's plane," the bright young man at the airlines office told us. And off we went, flying the thousand miles to Santiago.

Chile is easy on geography. The country is just a long string-bean, 2,600 miles long. If laid across the United States east and west, it would stretch from Seattle clear to Boston. In width it is laughable. Sometimes it's 250 miles wide, as at Antofagasta in the north. Sometimes it squeezes together into fifty miles. The average is about a hundred. Chile is so long and thin that maps of it have to be printed in columns like a newspaper.

There are three main parts, easy to remember—the North, the Middle and the South. The North is a thousand miles of sheer desert. Here are the copper mines, the borax deposits, the nitrate beds. Formerly, 95% of the world's nitrates came from here. Now they can be chemically compounded in commercial quantities. The rest is dry sand and a few people. Antofagasta is the big city of the North.

The South is a thousand miles of islands and snow and penguins and mountains reflected in cold blue lakes, as in Switzerland. It's great summer-resort country. The only business is sheep-raising; the wool grows especially long and heavy here as God protects the shivering sheep from the cold.

It is the Middle's six hundred miles which make Chile. Here are the rich wheat farms, the beautiful fruits and vegetables renowned all over South America, the green valleys lying at the foot of the snowy Andes. Here, too, are 85% of the people. All our missions are in this middle part, strung into line south from Santiago, each about 150 miles apart.

Down the entire length of Chile, run two mountain ranges. Behind it are the great Andes, back bone of the country. On the Pacific edge are lower mountains called the Coastal Range. The valley runs between them.

So you can see that Chile is like a shelf, a long, thin shelf which dips very far South. Indeed, much further South than Australia or Africa. Chile claims even a slice of Antarctica pointing like a piece of pie straight to the South Pole. Twelve Chileans live on it, too.

◆ 13 ◆

CHILE—THE CHILEANS LIKE IT!

"Buzeta? You want to go to Buzeta?" The taxi-man stopped his decrepit cab abruptly.

"Yes. Buzeta," Sister Marie Estelle said wearily. "Our school is in Buzeta."

"You will have to walk there, then, Madre," responded the cabbie firmly. "I don't go to Buzeta in the daytime. Much less in the evening."

"But the streets are not so bad now," Sister pleaded. "Why, the mud holes in front of our house were drying when we started out shopping this morning. I'm sure you can make it. But if you don't want to risk getting stuck in the mud, you can let us off at the main street and we can walk down the alley to our house."

But the man shut his mouth more firmly than ever.

"I'm not thinking of the street, Madre," he said. "I'm thinking of the people. A lot of tough characters live in Buzeta."

And he would not be budged. We had to get out, unload our packages from the car and hail a slow horse-vehicle to take us out to Buzeta. That's the kind of reputation the Buzeta district of Santiago enjoys.

I know there are a lot of tough characters in Buzeta. I had a vigorous battle with one on a Sunday morning. He was a duck we were to have for dinner. I had to call in reinforcements or he would have won the skirmish.

With only three Sisters in a house, it's a little hard to find time to do all the nice things one would like to do for guests. Especially when you have to play for the Sunday Mass, lead the choir and teach Sunday School as well. So I volunteered to cook the duck

135

for Sunday dinner while the three others flew around doing parish duties.

All went well until five minutes before the bell, when I started to carve the duck. Five minutes, ten minutes after the bell—while the others had finished grace and were sitting down—I was still in the toils. I was trying to wrench off a leg. But Buzeta ducks hold on to their parts with uncommon tenacity. I called for help. Sister Ann Walter clutched a wing, Sister Marian Therese the leg and I steadied the middle with a fork while they pulled with might and main. Eventually, outnumbered and outmaneuvered, the bird parted company with himself. He was Shredded Duck when we brought him in triumph to the table.

The exercise did me good. Santiago gave us our first touch of Old Man Winter as he hits Chile in June and July. He hits without mercy. The cold sinks right into your bones. You can pile on sweaters and prop your feet against the pot-bellied wood stove, but the cold stays in your bones. I burned the sole off my shoe that way— but my feet stayed cold as ice. Flannelette sheets and a hot-water bottle are standard equipment at night. Long woolies and sweaters inside and outside keep you going in the daytime.

At first, I thought the Fathers were always either just coming in from, or going out to, a sick call. They wore overcoats and mufflers all the time. Then I realized that in Chile, the priest dons his over-coat in the morning when he dresses and takes it off only when he goes to bed—if then. "I don't," Father Smith said positively. "I put it on top of the topmost blanket at night."

They tell of an Irish Columban who always said Mass with his overcoat under his alb. This sort of thing might account for the fact that the Sisters all look so strong and healthy. It's a bit hard to know, though, how much is Sister and how much is sweater.

In Chile, the law requires that children wear a white pinafore to school. Our children at Buzeta come to school wrapped in sweaters fore and aft, with the white pinafore over all of it. It's not a bad idea. The children are sewed into their clothes in March and ripped out in September. The white pinafore keeps the multitudinous sweaters a little cleaner than they would be without it.

Buzeta is a new section. So new, that it's just a collection of huts and shacks and tumble-down lean-to's that people put up until they can afford something better. About the handsomest thing in the district is the St. John of God School, put up by the Maryknoll Fathers as the parish school and opened in March, 1953. About 650 children attend, the boys in the morning and the girls in the afternoon. Three of "ours" (as the Jesuits say) are staffing the school together with many lay teachers.

But we do not stay in the nice school. Our business is to penetrate into the homes—to bring to them the material and spiritual help they need. For this reason, Sister Marian Therese took me on her rounds.

Sister is made of pioneer stuff. She comes of a large family in Willow City, North Dakota. A registered nurse, she visits the homes in Buzeta.

Off the street, we ducked through a narrow alleyway and found ourselves in the most noisome court I ever saw. Some twelve years of mission life in Asia and Hawaii had prepared me for this, but it could not be surpassed for utter destitution. A number of haphazard shacks faced a single yard, indescribably dirty. A horse stood in a pile of manure in one corner; an ancient car, bereft of tires and much of its body, stood beside one of the huts. It looked like a long-dead monster well-plucked by vultures. Three children under five stood near a puddle, blue with cold, for their little legs were bare and shivering. Their sore little noses needed wiping badly. Their hands were so chapped! A woman wrapped in a ragged sweater was hanging up clothes on the inevitable clothes line. Her hands were cracked with the cold. Several other women were puttering around their small wood fires trying to cook in large tin cans or broken pots. Their wooden-soled shoes squooshed in and out and around a muck compounded of rubbish, garbage and mud. It made one sick at heart to know that human beings have to live thus.

We were bound for Julita's house. The women were quick to help. "Right there, Madre!" they called, pointing to a lean-to holding itself up against the blank wall of a stable which faced another street.

Julita came out with the shouting. Her place was built like the traditional Christmas crib. Two walls were open to wind and rain. She had hung some dirty canvas from the corrugated tin roof to shut out some of it, but it was almost a useless gesture.

"Come in, come in!" she said, graciously as a queen, pulling aside the canvas to make an entry.

Benito—four years old—was lying in bed in a corner. He was wrapped in sweaters and wore no less than three woolen caps. His eyes were bright with fever. He was too sick to care much about anything outside his hot little body.

Julita was bundled in sweaters, too. On top was an apron with once-pretty ruffles which had been washed beyond all hope of bright color. Her eyes moved anxiously from Sister to the child and back again. Then, mindful of her duties as hostess, she threw a stick of wood on the open brazier and fanned it into a flame. She returned to the bedside and watched with her heart in her eyes.

Thanks be to God, Sister was able to look up with a cheerful smile. "He'll be all right in a few days, Julita," she said. "Just give him this, night and morning."

The other women crowded around the house. They had a few things to ask Sister, too. We had been in the district only a few months, then. It takes a while for neighbors to get to know you —and trust you.

It's not as easy as you think to gain the confidence of the poor. They have their standards. Oh, yes, they will swarm around and take your material aid and even—poor souls!—do a little bowing and scraping to please you. But you will not sweeten their bitter bread. Indeed, bitter bread is all the bitterer when it comes without love. The poor look through your eyes and read your soul.

St. Vincent de Paul, the great apostle of charity, knew the poor well. The movie of his life "Monsieur Vincent," quotes him: "You will soon learn that charity is a heavy burden to carry, heavier than the kettle of soup and the basket of bread—that you must keep your gentleness and your smile. It is not enough to give soup and bread; that the rich can do. You are the little servant of the poor, the maid of charity, always smiling and in good humor. They are your masters, terribly sensitive and exacting, as you will see. But, the uglier and dirtier they are, the more unjust and bitter, the more you must give them of your love.

138

"It is only because of your love—only your love—that the poor will forgive you the bread you give them."

For several months, Buzeta's women had been watching us. They saw us leave the big school each morning and walk the four blocks to church. They stood by stolidly when we tried to make friends with their children. It was a red-letter day for us, the morning that first little ragamuffin ran across the muddy street shouting "Madre! Madre!" running to throw herself into Sister's arms. From then on, Buzeta's tough characters began to soften. Like the folks from Missouri, they had to be shown.

The school helps a lot. You can form a bread line, or give out clothes, or run a clinic. Then poor people come to you, take what they need and go away. They are too involved with their own troubles to bother much about you. But in a school, they are touched in their family loves. A sweater given to Juanito quietly because Sister noticed that Juanito was shivering in the school yard—ah, that's a different sweater than the one Mama got when she stood in line at the relief agency. Sister's personal love for Juanito has gone into it.

One by one, the Juanitos and Juanitas have been led to the storeroom on the second floor and there outfitted with what they need. One by one, the Julitas have had help for their sick little Benitos. One by one, the poor women and children of Buzeta have come to realize that the Maryknoll padres and madres are there in Christ's name. And (which is the idea behind it all) they have found that God loves them each—each one, personally and intensely. In that, lies happiness and security.

Father Manning, in Talca, told us a story about his Boys' Town there. He was coming down from Santiago to Talca with a large number of blankets he had bought for his boys. The bus-man was grumpy about the load of blankets and almost would not let him come on with them.

"They are for poor boys in Talca," Father told him.

The bus-man grunted and sneered, "When did it happen that foreigners ever cared about the poor?"

Father said nothing. With bad grace, the man let the blankets be stowed in the rear of the bus.

Halfway to Talca, a bridge had been swept away by flood. All passengers and baggage had to ferry across the river where another bus waited to take them the rest of the way. Some boys were there, eager to pick up a penny as porters. The bus-man said to Father, "You'll have to leave those blankets behind. There aren't enough porters here for everybody."

One of the boys said, "We'll take the padre's blankets first and then come back for the other passengers' things."

"Oh no, you won't," the driver said. "We can't take the time for two trips on the ferry."

"Then we won't take anybody's," they said and sat down.

The bus-man soon capitulated. The boys took the blankets and came back for the rest of the baggage. They had lived at Father's Boys' Town in Talca at various times and told the bus-man a thing or two.

From that time on things were wonderful. The bus-man insisted on driving the bus right to the padre's front door and helping him off with his blankets. As he saw the boys eagerly seize them, his apologies to Father Manning would fill many a book.

Chilean people are cheerful. There's "Singin' Joe" for instance. Joe is handyman at the Chillan mission. His warblings enliven the atmosphere of labor. You never need to ask "Where's Joe?" Just follow the music to pantry or sacristy or rooftop. Joe doesn't get much done, but he's awfully good for morale.

In Galvarino one night as we walked home from church in the dark, we passed a young lad whistling a merry tune as he came home from work. Another time, our train slowly went over a make-shift bridge which had been constructed hastily after a flood. Two-thirds of the passengers—and that includes me—were leaning out the windows to watch the proceedings. I suppose we wanted to be partway out at least if the slender supports were to give way. The workmen who stood aside from the tracks had a gay time joking with us passengers about it.

There's such vibrant life and gayety in Chile!

Chilean gayety reaches a climax in the beloved *Queca*, the national dance. When you get a gayly dressed *huaso* and a vivid Chilean girl facing each other, quite spontaneously they break into a *Queca*. Others stand around, one strumming a guitar, while the two dancers wave their handkerchiefs at each other and stomp out the fast rhythm. At a certain point, everybody claps his hands in time while the dancers dance furiously.

You think you know Spanish? Come to Chile and take a tumble! Truly, one would think that everybody in Chile was talking through a mouthful of hot mush. Final s's do not exist, t's, b's, p's and d's are all the same. Even Sister Marie Estelle, after six years in Nicaragua, found it impossible to understand Chileans, at first.

Everything is "—ita" in Chile—even things far from little. After a while, you get used to drinking *cafita* (a little coffee) and *aguita* (a little water), to calling for a *cochita* (a little coach), and being a *Madrecita*—no matter how tall you are or how much you weigh. But, to the end, it is still a jolt to hear folks wish you *Buenas Dias-ita, Madrecita* (a little Good-morning to you) and, when they leave, *Hasta lueguita* (a little good-bye).

Sister Victoria Francis and I have a further grievance. During our stay in Chile—well over six weeks—she was known as *La Viejita* (The Little Old Lady) and they called me *La Bajita* (The Little Shortie). That simply didn't seem kind, even though they meant it affectionately.

No doubt of it, Chile has charm.

It does something to you to see broad fields, in which the curving lines the plow has made, stretch far off to a splendid line of poplar trees marking off one neighbor's farm from another. It does you good to see the two-wheeled carts piled high with big cabbages, carrots, radishes, and onions that make your mouth water; to talk to men riding majestic horses and wearing the *manta* which might well be an emperor's uniform; to sink your teeth into beautiful apples and oranges. And then almost anywhere in Chile you can lift your eyes to a panorama of snow-covered mountains. It is as if God has put a fence around Chile and said, "This much is My special property."

A great part of the charm of Chile, I've come to think, is that every Chilean thanks God from the bottom of his heart that he is a Chilean. He is tickled to death at his good fortune,—being born in that lengthy country which clings to the western edge of South America like the rind on a bacon. Or, as he would put it, like the gold leaf on the edge of a book.

The Chilean, no doubt about it, is very fond of Chile. And he doesn't mind saying so, as often as you will listen to him. Other South Americans want to hear about the States, but the Chileans begin with:

"Well! So you're a stranger! What do you think of Chile!"

He lets you murmur something about how beautiful it is.

"Yes!" he agrees. "The mountains and the sea! Have you seen our national flower, the *copihue?* Isn't it lovely! Everybody in Chile loves the *copihue;* we have it everywhere."

"The Chilean people are very progressive," you put in.

"Absolutely! You don't find people like that elsewhere, do you!"

There's no use trying to keep up with him. You only feed the flames of his enthusiasm. You have to admit, too, that he has a lot to be proud of.

Nonetheless, Chile has deep social problems. The same abysses which separate high and low, educated and ignorant, rich and poor in other countries, cleave Chilean society into the "haves" and "have-nots." Five or ten seconds in Galvarino, or Chillan, or Talca, or Antofagasta, or in wretched Buzeta, will show you that.

I saw a face in Chile which haunts me. It is the face of the corpus on a crucifix in the Augustinian church in Santiago. The story is that the crucifix once hung in the house of a Dona Isabel—a perfect harridan, the sort whose "piety" harms the Church. This immensely rich woman was noted for her temper and her strong right arm, with which, whip in hand, she used to beat her servants.

One day, she was beating a slave over nothing at all, when the Christus on the crucifix lifted His head and looked at her in righteous anger. I can well believe it. The life-size figure, nailed to the cross, has turned to the left. The eyes blaze, the brows are contracted, the lips are stern. It is the face He wore when He drove the money-changers from the temple with a scourge. It is His face as He said, "Ye hypocrites! Ye brood of vipers!" The blaze in those eyes scared Dona Isabel right down to her toes. I would love to have been around when it happened. The story is that Dona Isabel was an exemplary mistress after that. I should think she would be! Nobody who has seen the Christus in Santiago would relish having Our Lord look at him like that on Judgment Day.

We went out to Don Joaquin's *fundo* near Chillan one Sunday. There you can see the new type of *fundo* administrator. Don

Joaquin comes from a tremendous family, sixteen children I believe, which was once very wealthy. But one-sixteenth of even a big fortune is not much, so Don Joaquin has struck off on his own. He hired himself out to manage other men's *fundos* and is now in charge of three big places—hundreds and thousands of hectares. In addition, he saved enough to buy a *fundo* for himself.

Don Joaquin spends most of his time driving along the roads which Chile is less proud of. With three brothers priests (an almost unheard-of thing here), he is an excellent Catholic personally. He and his family are exemplary in Mass attendance and helping to support the Church. But what is more significant is his sense of Social Justice. There are other men who will let you bring poor children out for a picnic on their *fundo;* there are others who will provide a lunch for them and even let you use the *fundo* truck to transport them. But few *fundo* owners in Chile will give personal service to the half-starved kiddies we teach at San Vicente's parish, Chillan.

Don Joaquin was in the middle of the crowd, handing out buns and meat balls, laughing, joking, encouraging everybody to have a good time. His wife and children too were everywhere doing all they could to make this one day bright in the memory of Chillan's poor children. And, as the trucks filled up to go home, there was Don Joaquin stuffing the ragged pockets with candy and bread.

Sister Philip John got into conversation with the *huasos* (cowboys) who work Don Joaquin's *fundos.*

"How is he to work for?" she asked.

"Wonderful! Marvellous!" they answered.

His personal interest in their housing, their food, their families made him the idol of their hearts. You could sense it, too. I took a picture of Don Joaquin's little boy on his horse, a piebald pony. The men who captured the pony from the paddock, those who brushed him down for the picture and the man who lifted the boy into the saddle were all united with Don Joaquin in his pride as he saw his son sitting like a small Crown Prince on his mount.

Later, in the evening, we sat in their living room—a comfy room, with the upholstery rather worn and the cushions well sat on. Don Joaquin's bookcase of agricultural books filled a corner; a nice painting of Our Lady dominated one wall. On the table was

143

an old-fashioned glass bell covering a few artificial flowers. With its all-too-familiar pot-bellied stove, it was very much like the best parlor of a comfortable farmhouse of years ago.

Don Joaquin's energy was infectious. He took down his guitar from the shelf and fiddled around to get it tuned up. Then, with a roar, he burst into song, strumming and singing and slapping and stomping his feet like a whole band in himself. The children took it up quickly. They sprang to their feet and whirled into the good old *Queca*. Dona Bernarda put down her sewing and clapped out the rhythm. It was a family beautifully united and happy.

Next morning, Don Joaquin showed us his vineyards and his winery. The big vats were like gasoline tanks. Then he took us to where his special wines were stored. Shelves and shelves of them in all stages and degrees of goodness.

"And this," he said, holding a bottle in his hand, "this is very special, indeed. It will be the Mass wine when my son says his First Mass, please God."

◆ 14 ◆

KEEP IT DARK!

Curepto should not be written about. It should stay hidden in its pocket of rolling hills and keep very quiet, lest some prowling agent of Hollywood find it. The utter simplicity of this town would go up in flames in the bright light of publicity. And when it had died down Curepto, too, would be just like the rest of this burnt-out world.

So I'm not telling Hollywood about Curepto. Keep it dark.

Curepto is the kind of town where they hang a red flag outside the shops if there is meat for sale, and a white flag if they have bread. It's the kind of town where you must manage to get sick only on Mondays and Fridays, because the doctor comes from a bigger town thirty miles away on those days and opens up his little consulting office on Main Street. It's the sort of place where a stroll in the plaza after Sunday Mass is the bright spot of the week, for the band plays and you meet your friends and say a pleasant word and get all the news.

In Curepto, you observe the amenities of Christian life. If you see the padre coming slowly down the street and behind him a solemn group of country people carrying a coffin, you don't just go about your business. No, indeed not. You get off your horse and remove your big flat hat and stand respectfully aside until the simple cortege has passed. Furthermore, you say a prayer for the soul departed in the hope that when you die, God will be a little near-sighted about the shady deal you are embarked upon right now. Then you put on your hat, mount your horse and go on with the shady deal.

It's plainly a horse town. A jeep or truck only makes folk pull their oxen or horses aside and hold them steady until the infernal machine has gone out of sight and hearing. A few months ago, they had a flood which washed several houses away and even lifted a concrete bridge off its moorings and pushed it 300 feet downstream. That was excitement enough. But imagine—the government sent a helicopter to Curepto with officials who took note of the damage! That helicopter, to many old ladies, was far worse than the flood. Oodles of people in Curepto have never seen an airplane.

"There were two sticks on top of it," Maria Assunta described it to us, although we had seen the helicopter plain enough ourselves. "And the sticks went around very very fast. There it was in the air, Madre. Nothing but air under it. And yet it did not fall. Such a thing is not right, Madre. The devil is holding it up."

There are two old-ish ladies in town, too, who insist on addressing us as *Su Caridad* (Your Charity), just as we talk to kings as "Your Majesty" and to judges as "Your Honor." They were hard hit by the flood. It took their house right down the river, and all but took their lives along with it. They escaped through a window into a boat just as the house broke loose. Their theology could not stand up under such a calamity.

"Tell us, *Su Caridad*," they asked Sister Vincent de Paul. "What great sin have we committed that God could let such a thing happen? Wherein was our fault? Surely, we must be great sinners!"

Su Caridad was just as serious as they. They hunched forward in their chairs and she solemnly explained that the good must often suffer for the bad. They were comforting words, for the two good old souls had been going through a terrific examination of conscience. One last point remained to bother them.

"*Su Caridad*, tell us. When the *carabinieros* warned us of the flood, they told us to leave our old home and flee. But we refused. 'God will not permit our house to be swept away,' we told them. Was that wrong, *Su Caridad?* Perhaps, presumption? What should we do next time?"

Su Caridad wasted no time on that answer. "Go at once," she said. "The *carabinieros* are sent by God to tell you in time. You disregarded His warnings. As a result, men had to risk their lives to save you. The next time, go at once."

But Curepto is not all simple old ladies. We have folks who can turn out a good chair with a seat woven of *timbre* (rattan). We have a *farmacia* and several inns to put up the people who come from the *campo* for a day or two. We make our own clothes right here in town. If your horse needs shoes or you want your plow repaired, it can be done at the blacksmith's place.

We have stores, too, some pretty small but one of them quite big. Big enough for the owner (who is also the mayor) to make weekly trips to Curico for buying supplies. He gets some mighty nice things, too, and brings them to us in Curepto. He has connections with very important firms, as well. If you want to take the plunge and sink several thousand pesos in a sewing machine, why, Senor Rafites can take your order and get the machine delivered to you within a month. Quick, like that!

But in any of the shops you can buy candles or cheese, or a meter of cloth, or a new charcoal iron. You don't have to buy more than you need, either. The Señor or his Señora will sell you one or two safety pins as graciously as if you were buying a whole dozen, like some rich American. Or you can buy three nails and even borrow the Señor's hammer for as long as you need it.

Some of our shops have fanciful names. One was *El Pobre Diablo* (The Poor Devil); the chap thought, I guess, that customers would reason that a poor devil would be willing to sell cheaper than a rich one. Well, folks took to leaving the Poor Devil strictly alone. Then, too, the children were soon calling his little girls and boy, "The Poor Little Devils," and no Christian likes that to happen in his family. So he renamed the store. Since flirting with devils had been bad for business, he turned completely around. The new sign said, *El Cielo* (Heaven). It was much better. Soon after, we were in there one day buying an onion for the supper stew. The Señor showed us his cash drawer and, as he played around with the pesos in it, he said, "All of this since three o'clock this afternoon."

We have elegant people in Curepto, too. I stepped from the school door one day into the bright sun of the street. Rounding the plaza were a man and his wife on horseback. Young and handsome, the man wore a sleek black *manta* and broad black hat; a loose leather thong hung under his chin. His spurs were silver; his stirrups of carved wood. His horse—so beautiful in himself that he put to shame the handsome harness of tooled leather.

147

The man was impressive enough—a figure from a technicolor romance. But even more so, was his wife. She rode side-saddle, dressed also in impeccable black, her flat wide *huaso* hat set on top of pretty curls. In her arms was their baby wrapped in a white blanket. She rode her horse and carried the baby with the greatest dignity. I watched the two of them as they left Curepto's one main street. They broke into a gallop on the dusty road which led over the hills to their home far away on some isolated *fundo*. Small wonder Chileans can ride! They get used to the horse from the day they are born.

The women of Chile all ride side-saddle. Their mounts, those horses of which Chile is so justly proud, are gentle, intelligent, and graceful. The saddles are works of art. Rich tooling, bright red inserts, deep fleece to protect both horse and rider. Here one rarely sees a badly kept animal; there are no sores, no miserable bags of bones, no sad broken-down beasts. The horses may be muddy, but they are well fed and kept.

In Curepto, you drop back a hundred years. It is there you begin to realize that for the rest of the world they have not all been years of progress.

Curepto has also a tremendous enthusiasm for politics. The curbstones carry strident evidence of the last political campaign. Some of the paint on the sidewalks have been worn off, but the fire of the campaign is there still. There's quite a little debate painted on the plaza curbing.

"Viva Alfonso! He is with the Catholics!"

And the answer is right under it.

"Take care! There are devils walking around selling crosses. Vote for Ibáñez!"

Somebody else comes up with, "Catholics do not sell their faith either to atheists or to wicked politicians who make a business of religion."

It's a good principle but I don't know what side he is rooting for.

Faith, everybody agrees, is a good thing to have. It's like a bank account for a rainy day. You might not want to use it right now, of course, and it may even interfere with regular Sunday morning business with the *campo* people. But it's good to have a priest in town and he should be treated with respect. After all, you never know when your horse might stumble into a hole in the road some night and throw you into eternity, as happened to Don Alfonso not too long ago.

Right now the town is ringing with wonder at the marvellous effect of one look from Padre Francisco McKay. This is the story as he tells it.

"I was leading a funeral procession out of town," he said. "And of course, we blocked the whole street. That is usual. The people here figure that when you're dead you have a perfect right to block the street. There's never any question of right of way with a funeral.

"But this time a truck, driven by some fellow from another town, was honking and trying to mow down the mourners. When we came to the plaza, he tried to speed around and get ahead. I was at the head of the crowd with stole and candle bearers. The truck didn't make it. As he tried to come out ahead of me, I looked the fellow right in the eye. I couldn't say anything, because the words I wanted to say aren't in the funeral rubrics. Under my breath I was muttering 'Take it easy, boy. You'll be in a funeral yourself some day.' He pulled on his brakes with bad grace and sat back to wait until the crowd was past. Then he trailed us to the cemetery, hitting the road for fair when we had passed through the gates.

"The truck was full of people, jammed and crowded in the back as they do down here. It was top heavy. Well, about five kilometers further on, the driver swung out to pass an ox cart. He was going too fast and swung too far. The truck swayed from side to side as he sped on. Then on a perfectly straight stretch of road it turned on its side, killing seven passengers and banging up all the others. The fellow's in jail now, facing a manslaughter charge for reckless driving. But Curepto people know that his chief offense was disrespect for the dead."

Yes indeed. In Curepto, folks still know that death is the big event in any man's life. We're all heading for it, and we'll all want help when we get there. For that reason, when somebody is dying in one of the hundreds of tiny hamlets lost in the hills of this immense parish, everybody joins to help until the soul is safe in the arms of Mother Church beyond the grave. The first concern is to send somebody galloping into Curepto to fetch the priest. In past years, the old priests here could not take distant sick calls, but since the Maryknoll Fathers came, people know that any call for the Last Sacraments will bring out the priest, no matter where.

Sometimes it's Padre Juan Moriarity. Tall, thin, serious, he gallops through the roads in black *manta* and black hat, a spectral figure if there ever was one. He runs a race with death, beating him to the dying soul as he brings the life-giving Sacraments.

Sometimes it's Padre Jose Cappell on his motorcycle. The Padre is partial to that motorcycle. The wags in town say that he speeds out to care for a sick man but often returns carrying a very sick motorcycle. His spare time and his spare money (both very spare indeed) are spent in trying to rehabilitate the monster. They tell a story on Padre Jose that, one time, he was lost in contemplation viewing a lovely scene with hills and fields and a creek running along. "Like the view, Padre?" somebody asked. Padre Jose started. "Eh?" he said. "Oh yes. Very nice. I was thinking how I could throw stepping stones into that creek so I could carry my motorcycle across in case of a sick call out in this region."

We were out at a *fundo* one time—one of those big farms raising grapes for wine and wheat for bread. It was 25 miles from Curepto. One of the *huasos*—as they call the cowboys—took sick suddenly and died around ten o'clock at night. A ruptured appendix, it seemed to us. His name was—strange but true—Oswaldo. He had never worked hard at being a Catholic, but his last words were a plea for forgiveness.

There had been no time to get the priest from Curepto. But the man had not been cold for fifteen minutes before a messenger set out on horseback through the night to arrange for a funeral Mass the next morning. It was like seeing Paul Revere start off on his famous ride, to watch them open the big stable-yard gate and, as the kerosene lamps and flares lit up the scene, let out this lone rider into the night. His horse's hooves pounded off into the distance. We returned to pray for Oswaldo lying so stiffly on his wooden cot in the bunkhouse.

The funeral cortege of almost a hundred horsemen started before dawn. The body lay in a small black coffin. This was put on a stretcher-frame of supple young trees. Four men on horseback carried it on their shoulders—not in any solemn procession but galloping in perfect unison. Not a bad way, I thought, for a cowboy to ride to his own funeral.

We preceded them in nothing more romantic than a jeep. We got to town ahead and went to the church. Pedro, the sacristan, was watching from the church tower. He saw a cloud of dust on the road over the hills. "They're coming, Padre," he called down. Padre Juan donned his black stole and with two altar boys carrying the holy water sprinkler, went with a lighted candle to meet the body.

At the edge of town, the cortege's pace had sobered down. The coffin was lowered; the escort dismounted and tied their horses to the many public hitching posts. Someone pulled a cloth from his trousers pocket. He rubbed the dust from the black coffin until it shone. Somebody else brought from his saddle bag the silver handles and screwed them on the sides. The silver-painted wooden cross was stood erect on top; a few ornaments were screwed on the front and back. Oswaldo was ready to make an impressive entrance into Curepto. This was his last trip to town. The padre was there to greet him even if the poor fellow had never set foot inside the church on his other trips there.

The hundred *huasos* removed their broad flat hats and straightened their *mantas*. Leaving the horses tied, they formed a procession behind the padre and the coffin. With the slowest of steps, they inched down Curepto's main street. I could understand the irritation of the wicked truck driver who, even then, was repenting at leisure in the jail. No doubt about it, a funeral blocks traffic. No use going down a side street to by-pass it either. That would involve you in more mud than you would care to get into. No, better pull your ox cart to one side and wait respectfully until you can move again. That's what everybody in Curepto does. Even the ne'er-do-wells step from the tavern and stand with hats off. A bit wobbly, but observing the Christian amenities.

Yes, Curepto's alcoholics are not as other inebriates. Principio, our washwoman's husband, can witness to that for he is one himself. "Madre," he said to Sister Christopher Mary, "it is true that I am often in the tavern. But I drink up only my own money; only rarely do I drink my wife's money. Besides," he added, revealing the height of his virtue, "sometimes I help her with the wash."

Such is Curepto. A gem, a real gem, because the modern fretful world has passed it right by. Thanks be to God, it has. No visiting diplomats, no tourists, no newspapermen out for a hot story, ever bother about Curepto. For one thing, it's too hard to get to.

You get off the train at Curico, 130 miles south of Santiago. There, you look around in the milling crowd until you see two black veils rising above the heads. These are Sister Vincent de Paul and Sister Christopher Mary, two of our tallest Maryknoll Sisters. They make a good pair for Curepto, especially while they have no chapel in their convent and must slide down-hill to Mass in the church in the morning and climb up-hill for breakfast after it. They are both around five-feet-ten but that does not stop a certain dear old lady from calling them always *Las Palomitas* (The Little Doves).

It was nothing for these tall, queenly Sisters to take us two little ones under arm and propel us along. Well, we may have been *La Viejita* and *La Bajita* to the Galvarinos, but I was not going to pant alongside while two statuesque Sisters took majestic strides along a railway platform.

"Where to, so fast?" I asked.

"To the bus-carril! The bus-carril! It's waiting. Hurry. Or you won't get to Curepto at all today." That was enough. Even *La Viejita* did a very dignified sprint.

The bus-carril is a sort of trolley-car affair which runs on rails but has a Diesel engine. It goes from Curico, a city on the railroad which runs like a backbone down the center of Chile, to Licanten. You have to take a bus, or a horse, or a jeep, or your own two good legs to get to Curepto, thirty miles further.

The bus-carril was filled with soldiers, chickens, suitcases, men with big flat hats and thick mantas, and us. We zipped along those tracks, rounded the hills, tooted our horn, skimmed over mountain rills. All too soon, we left the sight of Chile's snow-covered Andes, and headed for the coast where rolling hills are all you can see of mountains.

Sister Christopher Mary was jubilant about the scenery, the people, the animals on the tracks. So was everybody. The whole carful took on a sporting event atmosphere. Killing cows seemed the objective. When the whistle tooted long and loud everybody stood up and craned to see what was on the track.

"Is it a cow?" the question goes around.

"No, only a turkey!" and the crowd begins to sit down.

"Did we get him?"

"No," looking out the rear door. "He's still walking around back there."

The bus-carril brought us to Licanten where Fathers Thomas McDermott and Francis Assenmacher are. They came two months ago to the most dilapidated church you ever saw. The rectory is just a shambles, a series of ancient rooms in a row, with a roof over them. Padre Tomasito is living in the parish office which alone has a lock and key. But he and Padre Francisco are working hard to put the place in order.

While the others were going through the overrun garden, I happened to find the parish books piled high on a table. I opened the old leather tomes expecting to find neglect, carelessness, and many gaps and so on. But I was amazed at the neat inscriptions. 1910, 1891, 1876, 1845,—back, back the books went with the handwriting changing but the items ever the same. Marriages, baptisms, burials all recorded faithfully.

"In the cemetery of Licanten, was buried on the 28th of July 1907, the cadaver of Juan Herrera, died yesterday, a native of Curepto, 55 years of age, husband of Crisostoma Mendez, legitimate son of Julio Herrera and Magdalena Gomez."

The sense of the Church as a vast body of souls, living and dead and yet to be born, came over me. Each individual personality created by God, each worthy to be recorded on the Church's books as it began and ended life, each a soul created fresh by God Himself by a separate impulse of His divinity—that's what we mean by the Church spanning the ages and embracing all men. So many of them, and yet each one so important! Here in this terribly unimportant spot of Licanten in Chile was the Church recording through the years, the beginning and end of every human life. And doing it faithfully for years and years on end. The church was a shambles, the rectory was falling to pieces. But the parish books were there and all in order. Small wonder that the Communist idea of The Masses—everybody in a big lump—is irreconcilable to the Church's ideas.

Padre Tomas, who is small and has a boyish face, has the nickname of *El Nino Jesus* wherever he goes. He looks so innocent, so young; but he can pack a jeep with dynamite. Into his all-weather buggy, he packed us four Sisters, himself and Father Francisco, as well as our baggage which had grown to alarming proportions as we collected souvenirs and would-you-minds along the way. Sisters Vincent de Paul, Christopher Mary and I (and the baggage, of course) squeezed into the back. As you know those two Sisters, you can understand how much of the seat was left for me. But I am not the complaining kind, thank God, so we went merrily over the hills to Curepto. At one point, we splashed through a little stream and took a jolt over a fallen tree. As I was putting my neck on my shoulders again and pressing the vertebrae back into place, I heard Sister Vincent de Paul exclaim with a deep breath, "Now, we're in our own parish! How good the air is!"

In no time at all we were rolling up the quaint streets of Curepto, 400 and more years old, with an old church, a postage-stamp plaza, and tons of men on horseback. A perfectly marvellous Spanish town. We saw a big crowd in front of one house. As we came along, the crowd broke into cheers. It was the welcoming committee consisting of children, priests, teachers, and the town band, blowing their hearts out with "Marching Through Georgia!" Blowing our ears out, too. But we loved it.

You never saw such a welcome. They made a legal holiday of it. They had to, because the Post Office had to close. Why did the Post Office have to close? Because some of the bandsmen work in the Post Office; they couldn't play in the band and work in the Post Office at the same time. Furthermore, they just had to play in the band because all the band's instruments belong to the Catholic School. In exchange for a more-or-less permanent loan, the band in courtesy plays whenever the Catholic School wants it to play. It's as simple—and as complicated—as that.

The mayor was there, too. Senor Rafites doubles in brass, so to speak. He is the leading political light, owner of the biggest store, and Curepto's best cornettist as well. He stopped tootle-ing long enough to step forward, shake hands all 'round, and then retired to his place in the band.

Sister Vincent de Paul and Sister Christopher Mary are so sold on Curepto that they thought we covered Lima, La Paz, Cochabamba, Riberalta and Santiago merely as way-stations en route to Curepto. To them, Curepto was our main objective when we sailed from New York four months before. And what we would cover from now on would merely be incidental stops on our way home. They couldn't see why we didn't settle down for a year or two, now that we had reached our trip's main objective.

You can't say anything too wonderful about the place. Sister Victoria Francis said, "What a nice plaza here!" Sister Christopher Mary picked it right up. "And you know," she enthused, "there's grass on it. Sometimes plazas in Chile don't have grass, but ours does."

Yes, such is Curepto. Not much of a town in the eyes of the big world; not much even in Chile. It has no great treasures of art or culture. No important products, no impressive personalities. But it has one thing it values highly. And that is the memory of Padre Tomas (Wellinghoff). He was their priest, Curepto's beloved young padre, who teased them and loved them and joked with them and corrected them until they gave their hearts and their souls into his keeping.

◆ 15 ◆

NOT A THING FOR HIMSELF

Know Padre Tomas? Of course, I did! He was my best friend. Absolutely, my best friend. Though, come to think of it, you'd be hard put to find anybody here in Curepto he wasn't the best friend of.

I was here when he came, a fresh young padre straight from the States, with the gringo accent heavy on his tongue. We weren't too happy then to have a foreign priest. He might change our old easy-going ways. I was here also on that sad Sunday morning when they announced in Church before the Mass, "Padre Tomas died suddenly of a heart attack half an hour ago. Please pray for his soul." I still hear the gasp that followed—the silence before we sank to our knees. It wasn't that the parish had lost a pastor. Each of us had lost his dear son. And yet, though it seems strange to say it, as we looked on that young face in the white stillness of the coffin, we knew we had lost a father too.

It's only on looking back that you can see how he was a father to us—correcting us, guiding us, pushing us firmly into the right path. You wouldn't think, to see him riding down main street with his cape flying out behind, with a hand lifted in greeting to everybody, from the smallest *chico* playing in the mud to the rich old mayor himself—you wouldn't think that he took his job as spiritual father seriously. He had the nicest way of doing it.

"You're just like my own mother," he told my senora, on his very first visit to our home. "Let me call you Mama!" I don't remember now that he even waited for her answer. We're not the priesting kind of a family. Don't know of any priests on either side, at all, at all. But from then on it was "Mama" every time he crossed the threshold.

156

My old lady's not so well. She takes medicine for her liver right along. I remember well that Padre Tomas got to questioning her about it. It was pretty plain, I guess, that we didn't have too much money and he probably knew (as everybody in town knew) that most of my pay went to the tavern. Heaven help me, that's the way it was! Well, Padre Tomas said to my old wife, "Mama, I'm going to Santiago next week. I'll get you some of that medicine there."

My back began to stiffen and so did Luisa's. We're poor and I have my faults, I know, but still we're not letting strangers. . . .

"Padre," says Luisa slowly, "my senor can buy what I need."

Padre Tomas laughed aloud. He came over and gave my senora a big hug. "Of course, he can!" he said. "Of course! But you're Mama to me here in Curepto, so let me have the happiness of getting medicine for my Mama."

Claro! It was so plain. A man has the right to get medicine for his Mama, hasn't he? You couldn't get insulted at that, could you? All the same, it stung me that my wife's medicine came from another pocket than mine. I thought of it the next time I went into the tavern. I thought of it—and marched right out the door with my pay squeezed tight in my pocket.

But that's the way he was. Never any sour looks. Smiling and laughing that big all-over laugh all the time, but firm and steady underneath. A number of fellows used to hang around outside the bar. When they saw Padre Tomas hurrying down the street, they'd call,

"Come over and have a drink, Padre!"

He'd wave and laugh. "I'm in a hurry now, boys. Can't do it. But I'll be seeing you later."

Everywhere he went people loaded him down with gifts. His pockets were always bulging. Then he'd go into Old Magdalena's home next door to ours and say, "Look what I found on the bush outside your door. You've got a wonderful plant there, Magdalena. It grows buns and oranges and meat loaf all on the same bush!" And Magdalena would say,

"Now, Padre, the people give you those things for yourself!"

"They gave it to the wrong fellow, then," he'd reply, filling up her cupboard as if he lived there and had a right to go to her cupboard at any time.

157

And so he had! He was in and out of our houses like he owned every one of them. No one ever thought to invite him in any more than you'd tell your brother he was free to come in. He knew it without anybody's word.

He knew us so well, he never stood on ceremony. Said just what he thought and never tried to act like a guest when we all knew he was one of the family. That's how he cured Maria Lopez of her quick temper.

Maria's a wonderful woman; don't let anybody tell you different. She's been a school teacher here for twenty years and supports her mother by it. What's more, her sister Josefina isn't quite right in the head, so Maria does sewing on the side to pay for Josefina's staying in an asylum up in Curico. Maria gets to know about many poor children in school. In a quiet way she gives them things they need; two of them she took into her house and brings them up as her own. So you see Maria's a fine woman. But she does get mad at people, and stays mad for a long, long time.

Well, Maria was real good to Padre Tomas. He liked to go over there for dinner and jolly up her old mother who's always complaining about her aches and pains. Then one day, Maria killed her pig and she sent Padre Tomas the head as a present. That's the custom in our town. When you kill a pig you divide it among your friends and they do the same for you.

Padre Tomas sent the head back to Maria with a note. "Why don't you cook it for me, too, Maria? I'm coming over tomorrow night and we'll enjoy it."

Now Maria's a good cook. She does things in the Chilean way. This head she was going to make extra-special so she put in a lot of *ahi*. *Ahi* is a small plant, but is it hot! Padre Tomas took one bite and all but spit it out.

"What are you trying to do, Maria? Poison me?" Then he started joking with her mother, "How I pity you, Senora! To live with Maria, the worst cook in Curepto!" and lots more of the same.

Maria started to boil inside. Poor thing, you can see her side of it. Working all day over a special treat and then being called the worst cook in Curepto. She flounced out of the room in a rage.

Padre Tomas thought she'd get over it, but things began to look serious when she did not go to Communion for three days. She, who was a daily communicant for years. So the Padre sailed right into the battle. That was his way when he saw things go amiss.

"I've missed you these mornings, Maria. You're in church but you don't receive Our Lord."

"I can't." Maria was stiff as a board.

"Why not? Come on, out with it, Maria."

"If you must know, Padre," she said, "I'm mad at you. Terribly, terribly mad. So mad, that it's a big sin."

Padre Tomas laughed again. "I'm not that important, Maria. Being mad at me is no big sin."

"I'd have to go to confession, Padre. And I won't go."

"Well, if being mad at me is all you've got on your conscience, don't bother to confess it. Lots of good holy people get mad at me. Go on to Communion, Maria."

She did, but she was still pretty stiff. A couple days later he went to visit her mother. Maria opened the door for him but disappeared right away. Padre Tomas gave her mother a crucifix. "This is for you, Mamita," he said in a loud voice. "And there's another for Maria when she learns not to get mad over nothing."

It was that night Maria sent him a big dish of pig's head—without *ahi*.

I don't think the man ever rested. He seemed to be going all day around Curepto or up in the hill district of this big parish. You'd see him in the morning after Mass visiting the school, giving out report cards or seeing about some rapscallion who was causing trouble. Then he'd be out meeting a funeral and walking down the village street in black stole. Next you'd see him chatting with the market women and going away with his pockets stuffed. (Poor fellow, he gave it all away; he ate like a sparrow when he was by himself, his housekeeper said.) His cassock was out at the elbows and his shoes were only uppers. "I like a man with his feet on the ground," he used to answer when we joked him about it.

Then you'd see him in the middle of a bunch of boys. He took them down to the seaside for two days, once, and spent 600 pesos for ice cream cones. The boys will never forget it.

At night, often, he'd thunder through town on his big white horse flying out to a hut 25 or 30 kilometers away, where some poor fellow was giving his soul back to God. Before he came to Curepto, we never called the Padre at night nor did we ask him to come long distances. But Padre Tomas let it be known that he wanted to be called. "Just let me know," he said. "Any time, any place, for anybody. We all need help when we're dying."

I went with him on a week-end trip, once. That's how I know he was a man of iron. I'm no softie myself, but I couldn't go at his speed. We left Saturday after he was through hearing confessions in the afternoon. We rode 40 kilometers through bad mud to *La Hornilla* (The Little Oven), arriving around midnight. I turned in, but Padre Tomas sat up awhile saying his prayers by the light of a candle dip. In the morning when I woke, he was busy hearing confessions before the Mass!

After breakfast, he started around visiting the sick who couldn't come. He knew all their names and all their symptoms.

"Let's go up to see the L-Shaped Lady," he said when I was all for getting back to have dinner and a bit of rest.

So we went. And went. And went. Climbing up a steep hill to the last house in La Hornilla. There was Old Juana bent, just like he said, to the letter L. Padre Tomas started emptying his pockets. "I know who has a sweet-tooth!" he exulted. "I got a package of candy from my folks in the States. 'This is for my friend, the L-Shaped Lady,' says I. So here you are—candy and cookies. That's what my good friend Juana is made of."

She was delighted! Padre Tomas was on his knees before her because the old lady was so bent over she could not see his face otherwise.

"Ay, Padre!" she cackled over toothless gums. "Sugar and spice and all things nice. That's me. But I'm not always so sweet, sorry to say. Oh, I knew you wouldn't come to La Hornilla and not be up to hear my confession."

That's the way he was. He heard her confession and we went back to get our mounts. We were due at Concepcion, 10 kilometers away, to hear confessions and say Mass the next morning.

It was dusk when we came into town. It was "Hello!" here and "Buenas noches!" there all along the street. "How's your baby?" to one and "Mass is at 7," to another. He was hardly down from his horse when he started off again to visit the sick and arrange to bring Holy Communion to them. Me? I was all in! I saw to the horses, ate a bit of supper and went to bed. I remember waking up during the night and hearing Padre Tomas and our host, Don Ramon, playing cards.

Does that shock you? Oh, Padre Tomas was a whizz at any card game. Don Ramon wasn't very much of a Catholic. In fact, hadn't been to church for years even when the Padre brought Mass right to his front door. But he loved cards and Padre could play them. He got him, too, over the card table. It wasn't a year before Don Ramon renounced his Masonry and came back to the Church.

The best trick Padre Tomas ever played came just about a month before that fearful announcement in church on Sunday, November 20, 1949. It was right that the Good Lord let him have that last fling, seeing as how He was going to take him so soon.

Each year in Curepto we elect a Queen of the Carnival—sort of a Queen of the May. For us, down south of the Equator, November is the month of Our Lady. Everything's springtime then. It's our loveliest month.

The Queen of the Carnival contest is run by the township to make a little money for the public works. Whichever girl can sell the most votes wins. With a system like that, it's plain that the richest girl will win. It's always been that way in Curepto and we common folk didn't mind it too much. We're used to it.

But Padre Tomas was different. He determined that a poor girl would be Queen. He chose a policeman's daughter, Teresa, a nice girl and pretty as a picture. For a time, in the early days of the contest, he let her work hard selling votes to her friends. But soon, she was running a very bad second to old Don Carlos' girl, because Don Carlos could hang a sword over many a man's head if he didn't buy votes from his daughter.

Padre Tomas went to the police chief then. "Look here," he said. "It's up to you *carabinieros* to put Teresa on top. But let's not let Don Carlos know. You get votes from every man on the police force for Teresa and I'll get them from the parish school. But we won't reveal them until the last minute. That way, Don Carlos won't have time to throw in more votes for his girl."

The last night of the contest everybody was in the town plaza. The mayor was getting in late votes and reading out the score. Don Carlos was away out in front; so far out, he felt mighty sure of himself. It was just like every other year. The contest was closing in another minute, when Padre Tomas stepped over to the rostrum and handed a packet of votes to the mayor. You should have seen his face!

"But . . . but . . . but . . ." he sputtered.

"No buts about it, Your Honor," the Padre said. "These votes are for Teresa and they're in before the deadline."

The mayor in a trembling voice read out the score, afraid to look at Don Carlos. Teresa's score made everybody else's look like a dead fish.

The town went mad with delight. We never knew before how much we really wanted a Queen from one of ourselves. Teresa and her court were everybody's darlings. There never, never was such a fiesta in Curepto. People came from a long way off to sit in our plaza and watch the happy faces of us all. It was a poor man's fiesta. As they say, God must love poor people because He made so many of them. That fiesta was the best Curepto had ever known.

Padre Tomas was tired, I guess, although he kept going the same as always. Every evening he had devotions in Church for *La Mes de Maria*—like the May devotions you have up North. He had funerals, weddings, baptisms, sick calls, and mission trips. Then on Saturday, the 19th, he carefully prepared his sermon for the next day. It was on the Last Judgment. He went to bed late, as usual. Around 5:00 next morning Padre Martin heard him call. It was almost too late to get the oils and administer Extreme Unction. In half an hour, Padre Tomas was dead. Dead, at thirty-two years! Padre Tomas was dead.

Can you imagine how we felt? Can you picture us in church as we came to Mass that Sunday morning and heard Padre Martin say,

"Padre Tomas died half an hour ago. Let us now pray for the repose of his soul."

They kept his body four days in church, dressed in the Holy Mass vestments. People came in and went out, came in and went out all day long. Me? I stayed there. In a corner of the church I watched them come and go. *Huasos* from the *fundos* far away rode up to the church door and left their dusty sweating horses tied to a pole while they knelt beside his bier. Children wandered in after school hours and said the rosary on their fingers for him.

"He gave me a haircut," one boy boasted as a group went out. "He pulled out this front tooth!" said another. Old and young women were there all the time looking at his clean strong features and thinking of his mother so far away. "He said I was just like his sister," I heard them say. "And I was like his aunt." I smiled to myself. Padre Tomas' relatives sure looked like a lot of different people!

Don Carlos came in, too. And the mayor. The two of them forgot all about the contest. Nobody was ever mad at Padre Tomas long. Not even Maria.

Wednesday we buried him in the little cemetery outside of town. The crowd filled our main street, and surged along the road up the hill. I thought of the hundreds of times Padre Tomas had climbed that hill to consign one of us in Curepto to his last resting place. And now we were trudging after his coffin. The Bishop of Talca was there and twenty-five of his fellow priests from Maryknoll. The Mayor and city treasurer, the *fundo* owners, the store-keepers, the school teachers and their children. *Huasos* and country people, farmers in their ox carts, and of course everybody who lived in Curepto. There were thousands in our town that day. It was the biggest affair Curepto had ever seen.

The band was out, too. Now we are mighty proud of our band. It has won more than one medal in the provincial contests. But when it was time to play while the body was being lowered into the grave, Pablo the clarinettist couldn't find his reed mouthpiece, and the band had to play on without him.

This was serious for Pablo. The mouthpiece is small and you can't get them anywhere but in Santiago. Poor Pablo turned his pockets inside out and searched the tall grass in the cemetery long after the crowd had gone. Juan the bandleader helped him search. A band without a clarinet isn't much good. But it was no use. Then a sudden inspiration seized Juan.

"Let's ask Padre Tomas to help us find it, Pablo," he said. "Surely, even up there above he can't forget us in Curepto."

Down the two of them went on their knees in the freshly turned earth. Then they turned to go home.

"There isn't much use looking," Pablo said as they plodded home in the thick dust which thousands had trampled that morning.

"And yet I can't help hoping . . ." And there it was, as plain as day, sitting on top of a rut in the road!

That's why, here in Curepto, when a child loses his school pencil the Mama will say, "Pray to Padre Tomas. He helps careless boys to find their lost things."

That's why, too, you will find in any hut in this wide parish a little picture of Padre Tomas tacked to the wall and sometimes there's a candle in front of it.

Padre Tomas lives with us still even though four years have gone by since he died so suddenly. His spirit is part of us. He never kept anything for himself. Not even the love we gave him. That, he gave to God. It was not because we loved him for himself that we went to Mass oftener and tried to live better lives. That's proved because we are still going to Mass and still trying, even though another priest has taken his place. No, Padre Tomas took nothing for himself. Not even our love.

◆ 16 ◆

ONE HORSE TOWN—ONLY IT ISN'T

Supposing—foolish you!—you took up a dare to swim around the world. Supposing furthermore that you were a little boy in the town of Galvarino in Chile, which sits squarely on the 39th parallel South. Let's call you Pedrocito.

Well, Pedrocito wades out into the icy ocean and starts swimming. He swims and swims and swims. He meets nothing. Absolutely nothing. In due time—that is, if he has had his Wheaties that morning and enjoys the athletic prowess they claim to produce, —he will skim along south of Australia. There is nothing but the island of Tasmania off New Zealand, between brave Pedrocito and the ice masses of Antarctica. Thousands of miles further on, he will pass far south of the Cape of Good Hope in Africa. Making a final dash for it, our hero follows the 39th Parallel until he is back home in South America, this time in Argentina, south of Blanco Bay. I hope his mother is there with a good cup of hot cocoa, for believe me Pedrocito will need something to warm up his little insides.

Pedrocito has proved nothing, except that the great big land masses on earth are all north of his home-town, Galvarino. By the time the Southern Hemisphere has gotten 39 degrees South, it has pretty well petered out. Up North, 39 degrees is right in the middle of everything. In the States it is around Baltimore, Kansas City and Denver and not too far from Sacramento. In Europe, it runs through Spain, Southern Italy, Greece and Turkey. There is a lot of inhabited land north of that!

The North Pole is jostled by any number of countries—Greenland, Canada, Russia and Scandinavia. They all crowd around it. But Antarctica sits by its lonely little self with only South America extending a cold finger of welcome as far south as 55 degrees. Why, in the North, 55 degrees is nothing! All of Scotland is above it. Germany is just below it. Denmark and Lithuania, too, not to mention obvious places like Alaska and Finland and most of Russia.

So little Pedrocito probably has earned himself only a scolding. Having gone completely round the world, he has seen nothing to boast about to his school mates.

Maybe because the South Pole is so lonely, he comes visiting in Chile around June and July. Between you and me, I think he sets his suitcases down for a good long stay right in the community room of our two-Sister convent in Galvarino.

You never heard of it. Of course! You can't find it on a map. Of course! Galvarino, like one of those stars scientists are always discovering, has to be located by mathematical deduction. You go 55 miles west from Temuco. At the end of the fifty-fifth mile, you may not see anything as yet, but you are in Galvarino. Slowly, the town comes to view. That's the way it was with us.

Father Joe Smith stopped his pick-up truck (a fiery red!) at the crest of a hill. He rested his arms on the wheel and turned to Sister Victoria Francis and me beside him in the cab.

"Well, you're here," he announced.

"Here?" said Sister Victoria Francis. "But I don't see anything."

"Look carefully down there," Father went on. "See that little river? Follow it. Along the shore you will see a white house. That's the biggest building in town. It's the Maryknoll Sisters' school and convent combined."

I wish I could call Galvarino a one-horse town. You might get a good picture of it that way. But, to say truth, there are plenty of horses in town. You see them tied up in front of the general store, or coming pellmell down the street with a slim boy on top, his colorful *manta* trailing out behind him. It throws you back to another era to wake in the night to the sound of hoofs galloping past your house. You feel like grabbing your trusty blunderbuss, and rushing to your neighbor with "To arms, friend Patriot; the British are coming!"

This is a town with no jeeps, no cars, no movies, and no pavements. It has a modicum of electric light (a mild blink for the night hours) and of wood-fires. But in a big way it goes in for friendliness, zest for living and bright-eyed children. Just between you and me I love Galvarino. I would be quite content to number myself among its 1,500 inhabitants, to spend my days walking around its mud puddles and my nights bedded down under a warm *manta*. And at the last, I would like my dying eyes to sweep over its rounded hills of wheatfields. Not bad living, I would say, and not bad dying.

There's something about Galvarino, as in so much of South America, which puts you back to Wild West days in the States. Maybe it's the hitching posts outside the stores on main street. Or the blacksmith shop next to the church. Or the sign showing a scissors and a hair clipper which tells the unlettered that here is a barber shop. It may be the big hats on the cowboys, or *huasos*. And the sight of a bearded old fellow coming into town from some hide-out in the mountains. They all add up to a definite Wild West feeling.

There are feuds, too. Sister Petrona came up from school one afternoon.

"That Romualdo!" she said. "Why didn't he tell me sooner?"

"Tell you what?" I asked.

"Just this afternoon he came late to school. 'I was taking care of my father,' he said.

" 'What's wrong with your father?' I asked. Then he told me. Last Tuesday in class, another sixth grader said to him, 'You had better go get your father. He was in a fight this noon. The other men left him all but dead over on Independencia Street.'

"Romualdo left right after school and, sure enough, there was his father lying in the mud of Independencia Street in a pool of his own blood."

"What was the fight about?" I asked.

"Oh, it's an old quarrel. A year ago his daughter, Romualdo's sister, went off with the son of a farmer's family. Her father says she was stolen but the other family insists she came of her own free will.

"Romualdo did his best. He got his father on a horse and took him home. The mother had gone away for a few days; the boy himself took care of his father. But he hasn't missed a day of school. Early in the morning, during noon time, and right after school, he nursed his father back to life. It was only today when he came a bit late that the story came out."

Another time, a man was killed in a brawl in a town some ten miles or so away. Chilean law requires that every dead man be examined by a coroner before he is buried. So the brawlers put the body upright on a horse and tied it to the saddle. Then they lead the horse the ten miles to town. I saw the cortege going past our school with the dead man's arms tied around the horse's neck and his head lolling in the horse's mane.

Things like that, however, do not make up the warp and woof of life in Chile. Like the early days of our West also, is the warm family spirit in the parishes. I noticed Sister Rose Andree (one-half of the Maryknoll Sisters' forces in Galvarino) frosting a cake one afternoon. But it was a mere sham of a cake—just an edge about an inch thick. And the frosting was only on one side.

"It's for the program tonight," she explained. "The Catholic Action group is putting on a welcome for the new pastor. One of the skits requires a cake on stage."

What a program! As I say, Galvarino boasts no movie theater. It has no civic auditorium. The only place is the big room which used to serve as the church before the modest wooden one was built about ten years ago. I think not one of the whole 1,500 in town was absent that night, jammed into this room.

Being visitors, we had seats of honor. I found myself sharing a small wooden bench with the Mayor's wife. I was never one to let the niceties of Spanish grammar interfere with getting information. In no time, we were chatting like old friends—just as if she knew what I was saying and I knew what she was saying. God is good! Often, just as I was going down for the third time in the rapid-fire Spanish, she would say something taken right from the Spanish-Phrase book I studied on the way down. An old friend like "What a pity," or "The child has four apples," or "In Chile, the mountains are beautiful," popped up in the conversation, and I could murmur a, "Si, Senora," with heartful gratitude.

There's one piece from that Spanish-Phrase book that haunted me. I was dying to use it and never had a chance. It was:

"Permit me, Madam, to assist you across this intersection."

To which, I was to answer,

"Thank you, Sir. You are very kind. One might easily lose one's life in the heavy traffic."

One can just picture the situation. I am a nervous little body standing on the curb and clutching my worn leather valise. The drays and horse cars, the whizz of bicycles, the heartless rush of a city's throbbing pulse, confuse me. Alone in the metropolis, I have no one to aid me. Then, a gentleman in derby hat, stiff collar and the most gorgeous handlebar mustaches steps beside me. And he says it!

"Permit me, Madam, to assist you across this intersection."

And I am right there with the answer in flawless Spanish.

"Thank you, Sir. You are very kind. One might easily lose one's life in the heavy traffic."

But, as I say, I never had a chance to use it. Usually, like now, I was seated beside a woman who talked Spanish like a woodpecker going at a tree, and there wasn't one word in it about intersections or traffic.

Behind us, the crowd was vociferous. Some few benches were sat on, but most were stood upon. Women and babies stood all along the walls. Young fellows hung from the ceiling, it seemed. Older men jammed in the windows, making them as air-tight as if they had been sealed up with bricks. It was winter, and most of the people had been sewed into their clothes in March and would not be ripped out until September. Added to that, was Mrs. Mayor's perfume which would have set her back a pretty penny at Woolworth's.

But this was the big show. Peanuts and cookies passed from hand to hand in grand good humor, even though many of the audience were parishioners by right of Baptism only.

Mrs. Mayor was one of these. At least, she gave herself dead away. When the two priests made their entry to the hall, she stood up and clapped like everybody else. Then she turned to me.

"Oh tell me, Madre! Which is the new pastor?"

The skit which starred Sister Rose Andree's cake, was really good. A wealthy man-about-town attired in wide flat hat and brilliant *manta* is seated at a table on which rests the cake. He calls his secretary and dictates a letter to his lady friend. It is to go with the cake as a present to her.

"*Querida amiga. Coma*"—he starts. Now "*Coma*" in Spanish means a comma, but it is also the imperative for "Eat!" Every time

169

the man indicates a comma, the secretary helps himself to a bite of cake. The business man has his nose in the daily paper and does not notice the cake slowly disappearing at each "coma." At last he says, "Take this cake and the letter to Senorita So-and-So."

"What cake?" says the secretary. And they do a good old Keystone-Kop-Komedy chase around the stage.

There was nothing of great drama about this—but the audience loved it. Loud huzzahs came from the ceiling and the windows and every bench in the room. Even the Mayor and the two priests, seated in state on three wicker chairs up front, went wild with delight.

Next came an orchestra—a guitar, castanets and accordion. Like three undertakers, they stood there not bending a muscle, while they played the jiggiest dance tunes you can imagine. One would think they couldn't keep their feet still. I had trouble controlling mine. They maintained funereal calm throughout. They were on the program for three numbers but tried to stop after only two, in spite of tumultuous applause. A woman's voice rang out from the audience—"*Falta una!* (They owe us one more!)" Everybody went into an uproar of laughter. The solemn-faced orchestra filed on stage once more to play another dance tune.

Next morning, Sister Petrona and I went for a walk around town. It was the Fourth of July. For the first time in weeks, God permitted a sunshiny day to happen to his loyal Catholics away down south in Chile. Galvarino knows how to appreciate a sunny day. Everybody in town brings a chair to the sunny side of the street and sits there to thaw out, chatting with the neighbors in an ecstacy of unexpected warmth.

For the worst of Galvarino is the cold in winter. This seemed so odd to me as a missioner. During my twelve years of mission life in Hawaii and the Philippines, my vagrant thoughts had always swung around the question, "How can I get a breath of air?" A cool breeze was something to make a novena for. But missions in Chile are different. Even the native Chileans live from dawn to dusk all togged out for a day in the Arctic. The teachers wear woolen caps, galoshes, thick coats and sweaters as they stand in front of the class. The children's hands are cracked with cold as they grasp their stubby pencils and try to write. The damp, dank cold plays havoc with their feet and legs, all too often bare as they stand in ice-rimmed puddles in the school yard.

So when God sent a sunny day to Galvarino in mid-winter, it was a day to be enjoyed. A day to let the sun's warmth sink right through your sweaters and deep into your bones. A day to hang out your blankets and hope they would get toasty dry. A day when you might pray that the muddy streets would harden a bit and the damp walls of the house dry out.

Small wonder, then, that we found all of Galvarino and his brother sitting out on the street on Fourth of July. We progressed from one jovial group to the next. A pharmacist noticed my cold and rushed into her shop for a bit of *tilo*. That's an herb which is brewed for colds in Chile. Then, a few doors further on, we stopped for an Hello with the ex-Mayor and his wife, a dear old couple sunning themselves on their doorstep.

Senor and Senora Gonzales have six daughters and two sons, all grown up except for the last who is a college student at Concepcion. A little reluctantly, Senora invited us upstairs. She was loath to leave the bright sunshine. We were loath to leave it too, but protocol is protocol, and in we went.

She ushered us into a big room with small rugs scattered here and there on the shiny floor. We sat in chairs conversing while our breath rose in steam to the ceiling. The little old ex-Mayoress wore a brown woolen dress, thick grey sweater and an imitation fur coat. Her hands were in woolen gloves, yet she kept hitting them together and blowing on them to keep circulation going.

We too stamped and blew and dug our hands into pockets. By this time, I was always wearing two pairs of gloves at once, cotton ones under and woolen ones on top. I wore a light sweater under my woolen habit and a heavy one over it. Yet, with it all, I felt I could never be anything but cold and damp. My feet? They were clumps of wood I stood on and walked on, but were away out over the horizon of consciousness. You could have cut them off and I wouldn't have known it until I wanted to use them again.

We were served lemonade. Then, after a suitable period, Senora Gonzales stood up and presented us with a piece of meat loaf as a present. I put it next to the *tilo* in my gadget bag, and we moved on.

It was the Turkish family which sat outside their store who were the next victims. Senor and Senora and Senor's old mother sat on chairs while the children frisked in the bright sunshine. "Do come in, Madre," Senor invited us into the store.

It was fascinating! Big thick *mantas*—as thick as the old-fashioned laprobes—maybe three-quarters of an inch thick, hung on two mannikins, who stood like cigar store Indians on either side of the door. Replete with mustaches and vacuous stare, they were obviously hand-me-downs from the days when 14th Street in New York was the main shopping thoroughfare.

Inside, the store was a jumble of everything under the sun. A single display case held crude iron pots, bits of harness, a few bolts of bright ribbon, photographic film (much out-dated), and several cards of jewelry and hair barrettes, all pretty dusty. From pegs in the wall, hung festoons of shoes. The tops were of quite stiff leather; the soles of wood rounded off to provide some little ease in walking.

I gravitated to the harness corner. This was *my* spot. The bridles! With little red inserts, with braided reins, with fancy doo-jiggers all of bright metal, they were a sight to revel in. Several saddles were slung over racks, each one more beautiful than the others. I could have stayed here forever, indulging in pipe dreams of other days. Even I, city-born and city-bred, have known the exaltation of galloping horse flesh beneath me, and the breath of purple sage in my nostrils. How would it be to pound over hills in Chile? How would it feel to handle one of these magnificent Chilean horses? But—could I ever ride side-saddle? Ay! There's the rub! I could ride like the *huasos* do, gripping the animal between my knees. But Chilean women? They could ride rings around me!

Senor Albar and Sister Petrona were calling me over to the Indian corner. "How would you like to wear this?" Sister said, holding up the breastplate and headdress of the Araucanian Indians.

These Indians are all over Galvarino. They were the last of the South American Indians to submit to the white man's rule. And even then, they did not submit. They signed an honorable treaty with the Chilean Government in 1888. For centuries, they had lived aloof in that cold strip of south Chile which ends in Tierra del Fuego. They dared the Spaniards to cross the Bio-Bio River which marked the dividing line. After 1888, the land was opened for settlers. That's about the time when Galvarino and other towns south of the Bio-Bio sprang into being.

The Araucanians are now around 30,000. Many live in the town and look like anybody else, but out in the country, they stick to the old ways. The women wear a heavy silver necklace, so bedight and be-hung with coins and chains and big pieces of metal that it covers most of the chest like a piece of armor. Around their heads is the heavy chain of silver, this also hung with coins, and tied in the front with bright bits of ribbon which trail down over the forehead. It was this armor-plate, Sister was holding out to me.

"Wear it? I'd love to!" I exclaimed with delight.

"It's yours, then. All yours!" Senor Albar's generosity was without precedent. Sister Petrona's jaw dropped. She was the faithful customer, but I got the gift! The necklace and headdress went into the gadget bag together with the *tilo* and meat loaf.

"I think you have enough loot for today," Sister said severely. "Let's go home." Leaving Senor Albar basking in the sun and in the thought of his good deed for the day "in the bag," so to speak, we turned our steps toward the convent again.

Halfway home, I stopped a splendid gentleman on horseback who looked as out of place in Galvarino as Cholly Knickerbocker would look in the African wilderness. He was elegance personified. The wide flat hat was immaculately brushed; the manta hung from his square shoulders in just the right folds; the silver stirrups glistened in the sun. He sat atop his splendid animal as the beautiful creature picked his way daintily around about our civic mud-puddles.

"May I take your picture?" I asked in not-so-good Spanish.

"Certainly, Sister, if you wish," he answered in flawless English. Educated in the States, he knew just what a colorful figure he was. He had a real Hollywood flair for posing. I was delighted.

"What a nice gentleman!" I commented as we passed on.

"The biggest Mason in town," Sister said. "He's always like that. Loves the Sisters and hates the Church."

Before we got to the house, there was one more incident. A woman in great distress came up to us. Her whole heart was in her eyes as she talked.

"Please, Sisters, come to our house. My husband is dying!"

"Surely," Sister replied. "I'll come at once." Then she turned to me. "Will you get the priest? I'll go with the woman now and commence the prayers for the dying."

I started off, but the woman's distress only increased.

"No! No! Don't go away, Madre!" she said. "It's you, we want. My husband is dying. Will you take a picture of him dying? I want it so much and he does too. Think! He will never do this again. We want a picture of it."

I had to assure her that if "La Madre Fotografia" came, it would be to pray for her husband, not to take his picture.

They lived away off at the edge of town. We told the priest and set off to put the man safely over the edge of eternity.

Here in Galvarino, our two Sisters and three lay teachers staff a school for 230 children. The two-story white concrete school is easily the biggest and most impressive building in town. The rest of the houses are of unpainted wood, all weathered to a most innocuous color. Perhaps that is why Galvarino is so hard to see until you are right in it.

Many of the children come from the *campo* or countryside, walking several hours every day to school. At noon they get a hot lunch of beans or soup. With this they munch the bread that they have brought in their pockets.

And here lies a tale of simple economics—typically feminine economics. But it works.

Sister Petrona two years ago was sorry to see the youngsters who had come so far, eating only a dry piece of bread at noon. They ought to have a hot meal, she was sure, but how to manage it? Then she evolved this system. Every Monday, each child brings a little sack of something—rice, beans, vegetables, meat, or what-have-you. Several are bound to bring rice. Well, on Mondays, all the rice is cooked up and the children all share in it. On Tuesdays, the beans collected for the week are cooked, and again everybody has a share. The meat and vegetables go into the pot another day and the whole crowd has stew. In this way, each child brings what he can afford and everybody shares in the whole.

This plan would have been in operation sooner, except for the pressing question: Who would cook the lunch? With only two

Sisters in the house, neither one could be spared for the work. But Divine Providence stepped into the breach.

An old lady, Fortunata, brought her granddaughter to school one day. "This is Rosa," she informed Sister Petrona. "She is the daughter of my daughter who lives fifty miles from here. My daughter wants her educated. Now, Madre, I have little, as you know, but I will give her food and lodging. Can she help around the school, to earn her school books?"

Rosa was a big girl—almost twelve and large for her age. She hadn't the faintest wisp of an education but she was certainly intelligent.

Now, Rosa cooks the beans or rice or soup every day. She enjoys a part of the capital, since her labor is essential to the enterprise. Sister also gives her clothes as her earnings. It's a marvellously simple example of investment and earnings.

In Chile, you see a progressiveness in legislation which is ahead of the United States in some ways. Chile was the first country in the Western Hemisphere to provide old age pensions and other social security laws. It's not so easy to administer these laws, though. In country places, old folks cannot produce a birth certificate. They have no exact idea of when or where they were born.

You will see the hills covered with regular rows of pine trees or eucalyptus. The government pays a peso a year per tree to anyone maintaining trees on his land. This is to offset the ravages of erosion, perhaps too late. There are already great cracks in the hillsides and much of the good earth has been washed away.

What concerns us most, is the "*subvencion*" paid by the government for each child educated in any approved school. This makes it possible for missioners to open schools with some little help from the government. It also makes it possible for nearly every child to attend school. We can afford to offer a Catholic education to many children who could not get it otherwise. Maryknoll schools are popping all along "the main stem" in Chile, as they call the railroad which runs like a backbone through the country from Santiago to Puerto Montt. In this middle part of Chile, where 85% of the population is concentrated, is the greatest need for an intelligent, well-educated Catholic laity. And that is where Teresita comes in.

I met Teresita at the blacksmith's shop. Sister Petrona wanted a hook made for the sanctuary lamp to hang from. We took our iron rod and went to the shop to have Victor hammer it into shape. Victor was a fairly young man, a real village smithy. A horse stood in the middle of the shop, with his hoof in Victor's leather-aproned lap. The owner held the horse's head; Victor was scraping the hoof down. With long iron pincers he reached over into the simple hand-blown forge for a gleaming red shoe. That's where I lost interest in the horse-shoeing. A pair of bright black eyes looked into mine over the forge. Teresita, nine years old, was cheerfully turning the handle which sent the wind rushing through the bed of hot coals. She was Daddy's little helper.

I met her next in the school yard, seated on a fallen log and rocking her dolly to sleep. Her wooden-soled shoes, her multiplicity of sweaters, her chapped hands were nothing beside the warmth of her smile and the light in those black eyes. Perfect innocence. Perfect simplicity. She hugged the doll to her heart as I came closer.

"May I see your dolly?" I asked.

She held it out to me. Just a stick, an ordinary twig, wrapped in torn cloth. Yet, how she loved it!

Teresita, listen to me. God sends us to Chile for you. He says to us: "Say good-bye to your father and mother. Give a last hug to your own little brothers and sisters. Put your feminine pride in your pocket and wear My livery. I have work for you to do, for there are Teresitas in Chile and Bolivia and Panama—and all over the world. Their black eyes are vacant now. I want you to fill them with nothing less than Me. My very essence, Innocence and Simplicity."

Besides Teresita, who stirred me deeply, Galvarino has another feature which aroused emotion. That was a bridge which made me tremble clear down to my toes. It's a suspension type bridge across the stream, but it swings from one high bluff to another, some thirty feet above the water. Three strands of wire rope support a boardwalk. The boards are as far apart as railroad ties. As you walk across this thing, looking down, you see the river flowing past. And yet you have to look down or you will slip through the cracks. Like walking sidewise on a moving belt, you want to keep stepping across your own ankles. You are awfully glad to see *terra firma* slide solidly between the boards.

Sister Vincent de Paul one time sent home a picture of herself walking across this bridge. The reaction was quick, brief and pungent. Her father sent a single sheet of paper and began without greeting or formality:

"KEEP OFF THAT BRIDGE! It was meant for squirrels, not *you*."

◆ 17 ◆

EARTHQUAKE HEAVEN

The South Pole has a peculiar liking for the community room at Galvarino; he comes with his icy breath around May and camps there until August. But Chillan is the favorite for Old Man Earthquake. The town must be sitting right on top of some subterranean jitterbox. If an earthquake is scheduled for another spot in the globe, nine times out of ten it changes its mind and comes around to shake up its old favorite, Chillan.

For all that, it's quite a neat little city of 46,000 people, with a tradition of culture. The newspaper in town dates back to 1870, and so do some of the venerable *coches*. The drivers sit up in front with tall silk hats, just like the sight-seeing carriages in Central Park. Chillan's pretty plaza is flanked by church, town hall and a modern hotel. We, of course, are in the more disreputable part where the people are poor, but we share in the general respectability of Chillan.

However, we did not arrive at any respectable hour—at 1:15 A.M., to be exact. It was the best connection we could make on the railroad from Galvarino. When Sister Victoria Francis and I finally stood on the station platform at 1:15 A.M. after a travel day which had started at 4:15 the morning before, we knew why St. Paul groaned about being "in journeyings often." He listed it along with shipwreck and "forty stripes save one" and being "let down over the wall in a basket," as a major claim to martyrdom.

We packed our things into a *coche*. The driver whipped up his sleepy horse and off we rumbled over Chillan's cobblestones. Inside the coach, Sister and I faced each other on two tiny seats, feeling like something out of Boswell's Life of Sam Johnson. At

178

any moment we should turn into the gate of The Boar's Head and meet Oliver Goldsmith and other cronies.

The horses clattered over the cobblestones in the blackness. Past the shops shuttered up securely for the night, past the traffic cop's stand with its umbrella spattered with advertising, past the deserted plaza where palm trees waved in the moonlight in the cold rain of Chile's winter. We were trotting through another century, surely. Then, suddenly we stood still before a little 4-room house, its windows bright with welcome. It was the Maryknoll convent in Chillan.

They were waiting for us—little Sister Henrietta and big Sister Philip John. We wasted no time in effusive greetings but went to bed gratefully between flannelette sheets as snug as a bug in a rug.

Life began in earnest the next day—or rather, the same day. We met the Catholic Action ladies. They attended Mass in a body that morning and offered their Holy Communions for us. The turn-out was marvellous, Father Walker said. Partly, I suspect, because the dear ladies wanted to see if we were tiny like Sister Henrietta or big like Sister Philip John. We were disappointingly medium in every respect. But that did not dampen their enthusiasm. They invited us to a tea that afternoon at the Grand Hotel, right on the plaza. This was an affair, indeed.

The plaza was very nice; the hotel was very nice; the tea was very nice. We sat at a huge table seating perhaps fifty women, the two Maryknoll Fathers in the parish and we four Sisters. I had a French lady on one side; a Spanish lady on the other. Since my French is equalled only by my Spanish—both slightly above zero —I got along as well with one as with the other. Indeed, sometimes I played both ends against the middle and gave myself a rest as they fought the battle of words over my prone body.

Horrified, then, I heard the chairman announce that I would tell the ladies my experiences in a Japanese internment camp during World War II in the Philippines.

"Only for God and Maryknoll, would I do this," I muttered, rising to the polite clapping that went round the table.

Well, my mother used to say as an antidote to almost any situation, "You have a tongue in your head. Use it!" I had no tongue in my head that day in Chillan. At least, I couldn't do a thing with what I had. But the Good Lord has given me hands at the end of my arms, and a couple of eyebrows. With these I pieced out the Spanish.

It was dramatic. The bombs fell, the planes crashed, Manila went up in flames. I was carried out of myself, remembering the history I had seen in the making nine years before. A waiter crouched behind a tea tray as in a bomb shelter and a couple of men put their heads out of the kitchen door to watch the burning of Manila. The ladies were terrified. It suddenly occurred to me: These women really don't know what a war is. They have always been on the sidelines. Their husbands did not get shot down; their sons did not die of fever in the South Pacific. In all that terrific struggle, South America lay calm in the back-waters. The only touch with war was to supply rubber, or oil, or metals, or some other raw product. The clammy finger of death and mutilation touched them not at all. For these women, there were no short notices from the War Department—Killed, Wounded or Missing in Action, Private First Class John J. Doe. Serial Number 692538472 to the Army. My boy Johnny to me.

How can you explain music to a deaf man? How can you talk about color to the blind? Of a sudden, my oratory collapsed. I finished the tale lamely and sat down. A sympathetic murmur ran around the table. They felt sorry for me. And I could not hope to explain to them that I did not feel at all sorry for myself, that there was nothing to be sorry about. Rather, that God had gone to a lot of trouble to teach us all what is essential and what is not. I, for one, have always been grateful for my three-year course at the School of Necessities.

Chillan, nevertheless, has known suffering. Indeed, the town was just coming to, after an earthquake less than a month before. It was the worst since the catastrophe of 1939 when ten thousand died. That visitation had come at night when honest folk were in bed. Fortunately, the recent trembler chose the noon-hour. People could flee from the houses in a hurry, munching dinner as they fled.

Our two were not so earthquake-wise. Sister Henrietta told me the story.

"It looked as though, for once, we were to enjoy that 'peace and quiet of the convent' people are always talking about. After eighteen months of hectic days in getting this mission school started, at last things were smoothing into routine. It had been a quiet morning and a pleasant dinner. Noon prayers and rosary said, we were sitting beside our wood-burning stove mending stockings and reading our mail together.

"Then my spool of thread rolled off the table. I stooped over to pick it up and all but fell on my head out of the chair. St. Joseph began jigging in his niche over the dormitory. The Blessed Mother wobbled off a small table and crashed to the floor. By this time Sister Philip John had sprinted to shelter under the doorway. She is from Los Angeles and has seen earthquakes before.

" 'Don't bother picking up the pieces,' she said. 'Come here with me.'

"Together, we stood under the doorway. Through the open window, we saw our neighbor's wall collapse. On the other side, the low mud-brick buildings we use as classrooms were jittering.

" 'There goes my Grade One room,' Sister Philip John said, as the building smashed right in like a crushed eggshell. Grade Three fell after it. Cracks ran down the walls of other rooms like streaks of lightning. We thanked God it was the noon-hour and no children were inside."

When I was there, the whole school was in an uproar of confusion, doing the best thing possible until the new school would be finished. Grade Three was holding classes in the small sacristy of the church, so jammed together that no one could hope to open the drawers of the vesting case. Every night, they had to pile the desks on top of each other, so that one could prepare for Mass the next day. In the other rooms, the walls were held upright by iron rods which ran across the room, so that walking down the aisle was like an obstacle race. The teacher was always stepping over or ducking under an iron rod.

But the new building was going up fast and all the parish hopes were pinned on it. You never saw such enthusiastic children. They were poor as church mice and often quite hungry and cold, but their zest for getting an education was magnificent.

Sisters were a new wrinkle to St. Vincent's parish when our two came in July, 1952. The children were used to lay teachers. They just gawked as Sister Henrietta and Sister Philip John emerged from the doll-house convent and crossed the schoolyard. Not any more; though. Anybody in a habit is fair target for a pack of children tearing across the yard to be first to greet you with *"Buenas dias, Maaaadre!"* They drag out that *Maaaadre* so! One afternoon, they backed me up against a wall and released me only when I offered to turn the jumping rope for them. At first, that was enough exercise for me, but illusions of youth crowded in. I offered to jump while somebody else turned. Three jumps—that's all—and I was ready to limp home.

Truly, man is a complicated creature. If you need any proof of it, glance through the typical convent library. The shelves at Chillan have many empty places, for the house is new and has not yet accumulated all the books it could use. Nevertheless, I ran my eye along the top shelf jotting down the titles.

First was the "Song and Game Book," evidently made for teaching kindergarten. Next was a goodly tome—"The Life and Revelations of St. Gertrude" and beside it the slim "True Devotion to the Blessed Virgin Mary" by de Montfort. Walsh's "Teresa of Avila" spread its bulk alongside.

Then, "Kon-Tiki," a story of sheer adventure. A paper-back *"Mujercitas"* (Little Women) of Louisa May Alcott. The next title asked impertinently, "What is Your IQ?" You did not have to answer for the next three were better, "Fanny Farmer's Candy Cook Book," "Martha Logan's Meat Cook Book" and "The 60-Minute Chef." And, if you overate, beside them was "The Red Cross First Aid Book."

"Character Education in Adolescence" was part of the Sisters' professional library and so was *"Los Majores Versos Para Ninos"* (The Best Verses for Children). The Spanish dictionary alongside was well thumbed.

The final book on that shelf was my Waterloo. A more fascinating volume has never been written. The title was simple enough, "Watkin's Household Hints." The contents—well, here are some of the chapter headings:

How to Get Out Stains: Grease, oil, dandelions, ink, indelible
                            pencil, beer, lipstick and champagne
How to Clean a Zinc Garbage Can

How to Relieve Corns
How to Care for Gutters and Down-Spouts
How to Read a Gas Meter
How to Prevent Discoloration of a Catsup Bottle Cap
How to Make Fly Paper
How to Darn Hosiery at Night
How to Prevent Tripping on Your Basement Stairs
How to Apply Floor Wax
How to Change a Sick Patient's Nightgown

Well, well! This was a find! I took the book in hand and went to the bathroom. There I surveyed the leaking faucet and turned quickly to the paragraph on What To Do About Leaky Faucets.

"Shut off flow of water," the oracle advised. "Replace worn washer with new one." That was all. Rome had spoken.

All very well, but how did one shut off the flow of water? Especially in Chile. I traced the pipes all the way back to the tank on the roof. There was nothing to turn either on or off. "Watkin's Household Hints" was silent on the subject, How to Find a Valve in Chile. I was climbing on chairs to investigate the tank on the roof when Sister Henrietta came in.

"There is no valve to turn," she said. "We just wait until next summer when the tank will go dry. That's the simplest kind of plumbing I know."

Up on the roof, there, I overlooked the home of Trini and her mother, Dona Julia, our neighbors in Chillan. Ay, there's a pair of hearts God must love!

I first saw them every morning at Mass. Dona Julia is an ancient, ancient old lady. Trini (short for Trinidad, I would guess) is getting on to 70 herself. Her mother is reputed to be 94, blind, and completely bent over so that when she tries to kneel, her head all but touches the ground.

Every day at Mass, just after the consecration, Trini began the process of getting her mother to the altar rail. She fixed her cane and all but lifted her to her feet. Then, with infinite patience, she led her up the aisle. Trini lifted her mother's head back so that Father could place the Host on her tongue. Returning after Holy

183

Communion was almost as difficult. But the two of them would get back to their pew and spend a full half-hour in deepest prayer. Then they walked around the corner to their house beside the convent. Did I say "house"? It was the merest shanty.

We left Chillan for ten days or so, and on returning found that Trini's mother had collapsed in the interim. Father Walker came every day with Holy Communion. One afternoon, Sister Henrietta took me over to see Dona Julia. We brought for her a warm shawl which had come in a shipment of clothes from Maryknoll. Being old friends and neighbors we came in the kitchen-way, just slipping across our yard and through the backgate in their wall.

Trini was fanning a blaze in the small stove in the corner; a pot of potatoes was boiling merrily. The walls were black with soot so that a big poster of the Eucharistic Congress of 1934 was all but blacked-out. With many exclamations of happiness at seeing us, she kicked open the door to the other room. The door was made of packing box wood and hung crazily on its one hinge. Two big beds were there leaving a very small space between. A small brazier of charcoal burned on the mud-floor but still the old woman shivered in her bed. We recognized on top of her Trini's coat and her own ragged shawl. The sheets, we would say, were dirty. It is true they were a dark grey. But they were as clean as hard work and cold water could make them. Even in the convent, we had no hot water except what was boiled on the stove. And that takes fuel which Trini could not afford.

I looked at this old woman who had lived 94 years in conditions like these. I looked at Trini as she rubbed her hands together and shifted from one foot to another in the effort to warm herself, because her one coat was on top of her old mother. I looked at the shanty they lived in. The cracks between the boards were stuffed with burlap or newspaper, and a wet spot on the mud floor indicated a leak in its tin roof. We Americans would say, "This is utter destitution." But to millions in South America it is just the ordinary way of life and they don't feel too sorry for themselves.

"What can I get for you, Trini?" Sister Henrietta said.

"Well, we have what we need, Sister," Trini said. "But if we could have some coal to burn on the brazier, it would make a warmer fire for my mother." Fortunately, we had just gotten some coal that afternoon and Sister Philip John ran back to the convent to get a sack of it for Trini.

I learned a valuable lesson in Chillan. That is: Keep quiet about what you like and what you don't like.

One afternoon Sister Henrietta took me shopping in the market. A wonderful place. The stalls were hung with a million things I should love to buy. Sister gave me about two dollars and put me on my own. I bought a woven grass shopping bag and set off to fill it. The collection was impressive in bulk, if not in value. I finished up with a pair of Chilean wooden stirrups carved with roses and shellacked to mirror sheen. Beside them was a pot for brewing *mate,* the South American drink, rather like tea. It was like a small tea pot of black clay and the cup to match had a horn in the side like a handle. Then came a jack rabbit skin which the jack rabbit had vacated all too recently. Rabbits are big in Chile. This creature must have been the granddaddy of them all. A drinking horn, nicely decorated, was in the bag also; it was simply a cow's horn hollowed out. Finally, on top of all were the onions. Such onions! Big, juicy white onions. The way to eat onions, in my humble opinion, is to boil a big one and serve it in solitary splendor with a piece of butter melting down into the crevices. Just a boiled onion on a plate. None of your fancy cream sauces; no camouflage or decorations. But a sturdy honest onion not afraid to be what God made it.

So I came home with a beautiful bunch of onions, talking long and loud about how to serve onions. So long and so loud that Teresita heard me in the kitchen.

Very well. At dinner, we four Sisters were served each an onion in solitary splendor. We laughed about it and enjoyed them. At least, the others said they enjoyed onions that way. The next day at dinner, we had boiled onions served in regal isolation. It was easy to detect a false note in the laughter. The third day, I sneaked out to the kitchen ahead of time to stave off a catastrophe.

"What's for dinner, Teresita?"

She gave me a knowing wink. "What you like, Madre! Oh you will like it very much!"

"Onions?" I asked warily.

"No," she said. "Onion. Just one. One big onion. All by himself. Ah, so good! So easy to make such a dinner!"

"Listen, Teresita," I remonstrated. "That's all right for me. I like it. But maybe, the other Sisters . . ."

"All right, Madre. I make something else for them. But you—you have just what you like. One big onion."

And I did. That day and the next and the next. The other three took keen delight in waving their hamburgers in front of me. I regret to record this of any Maryknoll Sisters, but there was a distinct flavor of "Let this be a lesson to you" in their enjoyment of a good meal. And I regret to confess this of myself, that I practiced deceit, extolling the onion and my appetite for it with no regard for God's sober truth.

But God is good to His weak creatures. He removes us from the fire when we have fried enough in our own confusion. We moved on to Molina.

From this point on, in Chile, until we landed at Santiago once more, we were at the mercy of the Maryknoll Fathers. We could have been in far worse hands. The train pulled into Molina at 8:30 P.M. in the pitch-dark cold of a winter night in Chile. Father Coleman was there.

Father is head of that interesting project, the agricultural school at Molina. He wears a jaunty little beret. He and Sister Victoria Francis sat on the front seat of his jeep, enjoying what there was to see of the town, while I and the baggage bounced around in the back navigating some of the worst roads these old bones have ever suffered. But all was forgiven when we reached the school. Out there they have pigs and rabbits, chickens, horses and cows. Just a short trip around that night and another jaunt in the early morning put me in grand humor once again.

"We have about forty rabbits," Father explained, showing the white bunnies. "There are the hutches and this field is their playground. Over here are the hens, and they have their play-pen over there. We're building a real rumpus-room for the pigs but in the meantime they have a good time in this yard. In fact, everybody on the grounds has a play-yard except the Fathers." Ergo, he showed off a big tract of land which the school had recently bought. There's nothing mincy about Chilean land-purchasing. Father's arm swept wide as he said, "It stretches from that double line of poplars straight across to the creek and beyond to that other line

Dressed up or not, the children of Nicaragua's gold-miners are willing victims for the camera.

Children stole my heart so often, I gave up any idea of keeping it intact. Here are just a few of the little rascals.

Easter hats on the Altiplano of Peru.

Araucanians are a cheerful race in southern Chile.

Lower left. School lads in central Chile.

Below. Serious business in Peru.

Chilean boys come bright—and lively!

No inhibitions here!   Puzzled Cochabamba miss.

Left. English-speaking Jamaican Negro children fill the slums of Panama City.

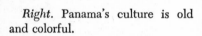

Right. Panama's culture is old and colorful.

Left. We help these youngster to come into their heritage.

The bridge at Galvarino. It was built for squirrels, not Maryknoll Sisters.

Left. "Como esta?" from Chillan's chief of police.

Right. Soup's on! Sister Petrona's smile is as welcome as her hot lunch.

Left. Chile's beggar lads roam the country living as best they can. Estimates say there are 80,000 of them.

Right. Kitchen chairs tied to the cart give that extra touch of elegance to an afternoon's ride.

Left. "Room for one more, Sister?"

Right. Buzeta's children. They have nothing to give but their hearts.

A HUASO DIES IN CHILE

Above. The funeral's advance guard rides into town.

Right. Fixing up the coffin at the edge of town.

Below. They carry him to the church.

A queer sense of timelessness fills the Altiplano. Confronted with the Andes, one knows without doubt that man was made to know and love Eternal Majesty.

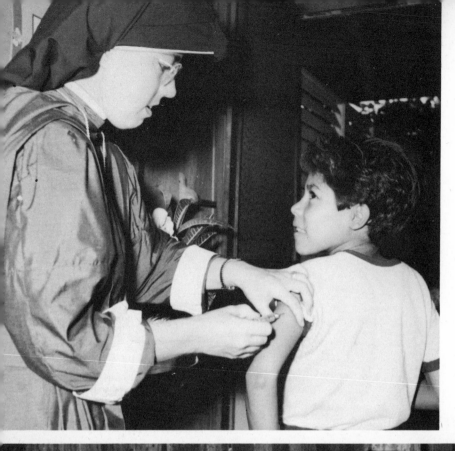

NICARAGUA

Left. A shot in the arm for Rodrigo.

Lower left. Hot tea and a warm smile. What more can anybody want?

Right. The hats are nice, but Margarita and Juanito need much more.

Below. Arts and crafts may help to change the social picture.

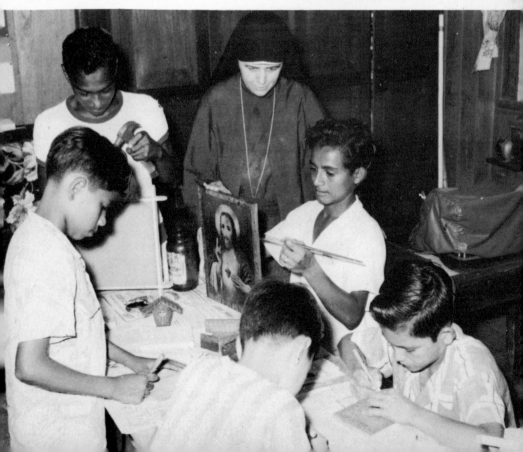

PERU

Left. Inca Indians, ancestors of this woman of Cuzco, built these walls which are the marvels of stonecutters today.

Below. A single faucet like this supplies water for 30 families in one of Lima's *corralones*.

Fighting poverty and discouragement is worse than battling dragons. Yet it must be done if Panama's depressed people are to have a chance for the better things, material and spiritual.

PANAMA

It isn't easy to give children a happy home life under conditions like this. Yet many courageous Negro women of Panama City have done it.

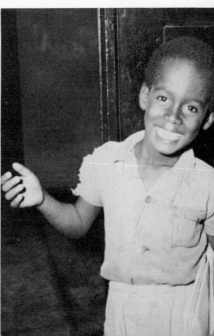

The Maryknoll Sisters are there to help them do it.

What is she thinking of, as she worships before her pot of incense? The Central American Indian retains much of the Church's customs and feastdays, but has slipped back to paganism for the most part.

of poplars." Fields are marked off by a double—and sometimes triple—line of lovely poplar trees.

At Talca, we fell into the charming custody of Father Garvey. He brought us, bags and all, to his rectory and then dashed out on a sick call, shouting as he vanished out the door, "Just make yourselves at home. The boy will serve you dinner."

We ate our lunch, said our prayers and wandered over to the church, a new one named for Our Lady of Fatima, and very tastefully decorated. That's how we met Eduardo.

He lay curled up under Our Lady's altar, one shabby foot tucked under him, the other stretched out in front. At first I thought him asleep, then dead, then sick. His rosary moved in his fingers with many long pauses. Once he opened his eyes and took a long look at us, but soon lost interest in two queer creatures disturbing his sanctum.

Father Garvey explained that Eduardo is religious but a trifle queer. He insists on writing letters to the Pope. That's all right, of course, but Eduardo won't write them on paper. He prefers to use chalk and scribble his messages to the Pope on the sidewalk. Possibly he thinks His Holiness takes an afternoon stroll on the streets of Talca and will read his message there.

At Temuco, we fell into the hands of Father Zemalkowski, one of the umpty-ump Maryknoll Fathers who confidently expect Maryknoll Sisters to arrive at the rectory door soon with the joyful message, "Here we are to stay." With all these priests, we enjoyed such lavish hospitality that we only wished we could produce Sisters out of a top hat—any number of them—and leave them behind to do all they could for their parishes.

Father Zemalkowski is ordinarily a humble man, but he leans to pride on the subject of ice cream. He claims his is the best in Chile. Cold though it was, we had to get outside of heaping plates of his pride and joy. Well, it wasn't so very difficult, I must admit.

It may have been the ice cream; it may have been the South Pole hovering around Temuco; whatever it was, Temuco could be awarded the Diamond Encrusted Snowplow as the coldest spot we knew in South America. The dampness ate into your bones. We were guests of the Santa Cruz Sisters. This order, originally German, made its first foundation in Chile in 1901, opening this boarding school. They have about 400 Sisters in Chile now of whom 80 are Chilean. Passing through Temuco, the metropolis for this section, our Sisters always find a warm welcome at Santa Cruz. Warm, I mean, in charity especially, and as warm otherwise as a wood-burning stove in your bedroom can make it. A generous supply of fuel is stacked under the bed and a hot-water bottle nestles between the flannel sheets. None the less, there's little creature comfort in Temuco.

One good thing, though. During winter time in Chile, the soap lasts a long long time, and the towels never wear out.

PERU

◆ 18 ◆

GOLD, BUT NO WATER

Francisco Pizarro loved Gold.

Not comforts nor luxury, not beautiful homes nor valiant ships, nor any other thing that gold buys. But Gold for herself alone. Certainly he loved her far more than he loved God.

For nearly sixty years he wooed her in vain. Steaming in Columbia's jungle coast, starved and shipwrecked on many a colonizing expedition, or roistering in Panama's *cantinas*, he had no luck with her at all. Then, he heard of her stronghold with the Incas in Peru. Gold—and Silver, too—lived high in the Andes. The fires of love burned in Pizarro. He would go through Hell to claim his Gold.

How else can you account for a man, almost sixty, riding, walking, staggering a thousand miles over Peru's desolate sun-baked clay? Where else did he get the courage to conquer 40,000 Indians with a force of less than two hundred exhausted men? The great Inca Empire, then just past its prime, fell like a house of cards before his treachery and his ridiculously small army. The last eight years of conquest brought him untold riches—and a knife in his back. "Thou fool! This night wilt thy soul be required of thee."

While Pizarro held the last of the Incas in prison, they came to an agreement on ransom. Atahualpa was to fill a room with gold. The room was 22 feet by 17 feet. The mark on the wall to which it must be filled was nine feet from the floor. Pizarro wanted to be able to swim, to drown, in his dear Gold. For months, the ransom poured into this room. Indian runners from Cuzco, the great Inca capital city, brought it on their backs—gold bars, gold ornaments, gold nuggets—even gold eyes plucked from their idols. The flood rose higher—7 feet—8 feet—8½ feet—9 feet! In May, 1533, it crossed the line and went beyond. Estimates of the value run between two-and-a-half and three-and-a-half million dollars, which is a lot of money even today.

In August, Atahualpa was executed. He was garroted as befits a Spanish nobleman, not burned as a heretic would be. That must have been a comfort to him.

They were a good pair, Pizarro and his Gold. One was as hard as the other. She led him a haggard life for eight years and finished him off, as the chronicler of the time puts it, "with no friend around to say, 'May God forgive him!'"

None the less, anybody who has walked or ridden in northern Peru would feel sorry for Pizarro. It is dry. Oh, so dry! It's terrifying, it's so dry.

Before landing at Callao, we stopped at two smaller ports, Paita and Talara. At both, we went ashore in a launch and took a look around. The towns are nothing; you soon walk through them and out into the surrounding country.

It was like a jaunt through pre-historic ages—maybe on one of those days of creation before God made any water. Nothing lives on the sun-baked clay. No trees, no shrubs, no flowers, not even grass. No coyotes, no horses, no elephants. Not even a bug. The only living wild creature we saw was a six-inch lizard who scampered out from under a few stones when we sat down. I wondered what he found to live on.

A merciless sun beats down on bare, bare clay, on deep *arroyos* and jagged cuts where it seems that the earth has cracked open for sheer thirst. Parched and split, begging for water. You expect to see a huge dinosaur humping over the dry hills, swinging his long neck back and forth, high and low, looking for even a fly to eat. Or a pterodactyl, one of those ungodly lizard-like birds who flew around millions and billions of years ago—you expect to see a pterodactyl circling like a vulture looking for some lone mud puddle and hoping that a little minnow might live there.

Northern Peru is the most desolate spot I ever saw. Compared to it, the deserts of Arizona and New Mexico are the garden of paradise, flowing with milk and honey. And yet, Talara is a town of 40,000 people. It's an oil center, owned and operated by the Standard Oil Company of New Jersey. The town lives for oil. As we drove around in the clay desert, every now and then, we came across a patient little oil pump, all by itself in the desolation, and yet faithfully going up and down just as if Mr. Rockefeller was looking at it all the while. In this No-Man's Land, it gave you the thrill you would usually get from seeing an unsuspecting bunny nibbling behind a bush, or a squirrel too busy storing up nuts to be scared of you. In Talara, automatic oil pumps take the place of bunnies, squirrels and such.

Some distance out of the town is the golf course. Bunkers, tees, roughs and fairways are all there, and not a blade of grass on any of them. It was as if you had taken a beautiful golf course and skinned it. Whoever played on that course loved golf.

Small wonder, that the taxi man said wistfully, "It hasn't rained here in 25 years! Once, when I was a little boy, it rained. I remember it well. But that was a long time ago." I looked at him sceptically; these taxi-drivers like to make up stories for tourists. But I guess it's not far wrong. The Encyclopedia Britannica says of this area that sometimes "in the summer there is a few inches of rain as in 1925." Water is brought to Talara by a 40-mile main running to the Andes. It comes to Paita in tank cars on the railroad.

We went to Mass at Paita, an old Spanish town of 4,000 people built on this same sort of clay desert. Old Spanish streets, over-hanging balconies, a light blue adobe town hall, two big churches (one of them very, very old), and a tiny plaza, postage-stamp size, a perfect riot of welcome green which rested the eyes like a soothing balm after the clay of the desert and the mud brick of the town.

We walked through the town nearly a half-hour early for Mass. There are no Sisters in Paita and yet the children ran to greet us in ragged little swarms. The padre was parading up and down the tiny little plaza, saying his office. He was a precise little priest, a man of few words. We were able to gain nothing from him but the time of the Mass and the fact that we were welcome.

The church was big and clean, light and airy. It was a pleasant surprise. Many ragged urchins scampered here and there. They gathered for curiosity but stayed to make the Sign of the Cross and diddle around, trying out our Spanish. But as the hour for Mass

193

came closer, the whole complexion of the people changed. The poor ragamuffins disappeared and, in their stead, came a whole churchful of nicely dressed people. Scrubbed-up children and women with stylish hair-dos and manicured nails. They drove up to the church in modern cars, waved good-bye to recreant hubby, drew lacy mantillas out of their purses and high-heeled their way up the middle aisle followed by one, two, three or even four well-turned-out children.

Where were the poor? They haunt the church most of the week, but leave it for their betters at Mass-time.

And where did the nice ladies come from? The town seemed gasping on the brink of destitution. After Mass, we saw them sitting around the little patio, talking in groups, chatting here and there and climbing back into their cars. Not only do they come through the parched countryside from places where they have haciendas hidden in the mountains' fertile valleys, but many live right in town. Pass behind these unpretentious mud brick walls which line Paita's streets and you will be in gracious Spanish gardens, complete with grass, flowers, balconies and dark-eyed Spanish beauties just as the tourist books describe.

But the cosmopolitan, brilliant, chatting groups paid no attention to us. We took our way through the poor streets toward the market, trying out our *Buenas dias* on everybody we met. These places had no gardens. Folks sat at their doorways smiling and bowing in the sunshine. Children peeped around their mothers' skirts, but when we stopped and held out a welcoming hand, they ran to take it. So,—as is usual—we Pied Piper-ed down the street.

A cobbler, old and bent, sat at his doorway for light. He gave us the grandest grin and pointed up the road at the right. "That's the road to Piura," he volunteered. Piura is quite a city in Peru, about seventy miles distant from Paita. Why he thought we were interested in Piura, I don't know. Perhaps he thought we were going to walk there on that hot Sunday morning.

We looked at the road. It shimmered in the sun, climbing straight up the hard clay bluff; no trees, no grass; and even the huts gave up half-way to the top and let the concrete road go on its way in sun-baked silence.

"Shall we?" said Sister Victoria Francis.

"We shall," said I with the thought in mind that Lent was well begun and we had done little penance as yet.

We started up. It was tough going, putting one foot in front of the other. Family groups and parties of young girls, sometimes a single man or a woman with a baby on her back passed us. Nearly all carried flowers in big heavy bouquets, all the worse for sun and heat. They were enroute to a cemetery to lay their flowers on the graves, built-up out of that hard clay. Heaven knows where they got the flowers; but everybody had quite a handful.

There were isolated graves on the roadside. Just a white wooden cross, above an adobe mound formed into a sort of squarish heap. Sometimes, in place of this, was a gasoline drum on its side, with the front sealed up with adobe and the flowers wilting on the white painted round top.

As we got higher, we began to look over the town and surroundings. Such a desolate place! I thought of the old Spanish missioners who had built that church years and years ago. How they must have longed for the green hills of Spain! But those who have lived their lives here do not seem to mind. Our eyes traveled over the low hills of dusty, dry earth, past a brick-kiln, past an ancient automobile raising a dust storm far away, and stopped. There, in that broiling sun, was a play field with men and boys getting ready for a football game. More power to them! Where did they get the energy!

Sister Victoria Francis and I weren't equal to walking to the top of that sun-baked road. We turned off into a side path and soon found ourselves on top of a bluff overlooking the town of Paita and the sea. We sat on some loose stones. A lizard scurried out from under and skittered over the dry clay. Four vultures with red naked heads swung in circles over a nest of houses below us and finally came to rest on a telephone pole, sitting with shoulders hunched and black wings folded awkwardly. They epitomized all that we had seen in the poor town below—poverty, smells, fish, hovels, disease, lack-luster eyes in sick babies, scabs and sores. Nothing stirred in the baking sunshine. The lizard was quiet again; the vultures watched in silence.

Then we saw a small boy coming up the hill, carrying on his shoulder a 5-gallon kerosene tin of water. It was heavy for him but he came along steadily. As he passed us, I thought, "He must live someplace nearby. This is his daily chore, to get water for the family." But to our surprise, he went over to a small wall of stones enclosing something about ten feet away; he poured all that water right into the small enclosure.

As soon as he had gone, we went over to see what was there. A very small coconut tree. Somebody certainly wanted a coconut tree badly, to plant it in that desolate spot and to keep it watered. I hope, ten years or so from now, I can go back to Paita. As we near the harbor, I'll borrow a pair of binoculars and search the barren shore for that symbol of hope—a coconut tree proudly flaunting its green crest on the hard clay cliffs of Paita.

Dreams come a-dime-a-dozen to missioners. It's a good thing they're cheap; otherwise, we might get too discouraged even to begin the task. If only we two Sisters had been able to say to the priest walking in the plaza, "Father, we are here to help you. Please put us to work!" If only we could have said to Pedrito and Jose and Conchita and Ramona, as they hung on our fingers and escorted us through the poor streets, "Come with your pencils tomorrow and we'll start teaching you about God. He loves you ten times, no twenty times, more than we do." How satisfying it would be to say to Senora Gonzalez and Senora Lopez as they sat on their sunny doorsteps, "Bring the baby to the clinic tomorrow and we'll start healing the sores on his head."

But it was not yet to be. Who knows when Paita will have Sisters?

They say the ground is fertile. A bit of water, a little cultivating and you can get wonderful results from this now-barren place. It's that way spiritually, too. So much good will, so much faith, waiting only for a handful of workers to bring it into beautiful flowering. One lone priest in Paita and all its surrounding country! How can he hope to delve deep into the lives of his people? The Paitanos are thirsty for God, as their land is thirsty for water.

Lima is thirsty, too. She may not admit it, being a proud old city, Pizarro's crown and jewel, mother of Saints, grand Capital of All the Americas! Her parks and plazas are floral masterpieces; her avenues are lined with palms and jacaranda trees. Even the bus drivers wear flowers in their caps. But that is old Lima, where the

Spaniards built mains to bring water from the Andes. We live out in the new part of Lima—the mud flats of Lobaton.

Not long ago, a rich old man owned a hacienda on the outskirts of Lima. It was a huge tract slowly being engulfed by the city. Street cars and buses raced along its edges; houses crowded against the fences. But "Old Man Risso" kept his mansion and his fields, dry though they were, in splendid isolation.

Then, in 1948, he sold the whole business to the city. The government moved in. It built streets and put up lamp-posts with street signs, and planted a nice little park. Then came the settlers. They were of two classes, almost half and half.

Fifty-three percent were of that almost unknown factor in South American life—the Middle Class. Neither rich nor poor, they built neat homes neither big nor small. Forty-five percent were poor. These built nothing. They merely moved what they had into one-room hovels built around a square, called *"Corralones."* What happens is that a man will buy a building lot. Then, while he is waiting for enough money to put up his new home, he hates to see the land non-productive. So he throws up these wretched hovels on his property and rents them out to poor families. As a result, you will find one of these collections of miseries right beside a very nice home. Nobody seems to mind; there are no zoning laws. You build what you like on your property and your neighbors can hold their noses if they don't like it.

I suppose you are wondering about the 2%. They are the rich people of the parish who do not bother us too much.

When Lobaton started mushrooming right after 1948, an old resident became alarmed. Her house was one of those that had crowded the railings of Old Man Risso's fields. She was Miss Rosario Araoz, as remarkable a woman as you will find on any of the five continents. She is remarkable in that she is commanding but not domineering; quick in action but not impatient; outspoken yet not flat-footed. Match that for a combination of virtues! They all stem from her chief one, a life-long dedication to furthering the rights of God in her beloved homeland, Peru. To hear Miss Araoz come thundering into the living room with a cannonade of Spanish, makes you want to run and hide. Her great dark eyes take your measure before three minutes are past. But, curiously enough, although you are sure you rate a 4-F in her estimate, you know that she will strengthen you gently, and bring to the surface, the best "you" there is.

Such is Miss Araoz. She was alarmed because all these people were moving into Lobaton and there was no church for them to go to. She went to the Cardinal. "I have no money to build a church there, and no priests to staff it," he told her. Nothing daunted, she arranged to have Masses every Sunday morning in the patio of a small Japanese school in the district.

She went around town asking priests to say Mass for them. That was how she met and fell in love with Maryknoll.

Now her ambition added a further clause. "We must have a parish church at Lobaton and Maryknoll must staff it."

"If you can get Maryknoll to send priests to Lobaton, so much the better," the Cardinal told her.

So Rosario Araoz set sail for New York, praying a blue streak the whole way. Sure enough, she talked Bishop Lane into sending priests to Lima. In November, 1950, Father John Lawler arrived, his red hair bristling with energy.

Father Lawler used to be a newspaperman in New Bedford, Mass. He has reformed in most particulars, but he still wears his hat on the back of his head like every police reporter in fact and fiction.

He took us to pay our respects to the Cardinal one day. I'm sure His Eminence had little idea of what he was running into, when he came into the audience chamber. Father Lawler had induced two young Maryknoll Fathers to bring 35mm cameras to record the event. An American army boy, sightseeing in Lima, was there with his movie camera, I had my Ciroflex, with flash attached. As the venerable old man entered the door, he faced a battery of cameras. All were to sponge in on my flash. Father Milroy counted, "Get ready, Get set, go!" and we all tried to click at the same time. Small wonder the victim was aghast. But Father Lawler sat him down gently and told him that the young priests were just language students and I had once been a news reporter and was therefore a little queer anyway. In no time, Padre Juan had reassured His Eminence. He even felt very happy about our visit and consented to pose for another shot.

Such is Father Lawler—one of the best salesmen Maryknoll has ever produced. Other priests build school and convent, and then wait for Sisters to come. But Padre Juan had nothing. He pointed to a large amount of emptiness as he showed Sister Angelica where the school was to be, and the church and the convent. Not a brick was laid on any of them. Yet such was Father's God-given gift of talk that he had Sisters by September, 1951. As soon as the last brick was laid, Santa Rosa's school opened its doors for any child in the parish, be he a member of the 53% Middle Class, 45% poor people—or 2% rich.

You can't imagine how revolutionary this was. Santa Rosa's is Peru's first and, to date, only parochial school. Rich and poor, Indian and white, it makes no difference. In the eager scramble to learn English and to be taught by American madres, many a prejudice is going by the board.

Sister Bernard Mary took me along one day as she visited the homes of her school children. But before I tell you about that, let me tell a story on Sister Bernard Mary. She and Sister Vincent de Paul, now in Chile, were friends in St. Louis. They met at a party one night and each learned that the other was thinking of going to Maryknoll. This made them fast friends in no time. They were walking home together from the party softly singing "Maryknoll, My Maryknoll." But Sister Bernard Mary wasn't sure of the words nor of the tune. She has always been a bit wobbly in trying to sing any tune. So they stopped under a street light. "I have a piece of paper," said the future Sister Vincent de Paul. "If we only had a pencil, I would write out the words for you."

"I have no pencil," said Sister-Bernard-Mary-to-be, "but I have this!" and she took her lipstick from her purse.

The two of them put their heads together under the street light as one girl wrote the words for the other. Then in practicing, they got so absorbed that their voices became louder and louder. At the end they were singing "Maryknoll, My Maryknoll" at a good volume. A policeman came along and suggested that they continue on home, like good girls. "That was the last of my lipstick," Sister Bernard Mary laughed. "I never bought another one. I couldn't have used it up in a better cause."

Well, Sister Bernard Mary and I started out to visit Ramon's home. He lives in a *correlon*. We were walking beside a mud brick wall. As usual, I was looking at everybody and everything. Then, of a sudden, I was alone. Sister Bernard Mary had ducked into an opening in the wall, just about as big as an ordinary room door. I ran back and ducked in after her. We were in a *correlon*.

It's a beehive of domestic activity. Washing, sweeping, chatting with the neighbors and keeping the children from underfoot goes on at a great rate. The narrow alleyway is cluttered with clothes drying, and loud with the chatter of women and squeals of children. Each family had a one-room mud brick shack with a basin and stand outside the door. The shacks are side by side like row houses so that a single side wall serves for two shacks. From thirty to forty families live in a single *correlon*.

How the children swarmed around us! Most of the women, too, stopped their work to gather round. Several of the "little brown bares" who had been washing their hair in a basin, hurried to wring it out and stand with dripping head and shoulders in the crowd.

The Spanish was flying around lickety-split. I caught a word here and there as it whizzed past and managed to look intelligent. That was at first. Then I found myself venturing out on a conversation and getting deep into the *"habla"* up to my neck and over. Sister Bernard Mary would reach out a saving hand as the waters of rapid Spanish closed over my head and I was saved for another five minutes or so.

But it's great! The children are so affectionate. They took my hand and divided my fingers among ten of them. Then the rest fought for the honor of kissing my medal and crucifix.

How wonderful a religious habit is! Just wearing the grey on my body and the black veil on my head, gives me a ticket of admission to every heart in that *correlon*. My habit tells the people right off that I am harmless if not actually beneficial to them. Other Americans had come on the boat with us. They were fully as well-intentioned as we. Yet they had no opportunity to talk to these poor people as people; they could merely see them from afar as picturesque and strange. Until they had proved themselves, they would have to stay in their foreign world of hotels and taxis and smart luggage. But me? I was just another wearer of the grey and black. They took it for granted that I had the same love for them that the other wearers of grey and black have. I needed no introduction, no probation period. Right away I stepped into the family circle of everybody in the *correlon.*

We found Ramon. He was flung across a pallet of rags, sound asleep. Poor lad, no wonder he was asleep; he had been out at the race tracks most of the night, begging, and most likely picking up what he could however he could do it. His older sister, Gloria, acted as hostess to us in the family's miserable hovel. Twelve years old, she already bore the burdens of the family. Both mother and father were drunk most of the time. Ramon and his three brothers were growing up wild. The care of the home—what care it received —devolved on Gloria's shoulders.

It is for Gloria's sake, that Social Service work has been established in Lobaton. Following a pattern already worked out in other Lima parishes, a Sister social service worker will direct a bureau which will help families to get on their feet. It's entirely a parish activity.

Some people like private cars. Some people like to walk. But give me a Lima bus, anyday. There is the zest of battle in riding on a Lima bus. Like most everything else in the city, the buses "go back to very early times—perhaps 16th century."

Sister Rose Jude and I joined a group of people waiting on the street corner. We were on our way to see the birthplace of St. Rose of Lima. The crowd of waiters, one by one shaded their eyes and craned their necks to see if a cloud of dust down the road might turn out to be a bus arriving.

When it did come, we joined in the free-for-all to get in. The bus was a veteran of many such assaults and stood its ground masterfully. The driver, too, was no tyro. An Indian woman with a shawl-full of vegetables tried to squeeze herself and all the vegetables into the bus.

"Wait a minute!" the driver cried. "You can't carry all those vegetables in here without paying for them."

She wouldn't. He insisted. She refused. Then she thought of a way around the point. Leaving the bundle outside, she wriggled her way inside the bus and through the crowd to a window. Then her friend outside lifted up the vegetables and she grasped the knotted corners of the shawl. Thus the Indian woman paid her fare for riding inside, and her vegetables rode free as she held them out the window.

The driver was satisfied with this arrangement. Once the bus had swallowed us all, it gave a heave and a jerk and went gallumphing down Avenida Salaverry like an ancient mule who had bitten a hornets' nest. Down landscaped avenues lined with flowering trees. Past stately plazas and majestic monuments. Beyond mansions of state dignitaries. Skirting the homes of the fabulously wealthy. Our worthy bus took us right to the door of St. Rose's family home.

It's very old. Very well preserved. Except for a few signs here and there and some paintings, it is just exactly what St. Rose saw every day of her life—thirty-one years. The room where she was born, the small enclosed garden where she took the air, the biggish room where she tended the sick—all things familiar to her. The picture of the Child Jesus, Whom she called *"Doctorcito"* (Little Doctor), hangs on the wall where the patients could see it. Outside, we walked the two blocks or so to Santo Domingo church, treading the very cobblestones, perhaps, that she stepped on 350 years ago on her way to Mass every day.

Such was the circuit of Rose's physical life. A house, a garden court, two blocks of city streets and a church. A very small range even in those days. Both Sister Rose Jude and I had lived years in the Orient and now we were away down in South America. "And what have we got in a spiritual way to show for it?" Sister asked.

St. Rose, so far as I know, never left Lima. It couldn't have been a big city then. Rose was born fifty years after Pizarro founded it. Yet she has influenced thousands of people who are far, far away from her both in space and in time. "How to Win Friends and Influence People?" Be a saint!

Even this narrow compass was too distracting for St. Rose. She and her brother built a hermitage in a corner of the garden. As I say, the garden is not large—no bigger than the modest back yard we had when I was little. In one corner is a mud brick chimney-like thing which you would suppose was an outdoor fireplace. Allowing at least ten to twelve inches for the width of the walls, the inside space is no bigger than the crate a household refrigerator comes in. Certainly, she could not stand upright, nor could she lie at length. In this cubbyhole, St. Rose spent most of the last years of her life.

Sinner though I am, I could understand it. Other peoples do not have the sense of elbow room that we Americans have. In a fair-sized home such as Rose's, there would be continual visits from relatives, servants underfoot or friends dropping in for two months' stay. Spanish adventurers, missionary priests, hacienda owners, must have passed through often. Besides these, the poor came clamoring, the sick came whining. Rose must have longed for the quiet of her packing-crate and the companionship of the Christ Child Who often came to see her in that tiny hermitage.

Not far from St. Rose's house, is Santo Domingo where the Blessed Martin de Porres, Negro wonder-worker, used to wield a broom in the corridors. Not far from there is the great bronze statue of Pizarro near the sumptuous Governor's palace. The bones of all three are held in high honor in Lima.

And well they might be! All three died well, although only two lived well. Pizarro, a poor fellow, spent his last ounce of strength as a Spaniard should. He raised his mangled body on one elbow and dipped his finger in his own blood. He traced a cross on the floor, already soaked in pools of blood. Then he bent his tortured body and kissed the cross saying the single word, "Jesus!" So, at the end, he cheated his mistress, Gold. When she had done him to death, he lifted his soul over the border into God's keeping. He was smart enough not to lose his soul simply because he had lost his body. That's a real Spaniard for you!

◆ 19 ◆

THE LLAMAS AND THE INCAS

The bright-eyed boy or girl who wants to be a missioner had better watch out. There are a lot of hazards to mission life which you will never read about in vocation booklets. Probably young Father Murphy when he was a boy in Gloversville, N.Y., never imagined that he would be almost strangled in Puno—and that by his loving uncle.

Puno is a symphony of old Spanish colonial days, high in the Peruvian Andes. Its houses are decrepit; its streets cobbled or mud. Stores are modest openings in mud brick walls and the few wares displayed are fly-specked. The cathedral is old Spanish, facing a plaza that is old Spanish and a town hall that is, oddly enough, likewise old Spanish. You gather, I presume, that Puno is a real old Spanish town. You expect to see Pizarro and his boys coming through the streets at any time.

We were picking our way down one of these streets at sun-down. Father Murphy, a pink-cheeked young priest, was leading the way. He was quite a bit ahead of us for he knew the cobbled streets well, whereas we were picking our way carefully to avoid the mud and dirt.

Around a corner came a troupe of Indians. Nicely dressed, but all in black. Strange, for the Altiplano Indians go in for color in a big way. No, these men wore black coats and hats; the women had big black skirts and shawls and topped off the funereal dress with black derbies. A sinister gang, I thought. Furthermore, they all wobbled a bit unsteadily.

"AY, YAY! Padre," yelled one of the first. He pranced across the street and enfolded Father Murphy in a tremendous bear-hug.

204

"He says he's my uncle," came Father's muffled voice from the depths of the bear-hug. "He says the whole tribe are my uncles and aunts."

The poor priest was passed from one to the other of his uncles. The first one now turned his attention to us, who were surely his nieces. He advanced ready to give us the same warm welcome but we held him down to a handshake.

Soon, very soon, they passed on, anxious to get back to their village before dark.

These were the Ichu Indians, a sub-tribe of the Aymará. They have quite a bloodthirsty reputation in Puno. One of the women is reputed to have cut up her husband. Since then, other Indians have shunned the Ichu village which nestles at the foot of a mountain some six miles or so from town. They cross themselves as they pass the side road which leads to the huddle of mud huts Ichus call home.

But Father McClellan, Maryknoll pastor of the Puno parish, thought of the Ichus in terms of souls. They were his parishioners. He approached the head-men and planned a series of evening instructions for the whole village so many nights a week during Lent.

Feeling like Isaac Jogues entering the Mohawk hut where a tomahawk waited to split his skull, Father McClellan rode his horse into the village for the first evening. A curious, not too hostile crowd awaited him in the quadrangle.

"We figure that if you're brave enough to come to the Ichu village at night, Padre," the leader told him, "then we're brave enough to listen to what you have to say."

Four hundred of them were brave enough, too, to go to Confession and to receive their Easter Communion that year if never before.

If Puno has a warm heart for Maryknoll, it has a cold outlook on the Andes. Puno is on Lake Titicaca, the highest navigable lake in the world, 14,000 feet closer to Heaven than the ocean is.

Puno was the end of a three-day trek which took us from Lima to Cuzco by plane and from Cuzco to Puno by train. It was Friday the 13th when we planned to begin. In Lima, Friday the 13th is celebrated as a Double Major with an Octave. We solemnized the day by arriving a half-hour late for the Cuzco plane. No more planes until Sunday.

Bright and early Sunday, we were off into a cloudless sky. The plane flew high over the city and headed out for the mountains. The words of the Psalm ran through my head over and over again. "The beds of the waters came into view and the foundations of the world were laid bare." The Psalm goes on to say that all this was done by the blast of the breath of God's wrath.

God certainly did something drastic to the country around Lima. We might have been flying over the Sahara. Sand hills and clay, heaped as the wind blew them! Now and then a river bed where thru long past ages the ever-thinning stream had marked off narrowing ridges until the last drop had passed long, long ago. It was so dry, so barren.

For a half hour I watched the plane's shadow passing over the dry hills below. Then, we banked sharply. The wing-tips pointed away up on one side and away down on the other. Looking out the west window you clutched your seat lest you slide off into blue nothingness; looking out the east window, you stiffened back as the wing-tip pointed down to the tree tops. Next thing we knew, the shadow was on the other side of the plane. We were going back the way we had come.

The hostess came through the cabin. She volunteered an explanation, which sounded pretty flimsy, "The luggage smells bad." Back at the Lima airport, we found she was only too right. Somebody had packed a bottle of ether in his luggage, stored away up front in the plane. The bottle broke and the fumes were escaping. The pilots had noticed themselves getting sleepy and decided to turn back to Lima.

Herewith, I present a modest claim to be the all-time Champion Jinx for travellers. Or at least I ought to get the solid rubber medal for Turn-Backs. In 1938, I started off for Japan from Honolulu; after two days at sea, a mutiny broke out and we were ordered back to Honolulu. In 1947, I went by plane all the way from Manila to Hong Kong; but fog obscured the airport. We cruised around for an hour and then went back to the Philippines, landing on the beach in northern Luzon. We stayed overnight and proceeded back to Manila the next day. Again I was going from Hong Kong up the West River in China by boat; we were wallowing in the only bit of rough sea there is on the whole trip, when fire broke out in the hold. Sister Cecilia Marie, who was with me then, came over to where I was stretched out on a wooden bunk.

"Can you swim?" she asked.

"Yes," I said.

"Good!" she nodded. "The boat's on fire. Be ready to jump."

The silly thing about it was this. I had taken off my cape. As I stood by the railing, I held the cape in my hand. The thought rushed through my mind: Should I keep my cape off and be able to swim better? Or should I put it on so that my body will be properly clothed when it is cast up on the beach tomorrow morning? Fortunately, I never had to decide. The men got the fire out and we limped back to Hong Kong for repairs.

And now, in Peru we turned back to Lima because the pilots started to be asphyxiated! The guilty bag was discovered and thrown off. We started off again. Up over the city of old Spanish churches and new Hollywood-style mansions and boulevards. Up over the sea which laps the golden beaches. Once again over the dry hills and long-dead river beds. Then came the first view of snow-capped giants. First, away off in the distance; then coming close. Clouds moved in. Through the rifts, we saw the deep snow piled by the wind and running into water streams in the sunny patches.

After the first range of snow giants, there were smaller mountains. But what was that on them? Sure enough, grass! Sparse and scrubby, but real grass. I felt the delight of a long-bald man who sees a faint fuzz on his head. Except for carefully tended patches in cities, we had not seen grass for several months.

We were flying at 30,000 feet. Each seat in the plane was equipped with a bit of rubber tubing connected with the sidewall. This was for oxygen. Not only were we told to use it and warned not to forget it, but the stewardess paraded up and down the center aisle to see that we obeyed. She herself wore a portable oxygen tank strapped on her back. A sleepy old fellow who looked like a veteran of many a junket over these Andes, was her special worry. He continually fell asleep and let the tube of oxygen slip out of his hand. At last, she could stand it no longer. She took a piece of adhesive tape and pasted the tube on to his upper lip so that the nozzle blew right into his nose. He didn't mind in the least.

Thus, in a super-modern conveyance, we came to Cuzco—one of the most ancient of cities on our side of the globe. Cuzco who, in her glory, fell victim to Pizarro and his 187 men! Cuzco, stronghold of the Inca Empire!

Just before the time of Christ, the highland Indians of Peru and Bolivia had a high civilization. This centered at Tiahuanaco, in Bolivia, on the south shore of Lake Titicaca. Here are the giant statues, the broken temple walls, which tell of a religion of years ago. The calendar was accurately divided; the equinoxes were noted so that the sun on March 21 and September 21 rose exactly outside the doorway of the temple and shone upon the gold in the calendar carved on the wall.

This civilization rose to new heights from 600 until about 900 A.D. After that, the Inca tribe of Andean Indians gained ascendency and by 1100 A.D. had developed Cuzco as the seat of a rapidly expanding Empire. By 1482, the Inca ruled an empire 1,800 miles long which included all of Peru, much of Bolivia and a goodish bit of Chile. No less than sixteen million Indians of the high Andes were their subjects.

It's amazing what they had—and what they didn't have. They had no wheel. They had no iron tools. Even the potter's wheel was unknown. They had not yet devised writing and they kept track of figures by tying knots in a cord.

On the other hand, they used a calendar far more accurate than the old Julian calendar that Pizarro knew. They terraced their fields with precise engineering. They built roads and suspension bridges across the mountain chasms. Their roads were their undoing. For 1,500 miles they stretched up and down Peru. Pizarro, so to speak, found the red carpet spread before him as he marched up to Cuzco.

Their stone-cutting is still the marvel of the world. So accurately cut are the huge blocks of stone, that not even a razor blade can be inserted between the stones in Cuzco's walls. How they did it, nobody knows exactly, for they had no iron or steel tools. Some think that they used an acid. In wool weaving, pottery and metal work, they were superb.

Best of all were communications. Runners could bring a message all the 1,500 miles of that road, in less than a week. Along the road were way-stations where travellers could rest—a sort of hotel-chain from one end of the empire to the other.

Furthermore, they had domesticated the llama and alpaca. Anybody who can bring a llama to terms is worthy of respect. They look something like small camels but without a hump. Though nice enough to the little Indians boys and girls who tend them, they look with disdain on anybody else, particularly tourists. Mamallama gives Sonny a lesson early in life: "When you see two-legged creatures come into the pasture, and they don't wear high white hats like all good women wear and they don't carry spindles, then you will know they are tourists. Especially, if they keep pointing a black box at you. Well, Sonny, you can have a lot of fun with that kind. You strike a pose and keep it, looking with dreamy eyes at some Andes or other,—any one of the majestic peaks that strikes your fancy at the moment. You'll see the tourist stalk up behind you with his little black box. He'll drop to one knee for what he calls an angle shot. That's when you skitter ten feet away and pose again. It's lots of fun. He'll try the frontal approach coming right at you. Well, look him square in the eye until he raises his black box. Then jump around so fast he can't find you in the view-finder. If he gets really annoying, spit at him."

Llamas are masters of the Disdainful Spit. They're so good at it that persons thus insulted even boast about it. At the hotel in Cuzco, a group of travellers were telling various adventures. One had walked out to the first of the wayside hotels the old Incas built. Another had gone mountain climbing; a third had spent the day in the old Temple of the Sun.

"What have you seen of Cuzco?" they asked a quiet little man.

"Very little," he said. "But I had a llama spit at me today."

This is the hotel where a sign is posted in each guest room.

THE HOT WATER

is effective at the following hours
6:30—10:00 A.M. and P.M.
We advise you to let the water run
during 5 minutes after which time
you shall get the water.

Cuzco is divided between the very old city and the new one built on its foundations by the Spanish. In addition, they had a severe earthquake a few years ago, and many of the Spanish buildings were ruined. Ramshackle housing and newer buildings tell the tale.

In many of the churches you can trace just where the Inca foundations stop. The large smooth stones, set together so solidly and yet without mortar, are unmistakable. Then come the mud brick or smaller stones and adobe—whatever has been used to complete the church.

At the monastery of *La Merced* (Our Lady of Mercy) a friar showed us one of the great treasures of the city, a monstrance valued at $2,500,000. Solid gold, it stands four feet high. It contains 1,500 diamonds from Brazil, 600 pearls from Panama and 46 pounds of 22-karat gold from Peru, all worked together in the most intricate and ornate designs. It was made in 1720, almost two hundred years after Pizarro captured the city in 1533. Wouldn't he have loved to see it!

But I never can get up much interest in gold and pearls and millions of dollars. To tell the truth, I've never had even a speaking acquaintance with such; they tell me though, that you get fonder of riches the longer you live with them. So it's just as well I never had much to live with.

Far dearer to my way of thinking are the hearts of the Indian people who walk through Cuzco's streets in their bare feet, carrying bundles of everything (including babies) on their backs. Hard work, few creature comforts, and the humiliation of being a long-defeated nation—these bring their lives close to that of Our Lord Himself.

St. Patrick's Day happened to fall while we were in Cuzco. We attended Mass in one of the beautiful big churches. It had been damaged by the earthquake and was being repaired. Scaffolding filled the church. High up next to the roof, the men were hammering and chiseling. A High Mass was going on at a special altar set up in the body of the church. The priest had a healthy pair of lungs. He had to. For, instead of the usual bell to announce the Sanctus and other parts of the Mass, a cannonade of firecrackers went off in the rear of the church. A band was back there, too. Both band and firecrackers went off at the same time, but the band won out in the end, for it was crashing and bugling away long after the last cracker had burst. Altogether, I would say, that if St. Patrick had had so much noise in his day, it would have been a great help to him in driving the snakes out of Ireland—and the Irish, too.

Sister Victoria Francis and I sat up in the front pew, as far from the band as we could get. I was trying my best to think up a few holy thoughts for St. Patrick's sake, or as least to suppress the uncharitable ones. Was there no one in Cuzco to give St. Patrick a nod of recognition by wearing a bit of green?

An Indian woman and her two little girls stepped into the space between our front pew and the sanctuary railing. She set down her bundle; it looked like our week's wash in pre-Bendix days when we put everything into a sheet and tied the four corners together ready for the laundry man to come. She was a young-ish woman, quite pretty. The two little girls put down their smaller bundles, too, and sat on their haunches quietly. Their mother took off the black scarf she wore over her head, folded it neatly and prepared to put it in her bundle. To my delight, as she put the black one in, she took out a solid green one—a real Kelly green. This she placed over her head, and let the generous green run over her shoulders and back. Yum! Yum! Surely this good woman must be named Patricia. Surely she must have something in her from the Emerald Isle, just as the great Bernardo O'Higgins, Chile's national hero, stemmed from an Irish father and a Chilean mother.

Patricia, poor soul, had much on her mind. As the Mass progressed, she began to weep. Soon, oblivious of everybody but herself and God, she was sobbing aloud. She told God about it in tones loud enough to reach the tabernacle. I understood not a word of her Quechua speech, but I knew her sorrow. More than once, I too, have felt as she did. But I didn't go to church. I would have been ashamed. No, I went to my room and cried it out there, instead of coming in simple faith to God's house and casting the whole sorrow at His feet. Patricia was a child. She brought to God the hard lesson He gave her to learn, and asked Him how she was ever to learn such a difficult thing.

Maybe that's why we get so tangled up in our minds, we Anglo-Saxons. We're ashamed to let anybody know that we have sorrows.

In the middle of Patricia's shower, an Indian man came over to her and put out his hand. He must have been her husband. She stopped sobbing long enough to fish around in her bundle for a bagful of coins. She selected one and gave it to him. He went off to a shrine at the side to light a candle. That little bit of business done, Patricia resumed her tears and lamentations.

We left Patricia to her sorrow, and went to catch a train. It was an English-style train running the two hundred miles between Cuzco and Puno, some of the most magnificent country God ever made. In this section live 2,000,000 of Peru's 8,000,000 people, the heaviest populated rural district in all of South America. And all of it next door to heaven, in air so rarefied that you are puffing like a steam engine after going up a very mild set of steps.

It's farming country. But the farms stand on their ears. Suppose you took a nicely laid out farm in Illinois and tilted it up 45 degrees or so. Fat cattle, herds of llamas, flocks of sheep and little colonies of donkeys and horses munch the grass without bothering even to look at the snow-covered peaks which fence them in. Here and there, Indian huts cluster around a woe-begone adobe church. This train is the big event of the day. Out to earn an honest penny, the women vendors in full red skirts and white stove-pipe hats crowd to the train windows to sell bread and fruit.

Puno is a stronghold of the Maryknoll Fathers. They were on hand in force at the station. We surrendered to superior numbers, gave up our suitcases without a murmur and followed meekly up to San Ambrosio school.

In spite of the warmth of the Maryknollers' hearts, Puno is cold. 14,300 feet above sea level, it is well above the timber line. The sun is nice when it's around, but it has a habit of going down every evening and leaving Puno like an iceberg. Most of us keep bundled up all day long.

We had dinner at the Puno seminary next day. Indeed, we sat at the table of the Rector Magnificus who is no other than a very unassuming young priest from Long Island, Fr. Charles Girnius. The Rector Magnificus dined with us, attired in cassock, overcoat, warm woolen muffler, riding boots and double thick wool stockings. In honor of the occasion, he had removed his thick black felt hat. The seminary is known as The Deep Freeze amongst the brethren in Puno.

The seminarians ate at a long table on a slightly lower level. Although they decorously kept their eyes down, they didn't miss a trick of what we foreign Sisters were doing. Food was passed through a window from the kitchen—a very austere meal, really. A bit of meat loaf, a few greens, rice and a very small orange, grown locally. Fit training for boys who will do heroic work for their country and for all of South America if they can "take it."

This is the situation, and this is the plan.

Puno diocese has a million people, practically all baptized Catholics. It has but 23 diocesan priests and 21 Maryknollers. Were it not for our priests, each of the 23 priests would have 46,500 persons to serve. Many of the priests are old; some are sick; nearly all are discouraged. A diocesan priest has a very hard row to hoe in South America. He is alone in an immense parish; he receives no salary from his bishop. Ergo, he is forced to find some means of earning a living. Usually he turns to teaching or some other profession. His parishioners either cannot or have not yet been trained to support him in his labors for them. Each parish has *at least* ten mission stations attached to it!

The more he teaches, the less time he has for administering the Sacraments. The more zealous he is, the more he wears himself out trying to cover his immense territory and at the same time support himself. There is little communication or community life with his fellow-priests. He sees them during the annual retreat, if then, and knows them not at all in a social way.

The plan is this: Maryknoll has already a minor seminary in Puno, with thirty students in it. In April, 1953, they laid the cornerstone for a major seminary in Cuzco which will serve all of Peru. Planning for 200 students, they look far ahead to the day when eager young Peruvians will be afire with apostolic zeal to bring the Faith to the furthest recesses of their mountainous country.

Besides the thorough pastoral training in both minor and major seminaries, the young priests will have from two to five years work with Maryknollers in parishes before they are out on their own. For this purpose, Maryknoll is taking over a number of parishes in the mountains, so as to get training grounds ready for the young priests.

Father Jack Byrnes from Dunmore, Pa., took us out to see some of these mountain parishes. We had hoped to get to Juli but mud and roads held us down to a snail's pace. We settled for Ilave, some fifteen miles short of it.

Ilave appeared to be deserted. In the plaza a lone little girl and her small sister played in the mud. They had appealing faces. Father had gone off with the officer in charge of the local garrison; they were seeing about some business or other. Sister Victoria Francis and I were alone in the jeep. "I'll just get out a moment," I thought, "and get a snap of those two children."

Fatal thought! I took the picture without mishap. Then I handed each child a holy card. Oh, oh! People came just pouring from their houses and side streets. A million eyes must have been watching me take that picture. In two seconds I was the center of a howling mob. "Give me! Madrecita! Give me a holy card!"

Sister was sitting in the car. She saw the riot. They came from everywhere, all converging on the holy cards. As in the California gold rush—men, women and children staked all in the mad thirst for a holy card.

I was getting scared. People could be trampled to death in a mob like this. The original two children were squashed tight against my legs. I didn't want to move lest the crowd mow them down. Already those near me were jammed by the pressure from the outer rows. Then I saw a policeman speeding to the plaza and thanked God.

He fought his way through the jam of outstretched hands and pleading faces. The poor people could not comprehend that I, the goose who laid the golden holy cards, had not one left. They still wagged their hands toward me and begged "Una stampita, Madrecita! Stampita!" The policeman came closer fighting through the mob. Then, as he came at last to me, he too put out his hand and said, "A stampita, Madre, please. Give me a stampita?"

"No tengo!" I shouted at him. "No tengo. Can't you see that I no tengo any more holy cards?"

The crowd realized at last that my bankroll was flat. They began to thin out. In just a few minutes the plaza was deserted once more.

Julita and her little sister played again in the mud, their precious holy cards already pretty well smeared.

Some enterprising religious should investigate the possibility of using holy cards instead of money in Peru. Better still, if he be a photographer. Then maybe he could get along with empty film boxes, silver paper wrappings, tubes for tropical packing and, best of all, burnt-out flash bulbs. Medals are also good on the exchange. You can collect a crowd anywhere just by putting your hand into your pocket and ostentatiously bringing out some.

The army officer told us this little tale of the Communists. One night they went out to a mountain overlooking the town. They uprooted all the grass in certain spots so that in the morning all the town could see "VIVA"—and a hammer and sickle etched on the bare rock. The tricky thing was that in a country with so little rain, it takes a long time for grass to grow over a bare place like that. The officer was stumped for a few hours. Then he thought of a scheme. That night he and his men went out to the mountain too. They converted the hammer and sickle into a capital P and added three letters, E, R and U. The Communists were chagrined to see that they had done most of the work for a beautiful VIVA PERU! now blazoned on the mountain.

If this young officer is a sample of Peru's up-and-coming army officers, then the future of the country is bright. He and his wife are roughing it here in this little outpost, high in the mountains. He is building better barracks for his men and trying to give them living conditions at least as good as the ones they left. It's an opportunity, he thinks, to give a young fellow some ideas of self-respecting discipline. Part of his program is to instruct them in their religion. He is anxious that the Maryknoll Fathers take over the poor old decrepit church at Ilave and fix it up. He is as zealous for his country as our priests are for the Church. It makes a good combination in Ilave.

Father McLellan from Denver, Colo., is the enterprising pastor at Puno. He has all sorts of schemes to make it a vigorous, self-supporting parish. Besides, he has the advantage of having been a noted all-round athlete in his day. With teams for this and that playing for cups and prizes, with Societies for Nocturnal Adoration flourishing, with contacts through the town business clubs, he still has time for big parish benefits. What inducement to bring the crowd? was a question for some time. They couldn't stage a card-party; for the people don't play bridge or canasta. Bingo is still, God be praised, a Thing Unknown in the Andes. But Father came up with a beautiful idea—a parish bullfight!

He was getting ready for it while we were in Puno. Bullfights are not as common as people think. Father had to refurbish the old bull-ring and hire a fighter to come. He had to get the bull, too.

I was all for staying on in Puno to watch this. I especially wanted to get Sister Victoria Francis to wear a red cape and sit in the front row. But she didn't like the idea much. So we packed our bags once more and left Puno.

PANAMA

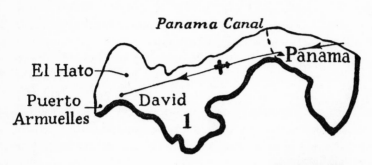

El Hato

Puerto
Armuelles

David

Panama Canal

Panama

1

AND
CURACAO

Willhelmstadt

2

KEY

◆ 20 ◆

UNDER ST. VINCENT'S WING

I first met the Panama Canal some years ago when I passed through on a freighter. Captain of the ship was a genial, likable man known up and down the West Coast of South America as *El Potensio* (The Powerful One). Not that he was so strong, although his short stocky frame was solidly upholstered with muscle. *El Potensio* was named for his voice; he could out-shout any able-bodied seaman from Valparaiso to Brooklyn.

El Potensio was as short of speech as he was of hair. The only covering he permitted his scalp was a quarter-inch fuzz. His legs were always braced for a gale whether he was in one or not. He was all of one color—tan. The suns of many an ocean had bleached the fuzz and browned his skin to just about the same khaki color as his shirt and pants. Only his blue eyes sparkled as he came out with his terse, quick sallies.

He had a real affection for his SS *Santa Olivia*. He seemed to think of her as if she were a horse under him. We had expected thirty hours of rough weather in the Caribbean; *El Potensio* was patient with her for that length of time. But when *Olivia* rolled and heaved for almost sixty hours, he felt that she needed a talking to. We were in his ship-shape sitting room talking about his little girl and boy in New Jersey. Cappie was trying to light his pipe, standing with his stocky legs firmly planted on the floor and his body swaying forward and backward as *Olivia* rolled from side to side. He was like one of those dolls you punch and can't knock over—only Cappie did it in slow motion.

"How now, *Olivia!*" he chided her as she took a good long roll. "This nonsense was supposed to stop long ago."

This mild reproof doesn't sound much like a blustering *El*

Potensio. At the Canal, however, we learned that he was well named.

The ship's laundry was taken off as we entered the Canal at Cristobal on the Atlantic Side. It was washed on shore, and taken by auto to the Pacific side that day. Eight hours later as we slid out of the last locks at Balboa and were ready to proceed on the Pacific, a dinghy came out from shore loaded with the laundry. A huge loading boom swung out over the side and a great iron hook was lowered to the boat which bobbed like a cork alongside. The whole crew from *El Potensio* himself down to Eduardo, the waiter, hung over the railing to watch the laundry come home. Every man there had at least a shirt due him. In the dinghy, the men put a canvas bundle on the hook and up she came! Once on deck, the men dove into it to get their things. *El Potensio* left the fracas early and strode toward the railing. As he passed us, he muttered, "Tablecloths! Sheets! Towels! Clothes for everybody on board! But not a scrap of underwear for me!" He leaned over the rail and yelled,

"Hey! You! Where's my underwear?"

The men paid no attention. Either they were hard of hearing or they hoped *Olivia* would be in mid-Pacific before the loss was noted. But *El Potensio* would not be frustrated. He picked up a megaphone and yelled loud enough to be heard on the Atlantic side.

"WHERE'S MY UNDERWEAR!"

There was no mistake this time. The laundry men realized that the stuff they had secreted belonged to nobody less than *El Potensio* himself. With a leap, they sprang to their feet and scurried around the dinghy, collecting a piece here and there hidden under boards and behind cushions. The loading arm swung out again and the small package was tied to the great iron hook. *El Potensio's* underwear arrived in state!

That done, *Olivia's* engines throbbed once more and we put out on the Pacific.

Panama is a crossroads. It is the halfway point for anybody going between North and South America, or for those bound from

Europe to Asia. Travellers pause here, get their bearings, and go off to someplace else.

Someday, somebody—not me, of course—ought to write a book on the Odd Folk who stop in Panama. Somehow or other, they manage to have the time and money to traipse around the world putting worry wrinkles into stewardesses' pretty faces and giving sleepless nights to passenger agents.

Our Sister Maria Pia can tell story after story about them. The passenger agents in Panama are sleeping better since they discovered Sister's talent for calming the ruffled waters. They will wrestle with some footloose oddity for a while and then call Sister on the phone. That's how we met Hildegarde Bugbee.

Hildegarde was trying to get a plane to the States. She had come on a ship from Australia where she was foundress of a new religion. This accounted for her wearing an outfit which was a cross between a Methodist Deaconess' dress and a religious habit. Beyond that, she volunteered no information about herself.

"If you can get Hildegarde out of our hair, Sister," the agent promised, "we will be your friends for life."

Sister drove her from the airport to the airlines office in town to arrange for tickets. Hildegarde's strong British accent wafted from the car appreciating Panama's strange birds and flowers.

At the office, the clerk said,

"Where do you want to go?"

"Why, to the States, of course!" she said quickly.

"But where in the States?" he asked. Then, since she looked puzzled, he went on, "To New York, Chicago, Los Angeles, Phoenix, Miami—?"

At Miami, her face brightened. "Miami! I think that's it. Yes, I'm quite sure of it now. I'll take Miami."

"Do you want a one-way ticket or round trip?"

"Well," she pondered over the decision. "Whichever is cheapest; whichever is cheapest, of course."

Since one-way was cheaper, she bought a one-way ticket. When the clerk was ready for payment, Hildegarde turned to him,

"I say," she said, "have you a jack-knife?" She began digging into a huge pocket in her skirt. The clerk fruitlessly felt his pockets, a little dismayed by the request, "A jack-knife? Well, not on me, at the moment."

"Never mind, never mind, I have mine here." She pulled out a big Boy Scout knife with multiple blades, nail file, corkscrew, bottle-opener and all attached. In the other hand was her money, neatly sewed up in a handkerchief. With the jack-knife, she slowly ripped out the stitches. The money counted out and change received, she pulled a needle and thread from the same pocket and sewed up her handkerchief again.

Sister sighed with relief as they left the office and stepped out into the street, but Hildegarde had one more thing to do.

"I say, do you mind halting for a moment?" she asked as they stepped out into the street. "I'll have to pull up my socks."

There and then, she bent over and adjusted her bobby socks which came maybe six or seven inches above her ankle. They were held up with men's garters. Sister hustled her into the car before she could think of anything else she wanted to do.

She stayed in our convent until her plane left that evening. She spoke a bit about the religion she was founding. A group of ten or twelve women lived together "something like you girls do," she said. "We persevere in prayer, helping one another and holding everything in common."

"They're such fine women," she reminisced. "And how hard they work! Dear me, all the day they work. And far into the night. Two o'clock, three o'clock, four o'clock, and still they're working."

Our Sisters feel that they work pretty hard but this was beyond them. "What sort of work, Miss Bugbee?" they asked.

"Why, confectionery, to be sure! Candy-making, you know. We're famous for it all over Australia." The group had been bombed out of England during the war and had gone to Australia to make a new start.

The only information she gave as to why she was going to the States, was that an uncle or somebody had left her some money in Canada, and Miami would be one of the stops enroute to her new fortune.

But people like Hildegarde Bugbee are not Sister Maria Pia's main concern in Panama. She is in charge of two branches of mission work. One is a variety of catechetical work—kindergartens, release time classes, special summer work, parish groups and a radio program. The other is St. Vincent's School in Panama City.

St. Vincent's was established for the English-speaking Negroes from Jamaica who had been imported to work on the Panama Canal. They were a distinct group in Panama City. The American Vincentian priests were asked to take care of them. They, in turn, requested us to staff a school for these children.

When four of our Sisters came in 1944, they found the school under the benign administration of Felicita. A dear old colored mammy, she had cleared out the basement of the church and set up benches facing a single blackboard. When the 150 little squirmers had said their morning prayers and sat down, Felicita used to fill the blackboard with the hardest and longest words she could find.

"Now, you chilluns copy them words into your notebooks," she would say. Then off she went to do the washing she took in as a side line.

Felicita was glad to see the Sisters come. She knew she wasn't much of a teacher; her only thought was that she could get the children to learn their prayers. She was only too happy to surrender the classroom to us.

With characteristic directness, Sister Augustine went to work. Sister is a born educator—and a born missioner. She has directed schools in Korea, Hong Kong, the Philippines and in Baltimore. She knew just what to do with these 150 unclassified little intellects.

She cut a roll of brown wrapping paper into sheets, and gave everybody a sheet. On the board was an easy test. Those who failed were in Grade One; those who passed, in Grade Two. Then, she passed out more wrapping paper and put a harder test on the board for the survivors. The victorious ones were elevated to Grade Three; the flunkers stayed in Grade Two. Thus, by the process of elimination, she soon had six grades of children but not much wrapping paper left. Some of the Second Graders were 19 years old. They minded it not at all, and neither did Sister.

The next question was where to put these separate classes. The basement was a single room. Four theoretical rooms were made when the classes were placed back to back and the Sisters faced each other. This made it hard for the youngsters to do shenanigans and easy for the Sisters to signal S O S in case of a near-riot.

Sister Socorro Maria took her kindergarteners up to the church choir loft. She played Jack and Jill on the organ while the youngsters danced around the pews. Her blackboard was placed between Our Lady of Perpetual Help and The Little Flower. "I was always afraid somebody would fall out a stained glass window, or climb over the railing into the church below," she says. She told the little black angels who crowded around her, "How lucky we are to have this kindergarten! We're almost in Heaven up here!" Then rolling her eyes and indulging in just a little white lie, she said, "Why, we couldn't imagine a better kindergarten, could we, children!" And the Recording Angel was nice enough to forget to note it down.

Things are better now. One new building is up and another is halfway done. But the roof's on and we hold class in the rough cement rooms. There's so much mud around the place that Sister lets the children slide into the classroom through the church window where it connects with the new building.

It's hard for us Americans to conceive of the background of these Negro children in Panama. We grow up with electric lights and loving parents and enough food and clothes. But these poor things have nothing of all that. Sister Martin Therese was telling me about a boy in her room who had not done his homework. "Why not, Julio?" she asked, a bit on the stern side. The story came out.

Julio's mother and her Current Husband had a falling-out. The Current Husband took to beating Julio's mother. Her yells brought the neighbors who tried to separate them. One of the neighbors in the fracas took a beer bottle and "bopped" (this is Julio's word for it) the Current Husband on the head so hard that he went out like a lamp. The police were on hand by that time and the whole tribe was taken to court, including Julio.

When the Current Husband regained consciousness, the police asked him, "Who bopped you on the head?" But he wouldn't tell because he didn't know. Julio's mother knew because she had seen it, but she wouldn't tell either, partly because she was glad he had been bopped on the head and partly because she would never tell the police anything, anyhow. Indeed, she got so indignant that the police should expect her to be an informer, that she fell on her C.H. like a wild cat, clawing and scratching him all over again.

The police were bored with the whole thing. They put Julio's mother into prison and dismissed the rest of them. Everybody dispersed. The C.H. took Julio by the arm and set out to celebrate the end of his romance for surely he would be involved in another in the two weeks before Julio's mother got out of jail. He took the sleepy little boy (only 9 years old) from one cantina to the next until the wee hours of the morning. At last, Julio fell asleep with his head on a whiskey-puddled table. When he woke, the Current Husband was gone from his life for good. Julio took himself home and put himself to bed. It was a very simple process after all, since he just threw himself into his usual corner of the room that he and ten other people called home.

And Sister wanted to know why he had not done his homework!

When you see Julio and others who have just as bad stories behind them, you marvel that they are as clean and neat, as bright and attentive as they are. Usually, there is at least one bright spot in the background—a grandmother who loves the child, a big sister who's trying to be respectable, a "real father" who still keeps an eye on his flesh and blood even though he is not living with the child's mother. These are the ones who bring their Julios to the Sisters and see that they stay in school. You only wish that the thousands of other poor little tykes in Panama had somebody to sponsor them and bring them to us.

Every child at St. Vincent's, thank Goodness, is not like Julio. There's many a conscientious family which has little in the way of comforts, but makes a sacrifice to send the children there.

To understand the situation, you must realize that there are two cities, two civilizations and two countries, side by side and overlapping as well. The American-administered Zone extends for five miles on either side of the Canal. The country of Panama extends beyond that. For instance, we live on Fourth of July Avenue in the Zone, but the other side of the street is in Panama.

The Zone is not unlike an army post. You may not live there unless you have some reason for so doing, and your application for residence must be approved. Once that is done, you are assigned a house to live in by the Housing Office. You may protest if you don't like it, but you may not go out and build yourself another house.

For ten years, our Sisters lived—well, a little oddly. Six of them were in the basement of St. Mary's Church. It was nicely fitted up. Once inside you forgot how strange it was to come out of church and duck down the cellar stairs to go home.

The seven others were assigned two small apartments upstairs in houses across the street from each other. They used to cook and eat and study in one and then walk downstairs, cross the street and walk upstairs to get to their sleeping apartment. It was disjointed living.

But now both groups are in an old Bachelors' Quarters. In the early days of the Zone, they built big barrack-like apartments for the single men—engineers, electricians and other types. Men who came for the duration of a special job and went away. These big well-constructed barracks housed 15 men on the first floor, 15 on the second and 15 on the third. That was all there was to the house—no kitchen, dining room, common room or library. Just 45 sleeping rooms.

One of these is now our convent. By taking down partitions, we have chapel, community room, study rooms, and all the usual appertenances of a convent. If one of the former tenants finding a key in his pocket should decide to come back some night, he wouldn't recognize the place, I'm sure. Can you imagine his face as he opens the door and sees the change?

Down by *La Boca* (The Mouth) where the Canal empties into the Pacific, there are people not so lucky. These are the Negro employees. They live in wooden barracks, painted a muddy grey and roofed with corrugated iron, much on the rusty side. Eight families are assigned to each barracks; each family gets 3½ rooms. One child, three children, five or thirteen children—it makes no difference. But there is green grass all around and the climate is easy on the nerves. Most of the time the children are playing outside and Mama has a chance to get her breath.

At La Boca, is Sister Francis Christine. She took over the basement of St. Teresa's church (we seem to run to church basements in Panama) and made a kindergarten out of it. Armed with needle and thread, and hammer and saw as well, she sewed up curtains and nailed cabinets together and sawed the legs off chairs to make them into low benches. Now, with 56 black angels there, she's quite in her element. And there are 56 mothers in La Boca, much relieved. They must go out and work all day; now they know that their little ones are cared for.

La Boca is one of three kindergartens we staff in both the Zone and in Panama City. One of these, in Chorillo, used to be housed in a very shaky little building. It had once been a Protestant church. Then we had our kindergarten in it. When we left, a sect of Holy Rollers took it. Carmen, one of our neighbors in Chorillo, was dubious about the whole business.

"Ah don't know how it will work out, Seestah," she said, shaking her head. "That old building is all right for Protestant services and for your Catholic kindergarten. Those are gentle religions. But the Holy Rollers are hard on their meeting houses. Some of these days, the old floor is just going to crash through."

◆ 21 ◆

THE BANANA AND I

Although I had often gone picnicking with him and many times had met him at breakfast, still I never really got to know The Banana until I met him face-to-face in Puerto Armuelles.

One sees him perfectly at home there. Not just a moment's cold study as he lies on your plate at the table and you note the slender form, the elegant color and aristocratic markings on him. No, in Puerto Armuelles, The Banana's inmost thoughts and feelings are laid bare. You see his birth, his happy boyhood with billions and billions of cousins and brothers, his sad cutting down in his youth, and his departure for that land of promise, The United States.

You see, too, the "rejects"—those poor bananas who made the grade all through but failed to pass the inspector's eagle eye at the last moment. Just as their comrades were being loaded on the boat, their secret faults were discovered. A brown spot here, a tinge of too-ripeness there. And the stevedore with the stem of guilty bananas on his shoulder, is ordered to stand that stem of rejects against the wall of a shack on the pier. Like many a lad who has flunked out in his senior year, the stem of rejects hangs around the pier, lurching against the wall every time a rough hand robs it of some of its glory. At the end, the naked stem is kicked into the sea, just one more piece of flotsam that didn't come out a winner in the Struggle for Survival.

We really didn't intend to pay a call on The Banana. But we were up at Cacuradi, near the Costa Rican border when the invitation came. You never heard of Cacuradi? Well, it is 4½ miles from El Rico. Don't know where that is? It's quite a good haul from Natividad. Dear me, you don't know Natividad! Why, that's a fairish town about 20 or 30 miles from David. And lest you show ignorance of even David, I rush to tell you that David has an airport and is an hour and a half from Panama City and the Canal, flying West.

There are four small cottages at Cacuradi. That's all. Kind friends in Panama City own one of them; they generously let us use it for rest from Panama City's heat and hard work. Mrs. Dicks leaves no stone unturned for our convenience. Here and there through the mountain cabin, there are notes pinned to curtains or left on top shelves:

"I hope none of you dear Sisters gets sick, but if you do, there are some simple home remedies in the bathroom cabinet. But don't touch the big bottle on the bottom shelf. That's special for our dog."

And: "You'll find the dish towels almost worn out but I got some new material the last time I went to the Zone. You'll find it on the top shelf in the kitchen. It won't take you a minute to run up some new towels on the sewing machine and I'll be awfully grateful."

Again: "I do hope you have a grand rest, my dears. But don't let Peppie play with that black dog who hangs around here. That mutt has fleas, I know. He's always around trying to get Peppie to play with him."

If Sister Victoria Francis had been a fugitive from Justice, she could not have found a better hideout than Cacuradi. But the Vincentian Fathers can track down a Visitor no matter where she hides. We had hardly arrived when an infernal racket and a cloud of dust on the road announced Father Grass. He had jeeped fifty miles from the Banana stronghold in order to convince Sister that the Catholic Church's future in Central America hung by a slender thread. The thread was—yes, you guessed it—that Maryknoll Sisters start a school in Puerto Armuelles. He invited us to see for ourselves the Banana's empire and its spiritual needs.

Consequently, a few days later, we piled ourselves and our baggage into Antonio's station wagon, which makes a twice weekly run picking up freight and passengers. With the Latin's innate courtesy, the other passengers left the entire back seat for us three Sisters. We shared it only with several huge cabbages, a live chicken and three bags of greenery. This was really luxury travelling; six people crowded into the middle seat and five were up front to keep the driver company. Ready? And off we started down the mountain trail for two hours into Concepcion.

Father Grass was there with a queer contraption. It had iron wheels and ran on tracks like a railroad car, but it had a Ford motor and an automobile front. The body was of iron with seats like a station wagon. Since there is only railroad through Banana country, company officials use these cars to get from one plantation to another. We climbed aboard and started off.

"Don't open your eyes until I tell you to," said Father Grass. "This isn't our parish and you might get ideas about starting a school here instead of in ours."

We went bowling along over the tropical jungleland. Beautiful heliconia grew in masses along the railroad tracks. Black birds with long tails twitched and twittered along the wires overhead. We sped over trestles looking down on tumbling streams. Now and then we came to a tiny town, just a few houses, a school and a store with several horses tied outside. "We're coming to a nice town; wasn't it?" Father quipped.

Often the driver of our little automobile-railcar had to stop and telephone ahead to see if the next piece of track was clear. Then, the people would gather around and just stare at us. "They have never seen Sisters before," Father explained.

After an hour or so of this, we zipped across a small stream and Father said, "All right, you can look now. We're in our parish!"

"Where are the bananas?" we asked. There was nothing but bamboo.

"The bamboo was planted here as a windbreak to protect the banana plants," Father said. "Here everything is for the bananas. They're the white-headed boys of this parish."

Soon we were surrounded by these white-headed boys. Bananas, bananas, bananas! Miles and miles, as far as the eye could see in any direction, the banana plants stood in even rows. Several times we saw Indians spraying them with blue copper insecticide. The Indian had a long stiff pipe away up in the air which sent out a blue cloud all over the top of the plant. The poor man was almost solid blue in color from the droppings. I dashed out to get a picture and was spotted blue for the rest of the trip.

"That's for the dread disease, *sigatoka*, known as the Panama Disease because it was first found on the company's other plantation at Almirante," Father explained. "If these trees are not sprayed every three weeks, the disease gains a year on them. Once it has gotten a foothold there is nothing to do but cut down everything in the area. That's why you will see large empty spaces here and there. In Almirante, where the disease gained such a hold, the company had to flood the land for five years. Imagine! They made a huge artificial lake of that immense plantation and kept it under water for five years, before the bug was conquered. Only just now are they beginning to get bananas from Almirante once again."

On and on we went speeding along the railroad tracks through a banana empire. It's all right to read about millions of bananas but what makes a lasting impression on the mind is to watch each one of the million speed past you. You get a feeling that it is not you who are moving, but the bananas. You are still—suspended in space—and an endless belt of bananas is going past you like the cleats on a caterpillar tractor. It's a dream-like state. The monotony of banana, banana, banana, half makes you afraid that you will never see anything else again.

But we did. For from time to time a loading station came to view. This is a concrete platform there in the banana groves. We saw mules, with a stem of bananas slung on each side, coming in single file through the trees. They congregate at the concrete platform; workers lift off the heavy banana stems and hang them, one after another, on a big crane. The stem swings around to a big barrel and is soused up and down in it. This is an anti-insect solution. They tell you with some pride that stories you may have heard about finding coral snakes and tarantulas in bunches of bananas are all poppycock. Any animal life that could survive that insecticide bath would belong to pre-historic ages.

After their bath, the bananas are gently laid on their sides on a carefully prepared freight car, lined with banana stalks, protected from the least shock which would injure their little sensibilities. "They're handled with kid gloves, those babies," commented Father Grass.

We had a whole day among God's little creatures, the bananas. We sped through the groves for hours. We had gone over the

Costa Rican border before we knew it. There were bananas on both sides of the border so it made little difference. Father brought us over to Costa Rica because this is one corner of their parish. He comes out here once a month for Mass.

More than a thousand workers are in this single section, living with their families in 1½ rooms per family, with outside kitchens and community toilets. They get $40 to $50 a month with commissary privileges.

It sounds worse than it is since the workers also get free rent and free hospitalization and the food is cheaper at the commissary. For instance, the company runs a cattle farm to supply the workers with meat. It costs 27 cents a pound to produce the meat; they sell it at 17 cents a pound. Also, the company will rent, for a dollar a year, a farm of two acres to any worker who wants to grow his own food. Still and all, the lot of the plantation worker is not soft by any means.

Everything is on railroad tracks in this vast banana country. There are no roads. The medley of conveyances has to switch and go into sidings and get permission by phone to go from one section of tracks to another. We passed or were passed by many station wagons on iron wheels, a hospital car, an ambulance, the school bus which takes the American children to their school, and many freight trains and passenger cars. The Vincentian Fathers are anxious to get a truck chassis and fit it up with iron wheels for use as a chapel car. In this way, they can get the Mass to every point in the plantation.

In all there are 20,242 people in this banana parish. At least 14,000 depend on the United Fruit Company for their livelihood. There are 7,000 employees here, most of whom are single men. They are brought in from Costa Rica and other countries; in many places there are three times the number of men that there are of women, which is bad for the moral situation—very bad.

The poor Fathers! They have a time of it trying to patch up a parish out of such varying people. They have itinerant banana workmen, poor families, company officers, and people from The Pig's Tail. Ah, that's the place, The Pig's Tail! It's a section out of town where cantinas and juke boxes wake up in the late afternoon and attain to a shrill maximum in the hours after midnight—where

sailors lose their wallets and many a poor fellow has lost his soul
—where the children have big eyes and skinny little arms.

Father Gleason, the Vincentian pastor at Puerto Armuelles, has
sallied right into the fight. Every evening he walks in procession
saying the Rosary through the streets of Pig's Tail followed by a
valiant little band of Pig's Tailers who don't cotton up to all their
neighbors do. For Pig's Tail was not always the red light district
of Puerto Armuelles. Once it was poor but respectable. Then,
driven from their usual haunts, one by one the shady business
slipped across the wobbly bridge which joins, or separates, Pig's
Tail and the company town.

The slaughterhouse stands beside this rickety bridge. A crowd
was gathered around it watching a sort of unofficial bullfight. A
bull had broken loose, the ring tearing right through his nose. The
maddened creature was being roped and gored and poked and
beaten to get him into the slaughterhouse. His eyes were wild, his
throat bellowed, his nose dripped blood all over. We skirted the
edge of the crowd and ran for Father's jeep.

Father Gleason and Father Grass are a grand pair of missioners.
They have the buoyancy which helps smooth the bumps every
missioner inevitably gets. They regaled us with story after story.

Because there are so few priests in Latin America, many quasi-
witch doctors operate in the country places. Recently one of these
came to the Vincentians at Puerto Armuelles with a business deal.

"Now, Padres," he said, "let's work together. When somebody
comes to me to get even with his enemy, I'll say to him, 'Why, you
go to the priest and get a Mass said against your enemy.' Then,
Padre, we can split any offering he gives you."

Another time, one of them was peacefully saying his Office in
his rectory when a man came in. That's nothing startling, for the
door is always open and people are running in and out all the
time. But this man had a basin of water, a cake of soap and a towel.
Without a word, he knelt before the priest and started to unfasten
his shoe laces.

"Hold on!" cried the priest. "What's the idea?"

"I have made a vow," the man explained. "I promised *El Senor*
that I would wash the feet of the priest."

Quick thinking saved the priest. "Fine!" he said immediately.

"That's a beautiful vow. I am not worthy of it. So, by the power of the Holy Roman Catholic Church entrusted to me, I hereby commute that vow to ten Hail Marys."

These informal "vows" are an honest attempt to do penance, although you can laugh at some of the forms they take. We saw a number of big boys with long hair playing ball and working around the workers' houses. A common vow, it seems, is that you will let your son's hair grow until he is fifteen. You are to cut it off, then, and send it to the Christus of Alanje, a reputedly miraculous statue which already has more hair than it knows what to do with.

We heard another story. It shows the sturdy caliber of the native priests in Panama. A politician, who had been in and out of office as revolutions permitted, was asked to be godfather at a baptism. The priest who was to perform the ceremony and the politician happened to be on the same train en route. Neither knew that they were bound for the same affair. The politician gave his views on religion in a decided fashion.

"Now, priest, I think all religions are alike. One is as good as another. As for me, I'm a Rosicrucian myself, but I get along with every religion."

When the baptismal party met for the ceremony, the priest recognized his travelling companion, standing up there ready to be godfather.

He forbade him. "You're not a Catholic yourself," he said. "How can you promise to sponsor this child in the Faith?" Furthermore, he stuck to his guns in spite of the politician's roaring.

When the tide of government turned again and our friend found himself in power once more, his first act was to get that priest banished from Panama. Which goes to show that there is more than one way to be a martyr. Modern persecutors toss you to political lions.

Benediction that evening was crowded—phenomenally so. The Vincentians—those villains!—had spread word around that we would be there. It was all staged. But so candidly and simply, that you couldn't do anything but laugh as Father Grass and Father Gleason jigged around the outside of the crowd which mobbed us in the plaza afterwards.

"These are the Sisters we want to come for the school," they told the people. "Go ahead! Be nice to them! Make them want to stay here in Puerto Armuelles!"

And it didn't take much urging. Young and old, the people swarmed around, shaking hands, kissing our medals, laughing, exclaiming, delighted at the thought. To them, it was a sure thing.

Wouldn't it be nice if missioners were like amoebae! All you'd have to do to get enough, would be to cut the existing ones in two. But—such are the heartbreaks of mission life. How we suffer! Tell the hard facts of the case to such lovable enthusiasts as the Puerto Armuellanos? Not we! Not that night!

Next day, as the good Fathers fed us for the last time—man-size sandwiches before starting off for the plane—they said, "We're holding our breath in anticipation of the big day when we stand up in the pulpit and say to our people,

" 'Tomorrow morning, I want all you men in the parish to come with your shovels. We're going to start the convent!' "

The Vincentians in Puerto Armuelles want nothing less than a major miracle. I, for one, hope they get it!

◆ 22 ◆

PIRATES MUST HAVE THEIR LITTLE JOKE

It's a little island, Curacao, and just as Dutchy as it can be. Going down the steep streets of Willhelmstadt (imagine a name like that in Latin America!) you might think yourself right in little old Holland itself. The houses line the street, each one a bit cleaner and brighter than its neighbor. The favorite combination is deep pink with windows outlined in blue. They must be newly painted every week; they're that fresh looking.

Queen Emma Bridge, spanning a canal which runs through the town, is lifted right out of The Tourists' Guide to Holland. Built on pontoons, it swings aside to let the barge-fulls of black oily mud from Venezuela pass up the canal to the refineries.

But one thing sure, Hans Brinker and his Silver Skates would have little chance to perform on Curacao's canal in winter.

Curacao is about 800 miles from Panama and just north of Venezuela. All its life it has lived on ships. The ships of Morgan the Pirate used to come in here laden with booty snatched from the Spanish Main. Morgan's headquarters were here when his pirate empire spread over the entire Caribbean. The peak came in 1671 when he captured Panama itself. Three years later he was appointed Governor of Jamaica and turned respectable.

But that was before the fabulous oil deposits of Lake Maracaibo in Venezuela were discovered. The thick gooey black earth from the bottom of the lake is brought on barges to Curacao, just 40 miles off the coast of Venezuela, and there is refined.

From a distance, one wonders if anyone lives or would want to live on Curacao. The buff-colored volcanic peaks and rounded humps are scarcely covered, and only with cactus and thorn trees at that. The scarred mountainside where the phosphate mine has

236

gouged deep ravines, shows up in the field glasses. Hundreds of oil storage tanks squat here and there on the hills. Someone must work under the hot sun of Curacao if life is to be pleasant in the far-off cities of the world. Or, even, if it is to be safe.

There were at least six large ships in the harbor as we edged around the promontory at the entrance. Another, going out, passed us; there was yet another waiting to follow. The ships of the world come here to re-fuel, in the shadow of Captain Morgan's castle. This yellow-brown adobe tower, bristling with Spanish cannon, stands on the hillside dominating the bay. To modern eyes it hardly seems possible that such a play-toy could have been a formidable defense even for a pirate's empire.

Our freighter was tied to great concrete piles, at least ten by fifteen feet, which have been sunk in the solid rock ocean floor about fifty feet from the shore. We were just at the mouth of the harbor, barely inside it, yet the water was as still as in a swimming pool. It must have been 40 feet deep, but in the green-blue depths even the bottom was visible. Hundreds of little zebra-fish swam lazily back and forth, now rising closer to the surface, now turning over to go below. They were quite unimpressed with the bulk of our vessel beside them, or with the loathesome length of huge hose which dipped into the water and rose to the pipes on deck, pouring into our tanks the black life-blood of industry, oil.

Eight shiny pipes (each about a foot in diameter) brought the oil from storage tanks on the hills nearby. Negro workmen turned the valves and operated the derrick which lifted the great black snakes of hoses.

During World War II, a million tons of oil every month flowed into Allied ships from the hoses of Curacao. In the office of the Shell Oil Company, (one of the six palm-shaded bungalows on a lagoon in the bay) there hangs a paper, signed by the King of England, thanking Curacao for its vital contribution.

The agent of the Shell Oil Company, a keen little Dutchman, came aboard. He was showing us Curacao's money.

"Here's a guilder, worth about half of your dollar," he said. "And this is a half-guilder and a quarter-guilder. This is our penny. And this," with a broad smile, "is a Coca-Cola coin—12½ cents of the guilder."

It was a copper slug embossed with a bottle of the good old stuff on one side of the cogent words, Drink Coca-Cola, on the reverse. Didn't I tell you that Coca-Cola has conquered the Southern Hemisphere?

It seems, according to the Shell Oil man, that the soft drink people were stumped when they tried to introduce their vending machines to the island. There was no coin on Curacao which fitted the slot. But they were not stumped for long. They minted these Coca-Cola tokens and sold them, two for a quarter-guilder. Now they are a standard piece of Curacao currency. Later, in Willhelmstadt, we bought fruit and candy for Coca-Cola coins.

Sister Victoria Francis has a yen for licorice. The little candy store was a dream of our youth. In the glass jars were mint leaves, hoarhound drops, rock candy, and long strips of licorice guaranteed to make your insides black all the way from your tongue clear down to your toes. No cellophane, no wax paper, no wrappers. No piece of cardboard which makes the chocolate bar look bigger than it is. Nothing of effete civilization whatever. Sister's eye lit up; she had found a jarful of "nigger babies," the kind that will keep you out of conversation for five minutes straight. Me? I like taffy, the pinker and stickier the better. We each pointed to our choice—"A Coca-Cola's worth of this, please."

The shopkeeper and his wife and his wife's sister and her children as well were on hand to wait on us. They got in each other's way rushing to be of service. Mrs. Shopkeeper, a solid Dutch housewife, disappeared into the back room for a moment and returned with a tin box of Dutch pastilles of milk chocolate, something very special indeed. It was a gift for us.

As happy as two kindergarteners coming home from a Christmas party, we Maryknoll Sisters returned to our ship each clutching a bag of our favorite candy. Oh, for the digestion of Youth!

Maybe it was the pink taffy; maybe it was just my poetic soul loath to waste the moonlit hours in sodden slumber. Anyway, I rose at four A.M. for a turn around deck to see if we were moving or not. On the pier, a single light burned over the oil valves and the sleepy Negro watching them. The great black snake still hung from the derrick connecting us with the oil pipes.

The moonlight penetrated the clear waters. Even at night one could see the bright black and yellow stripes of zebra fish, moving lazily down below. What do they think about, those creatures of beautiful bodies and no brains? Have they any sense of their own beauty? How silly they are! Bathed in moonlight, immersed in crystal water, surrounded by shimmering beauty—and all they're interested in is a worm for their tummies. Well, aren't we all that way!

Next morning, we were still loading oil.

"How about exploring Morgan's castle?" one of the passengers proposed. We were only eleven passengers, a very congenial group although you would not think it from a reading of the line-up. An Anglican minister, two Protestant girl missionaries, a Chinese business man, a Filipina student, a couple from the mid-West on their Golden Wedding honeymoon, a Colombian couple and their two children and we two Maryknollers. We got along beautifully, too.

We all set out for Morgan's castle.

It was an adobe wedding-cake, built in four tiers. You walked an easy ramp to the first level. You mounted mud brick stairs to the second level. A wooden stairway, quite decrepit, put you on the third level. To get to the topmost peak you entered a recess in the masonry and climbed a very shaky ladder to the top. You emerged into the sunlight from a hole maybe four feet wide and twelve feet deep, just like a worker climbing up a manhole in the street.

It was wonderful up there. Some Dutch soldiers were sunning themselves. The rest of us viewed the bay and ships, and fiddled around with the old cannon poking their noses through notches in the parapet. Old Morgan had good reason to keep a sharp lookout on the bay. Some of his old friends might want to pay him a return visit.

"Yes, they might!" said a voice beside me.

I turned quickly. There was a gentleman beside me. Quite a gentleman! His long black curls flowed from under a plumed hat. His wrists were covered with frayed lace. He wore a patch over one eye but the other gleamed with friendliness. I knew him right away.

"Captain Morgan, I believe?"

He bowed in acknowledgement. "At your service!"

"You have a beautiful view here," I said a bit lamely.

"Charmed, that you enjoy it! Others, standing where you are now, have not found it so pleasant."

"Oh, anybody would like this!" I exclaimed.

He smiled wryly. "Not if you have a lot on your mind. For instance, if you are wondering when—or even if—your friends will get around to paying your ransom. Then, there were hostages kept up here, too."

"What did you do to them?" I was almost afraid to ask this.

"Well, my dear Sister," he said with an exaggerated shrug. "After all, a poor pirate like myself can't afford to feed a lot of hostages forever. After a reasonable interim, I . . . well, I . . ."

I lost patience.

"Now, Captain Morgan, is that nice! No wonder your memory is not held in honor. You know, don't you, that children growing up today think of you as having been—well, kind of wicked?"

He laughed aloud.

"To my enemies, I am wicked. To my guests . . ." and he swept a grandiloquent bow at me. "After all, Miss Self-Righteous, I have a few virtues, too. Look how I let you passengers come up here and see my view for nothing. Doesn't my hospitality cancel out a little . . . bloodthirstiness, if you want to call it that?"

Of course, it didn't. But what's the use of scolding a poor ghost who can't do anything to rectify his character anyway?

"Come," he said in more lambent mood. "Let's drop the theology. Enjoy the view. Oh, you have a camera! Now, I'll show you just how to get a magnificent picture. Step back a bit so as to get a cannon in the foreground. Now back a little further."

Eyes absorbed in the view-finder, I stepped back. Twice. A third time. Just a little more. I took a fourth step back—and my foot went right down the hole where the ladder was!

Had I been a circus clown, I couldn't have done it better. I went over like a plank bridging the hole. I remember thinking with mild surprise as I fell back so stiffly: "So! This is how I'm going to die." Then I found myself flat over the hole and staring into blue sky, not dead at all.

"I'm kind of wicked, you said?" a mocking voice whispered. "I think you're kind of silly right now!"

There I was, stiff as a board, with one foot pressing against the edge of the hole and the other dangling down. My shoulders rested on the other edge. And twelve feet of space under the rest of me!

The camera was still in my hand. "Shall I drop it?" I thought. "I'll probably need both hands to get out of here."

"No. No use dropping it until I'm sure I have to," reasoned the canny old Scotchman inside of me.

Of course, everybody came running. The Dutch soldiers and the men of our party each had his own rescue plan.

"Get underneath and hold her up!"

But the hole was twelve feet deep.

"Put a board under to support her."

But there was no board around.

"Get her from the sides!"

But they couldn't reach over that far.

Frankly, I am not accustomed to being a human bridge over holes. That point is slighted in our novitiate training. In another second or two, I was ready to cave in and finish my earthly career then and there.

I lifted both hands, with the camera still clutched in one.

"Take my hands and pull me up," I said in a strangled little voice.

Held by a contingent of soldiers in the back, the Anglican minister and the Chinese business man reached over. I grabbed their hands and they raised me upright again. I made a perfect arc with my good old foot as the center of the circle. As good as new, I snapped the camera on that picture.

Isn't God good! Or, do I have a super-special guardian angel! I hope he got a merit award or a promotion in the ranks for his care of me that day. They say that angels have special charge over fools and little children. I don't know which of those categories is mine, but I must come under one of them.

In spite of my gratitude, Guardian Angel spoke his mind that evening as I lay down to sleep.

"Let that be a lesson to you, not to talk to gentlemen with patches over one eye."

NICARAGUA

Puerto
Cabezas

Siuna

Rio Grande

Managua

*Lake
Nicaragua*

1

AND

YUCATAN

Merida
Chichen
Itza

2

KEY

• 23 •

THE MOUNTAIN THAT USED TO BE

From fire, flood, thunder, thieves, schisms, heresies, earthquakes and sudden and unprovided death,—spare us, O Lord!

I used to think that this list of misfortunes couldn't possibly all happen to one person, nor all in one place, but Siuna, Nicaragua, has everything. Sister Virginia Therese goes down the line-up of children marching into the classrooms and tells the story of several. Teresita's mother was killed in a blast from the mine. She was walking with the child along a road when dynamite went off prematurely. Pedro's father was murdered right after payday. Clarito's brother is in jail at Puerto Cabezas now; he went berserk and badly wounded his best friend. At least, they had always been best friends before.

It's that kind of a town. A gold-mining town. The 4,500 people here are engaged in the rugged job of grinding mountains to powder in order to extract gold from them. The finer things of life are apt to be ground up, too.

In the nine years she has been in Siuna, Sister Virginia Therese has seen the mountain across from the convent disappear. There are mountains on either side of it. They were lucky; they had no gold in them.

We were watching the moon rise between a cleft in the mountain range which faces the convent.

"When I came here," Sister said, "you couldn't have seen this. Then, there was no cleft. It was a solid range with three peaks. We used to climb to the top just for the view.

"But in these nine years, I have seen the middle mountain die a slow death. Dynamite blasted it, bulldozers hacked at it, steam shovels scooped it up and ten-ton trucks carried it away. That little mountain 800 feet high has been ground to the consistency of face powder in the gold mine. One-tenth of an ounce of pure gold was squeezed out of every ton of mountain."

"What happened to the rest of it?" I asked.

"The fine powdery stuff floats, a grey scum on La Luz creek. The heavier parts and the rock strata were crushed to rubble and make the foundation of a road the company is building."

Next morning we walked over to The-Mountain-That-Used-To-Be. Not only is the mountain gone but there is even a 200-foot hole where it once was. Four giant steps, each 200 feet high lead to the top of the ridge where the neighboring mountains still rear their lofty crests. Down below us, at the bottom of the open pit, a steam shovel buried its bulldog teeth into the side wall.

A siren wailed. Shovel operators, truckmen, laborers began to move away from the open pit.

"That's the blasting signal," Sister explained. "We had better go inside the house."

"Oh, it's very far away," I demurred. "Let's stay and watch the fun."

"You can, if you want to. Not I. You're standing right where Teresita's mother was when she was killed. And see that new patch on our roof? Just last month, a rock was blasted right through the roof into Sister Concepta Marie's classroom."

I gladly went in.

If you take a map of Nicaragua, you will notice at once that all the black dots are on the Pacific coast side. For 50 to 75 miles in from the Pacific there are cities, roads, towns and railroads. But the whole Caribbean side of the country is quite blank. Just a few dots along the rivers.

That is why the people in Siuna take a plane as casually as you or I would step on a bus. There is no other way to get around. The NICA airline operates a daily plane which hops from Managua, the capital, to Siuna, 160 miles over the mountains, as rocky a ride as any jeep jaunt. This is for the benefit chiefly of the gold mine. Trucks, shovels, conveyor belts, ore crushers, elevators and equipment for the underground mines—if they are to get to Siuna at all —must be flown in. An expensive transport. It takes Big Business to grind a mountain to face powder.

Everywhere we went in South and Central America we came face-to-face with—of all things!—Modern Industry. You would think that away down in isolated places one would be free of all that. But here you come to grips with Raw Materials,—rubber, copper, coffee, nitrates, oil, bananas, and gold. All that sort of thing is controlled by Big Business. Unless you can engage thousands of workers and can sink millions into the equipping and building of an immense plant in some God-forsaken spot of the world, you might as well give up the idea of supplying any part at all of the world's raw materials. In the modern world a man may use individual enterprise and run his own service station, selling rubber tires and gasoline. But in the producing of the rubber and the petroleum, the little operator can do nothing.

All over South and Central America, then, we have come across this situation,—a COMPANY, be it Standard Oil, United Fruit, Anaconda Copper, Ventures Mining Co., or even what, controlling hundreds of square miles of land and thousands of human beings with a power unheard of by the ancient Pharaohs of Egypt. The COMPANY controls everything in that entire area. We cannot conceive of it in the States. For instance, I imagine that The General Electric Company exerts considerable influence in Schenectady, N.Y. But it does not tell its employees where they must live, what food they can buy, what clothes they must wear. Somebody not employed by the company is free to come in to Schenectady and set up a little store, or operate a shoe repair shop, or organize a taxi service. If a new Catholic church is going to be built, the pastor buys the land, hires his architect and never thinks of consulting the General Electric Company about anything.

In these towns, however, the COMPANY has bought or leased tracts which can be measured only by square miles. It must grant permission for a priest to live in the territory. His house is allotted to him; his baggage and supplies usually come in on company transport means. If the priest is diplomatic and works well with the company official in charge, he can often make great headway. On the other hand, a change in officials can hamper his work considerably. Worse still, if the COMPANY decides to abandon the site for some reason, the priest might as well pack his bags and leave; his congregation goes off with the COMPANY.

Officials of these huge international companies frequently feel responsible for the welfare of their people. They reason that if you bring several thousand workmen and their families to the middle of a jungle, you ought to bring in the necessities of life for them, too. The COMPANY builds houses; it supplies light and water; it makes what roads there are; it enforces at least a minimum hygiene. It frequently maintains a hospital giving better medical care than the workers could possibly get in their own villages.

In order to feed the workers, the COMPANY sets up a store. It has a herd of cattle for meat and milk. It operates a little shoe factory. It has a farm for growing vegetables. I talked to Mr. Wolff at Bonanza, another gold-mining town in Nicaragua. Mr. Wolff sells meat for 15 cents a pound although it costs the COMPANY around 35 cents to produce it. He sells heavy shoes for a dollar a pair; but they cost $6.00 to make. Other below-cost items are things like milk, rice, beans, cabbage, cheese and other essentials. On no less than 15 items, the COMPANY takes a terrific loss. On items like perfume, cosmetics, canned food, fancy pillows and so on, the prices are high.

The idea is, of course, that the workers can buy good food for almost nothing. Their pay is very low because the COMPANY feels that if they were paid more, it would only go for liquor and dissipation.

It's a ticklish question for sociologists. The situation is much the same as in the days of slavery. Many slaves under good masters were better off than some negroes are today. Does that justify making them slaves?

On the other hand, suppose you were in charge of a large COMPANY, sitting almost on the throne of God Almighty to some 8,000 people. Would you pay the miner a good wage and watch it go to fatten the barrooms? Or would you give him a small amount of spending money and make it up to him with good milk, meat, rice, beans and other things he needs? I think I would take one look at the wives and children and decide to be paternalistic. At least, until I could educate him to the point where he can handle his own money.

Some 8 or 10 years ago in Hawaii, the big sugar and pineapple plantations did away with this system of perquisites. Some of them sold lots and homes to the workers. A man's rent, light, heat and gas were not given to him free. He had to pay for them from his increased salary. For about six months, things went haywire. But before two years had passed, the workers had learned to manage their own money.

The situation here is different. In Hawaii, nearly all of the workers could read and write. Only the new ones imported from Porto Rico or some old Filipinos were illiterate. Also they had absorbed much of the American way of life. It would take many years of careful education before the South and Central American workers can be safely freed from slavery to a COMPANY, benign as that company may want to be.

There's another kind of mountain in Siuna which is levelling slowly and with much greater effort. Just to compare the figures of ten years ago with the present, is encouraging. In 1944 when Colegio Maryknoll first opened its doors to Siuna's young intellectuals of 16 and 17 who were avid to enter First Grade,—in those days, I say, more than 90% of all the children registered were illegitimate. A gold-town is never a Sunday School town, to be sure, but Siuna was mired deep in the stickiest, gummiest mess of immorality we had ever seen. Now the illegitimacy rate has gone down to 66%.

Even the old die-hards were trying to conform to the new notions of respectability. The Sisters imported a piano into town; the only one in town. Having a piano, of course they gave music lessons. Soon the thin ranks of music pupils were ready to give their first recital. Mamas and Papas came all dressed up for the occasion.

We were surprised at Marita. A thin nervous little girl, we had expected her to blush and stammer all over the keyboard. But instead she tackled her jig tune with vigor and saw it through to a gory victory. Later, I said to her father whose eye was a bit watery with proud affection,

"Marita did very well. She didn't seem at all nervous."

"Oh, I saw to that, Sister," he assured me. "I gave her quite a swig before we left the house."

Speaking of music—! Tippy's Band serenaded us one evening. Tippy is so called because one leg is shorter than the other and he walks tip-tilted. His band is famous. One of the instruments is an inverted washtub in which is planted a broom handle. A wire stretches from the top of the handle down to the edge of the wash-tub. Tippy modulates the tone by putting his foot on various parts of the tub. It sounds rather like a bass violin. Another instrument was a saw played with a violin bow and very sweet.

Besides instilling some notion of the Ten Commandments, the Sisters have been hammering home various points in hygiene. When I was there, the current battle was against runny noses.

"Everybody should have a handkerchief," they thundered in the classrooms. "You can all get a clean rag of some sort to use as a hankie even if you can't get a real one."

They soon saw results. A little more than they expected. As the children stood in line one morning, waiting for the bell to go to their classrooms, a horseman was seen tearing up the main street frantically waving his hand.

"My stars!" Sister thought, "he must be bringing news of a flood, or a fire coming this way."

The rider pranced up to Sister Virginia Therese and threw himself off his panting horse. Then he pulled from his pocket a long piece of clean white rag.

"Conchita forgot this, this morning," he said. "She said she had to have it for school."

Sometimes the children get their hygiene lessons mixed up with theology. The Sisters waged war against spitting. The youngsters do it all the time. Just before going to confession, little Victoria came to Sister Rose Anna with a problem.

"What is it?" Sister asked.

"Is it a sin to spit?"

"No, Victoria. That's a bad habit, but it's not a sin."

Victoria went away but she was not satisfied. In ten minutes she was back again.

"Madre," she said, "if I spit 50 times, wouldn't that make it a sin?"

"Fifty times nothing is still nothing, Victoria," Sister said, enlisting arithmetic to prove the theology. "But your punishment for such a bad habit would be a very dry mouth."

A few minutes later Victoria came beaming out of the confessional. We are wondering if she checked with Father on the point.

The Fathers in this section of Nicaragua are American Capuchins under the leadership of Bishop Matthew—as dutiful a son as St. Francis ever had.

He loves birds and animals and children. We found his little house full of all three. Two parrots and a *lata* perch on his shoulder and chair as he reads his office. The children are running through the house all day long, playing the victrola, studying their lessons, writing on his wall, or playing hopscotch on the colored cement walks in the garden.

"I open the door at seven in the morning and close it at eight at night," the Bishop said. "It's never closed otherwise. See the colored stones in the path? I had them put there for the children. I tell them, 'I will give a piece of candy to the boy or girl who can go up and down the path hopping only on the blue stones. Or the red ones!' It's lots of fun for them. And for me, too. I've tried to do it myself but I've never won a piece of candy."

The school bell rang and all the children ran out. The Bishop and we settled down to talk business. But soon a little girl came to the door, hesitated, went away, and came back. This happened several times. Then the Bishop said,

"What is it? What do you want, Erlinda?"

The child ran into the room and picked up her school books from behind the cupboard door. Then, swift as lightning, her bare feet ran out the door to school. The Bishop laughed with pleasure.

Sometime later, I saw a mouse creeping along the floorboard. The Bishop saw it too.

"Oh, I forgot," he said and hastily went out of the room. He was back soon with a few crumbs of bread.

"The poor little mice, they come for food. I used to chase them away. Then I thought 'They are only hungry as others of God's creatures are.' So I give them bread every day and they are content. They never bother me any more. Sometimes when I have time, I let them run up my cassock and eat the bread from my hand."

I don't think Bishop Matthew would ever be disconcerted. He has a beautiful simplicity.

"When they were building my house I was living in what was up. Part of the wall was only a piece of burlap and one night while I was sleeping, the burlap fell down. The next morning was Sunday and all the people coming to Mass could see me in bed. Quite a crowd had collected outside the house by the time I awoke. I sat up in bed in my pajamas and extending my hand bestowed on them my episcopal blessing. I wanted to give them something, and it was all I had at the moment."

In Bonanza, we met Father Crisostomo—one of those story-book Franciscans with lots of beard, lots of friends and lots of twinkle in his keen blue eyes. He has a school of 240 children and—of course!—wants Maryknoll Sisters to run it for him. It is practically the only school in the place for very few attend the public school.

As we took a tour through the classrooms, we came at the end to the sixth grade room. Here were the eight or nine children who had been able to stay that long in school. A Chinese girl, Paulita, caught my eye, tall, thin and serious. We went through the room talking to one and then to another. I asked this girl where her parents came from. She said, "Hong Kong." She seemed to me too shy to enjoy my advances and I went on.

However, a few minutes later we were out in the play yard surrounded by a little horde of curiosity-seekers. Paulita came to the edge of the crowd and slowly worked her way in.

"I want to talk to you," she said in English, slowly and deliberately.

"Go ahead," I answered, "I don't think anybody else here understands English."

She hesitated still. Her sweet face was so serious.

"I want to be a nun," she said slowly. "But I'm not even a Catholic."

I was stunned. "What are you, then?" I asked.

"My parents want me to be a Moravian and I have to go to their church every Sunday. But I come here to the Catholic Church, first."

Paulita had never seen Sisters before. "What makes you want to be a Sister?" I asked. "You don't know anything about our way of life. How do you know you would like it?"

"All I know," she answered, enunciating each syllable, "is that they serve God. And that's what I want to do."

My heart went out to the girl. What a long, long road lies ahead of her before she can serve God as she wishes! She cannot go on to high school as yet, she told me, because her older sister has been waiting for her to finish the grades; only one of them can go to school at the same time.

I told her, of course, to tell Father Crisostomo and see what he could do to get her baptized, first, and then lead her toward her ideal. Isn't it marvellous the graces one finds in these bleak little towns?

Bonanza *is* a bleak town. Its shacks of dingy wood and rusted tin huddle together in a mountain pass scarred by the blasting and digging of men who have staked much in the thirst for gold. To look at it, you would think Bonanza a wretched place to live. But a nice spirit pervades the town.

For one thing there is no segregation of the "staff" in barbed wire enclosures, sacred to Americans or Canadians or other Nordics. In Bonanza, about half "the staff" are Americans and the other half Latins—that is, from Central and South American countries. They live here and there throughout the town in wooden houses nicely furnished but very unpretentious. There is a good deal of friendliness among all parts of "the staff" and also with the Chinese store-keepers and others in the town.

"Silvestre has a good head," Sister Concepta Marie was saying as I joined the group around the table in the community room. "But I don't think the boy opens a book from the time he leaves school until he comes back the next morning."

"Maybe he can't," said Sister Virginia Therese. "Why don't you go see his mother? She might be able to help him study at home a bit."

We set off right after school, Sister Concepta Marie and I. Siuna has no paved streets nor even wooden sidewalks. We took the center of the road like everybody else. Just an hour before, it had stopped raining. The air was fresh and clean. But the street was a mire of mud.

253

"Where does Silvestre live?" we asked many who passed us— women with a basin-full of laundry on their heads, children carrying pails of water, men lounging against the store-fronts.

Nobody seemed to know the small, thin, little boy with the "rubio" complexion (meaning a fair skin). Several wild-goose chases led us up muddy alleys and over goo-ey fields. Then we met Margarito, a second grader.

"Yes, Madre, I know where he lives. It's a little far. Follow me!" and off he went with us trailing behind.

Margarito's bare feet went through the mire briskly. We limped along after him, slipping up and down the narrow path which trailed across the hillside. I left my rubbers behind me several times, sucked off by the wet clay.

At the end, was Silvestre's little one-room shack.

He was at the door, fairly jumping out of his skin with excitement. "Madre! Madre!" was all he could say.

"Is your mother inside?" Sister asked him.

He stepped aside to let us pass. "She's sick," he said.

Inside the bare damp little room, there seemed to be nothing at all,—no mother nor even a piece of furniture. We soon made out something in a dark corner. Two boxes and, lying on them, a very sick woman. She was less than five feet, but the two boxes were so small, she could not lie flat. Her feet were drawn up against her body. An old rag that at one time might have answered to the name of a dress, clothed her. Only a towel around her shoulders protected her from dampness. Swollen legs, swollen ankles. We easily guessed that she had beri-beri.

"Yes," she said, "beri-beri."

"How long have you been here like this?"

"Six weeks, Madre."

"How do you live, Senora? You must need food."

"We have a small farm. Away off in the mountains. My husband comes on Sunday with enough food for the week. Don't be concerned, Madre. We get along."

"But Senora, why don't you go back to the farm where, at least, your husband can care for you?"

"No, no, Madre! I cannot go back. Silvestre must go to school. He must learn to read and write, to do figures. He should not be what we are—poor ignorant folk. I came to Siuna to live here, so that Silvestre could go to your school. I will stay."

Well, our purpose for coming was answered. Silvestre could not study at home. Outside of school hours he was cook and nurse for his poor mother. When darkness fell, he had no light. Who can study by the light of the moon? Without asking, we knew where he slept. There was no other place but the bare floor.

We made arrangements for two men to carry the mother to the company's hospital. Another followed, carrying her pathetic boxes. How we wished she might exchange them for a bed! But the hospital here is so small and so poorly equipped that only those in need of operations rate a bed.

Silvestre went with her. As is the custom here, he will sleep on the floor beside her. But at least, it will not be on bare ground. He also will have to prepare her food and bring it to her.

As we walked home, slipping and sliding once again in Siuna's muddy lanes, Sister Concepta Marie was strangely silent. I knew what she was thinking. Our convent is poor in Siuna, as elsewhere. But it is clean and dry. Each one of us has a bed to sleep on. We can be sure of breakfast, dinner and supper. We have sheets and blankets at night.

For most of us, destitution such as Silvestre's brings on a virulent attack of what the wise ones call "imprudent zeal." It would be such a satisfaction to give one's bed to the sick woman! And to run out with your hot meal to the family eating cold rice and beans next door! How good it would be to wrap your blanket around some old lady, and shiver through the night yourself!

But that would be to miss the forest for the trees. These people in Siuna have known this sort of thing all their lives. True, they need immediate help, and we give them every bit we can. But the long-term need is for education, steady and sure social betterment, a deep grounding in the Faith. Of what value is it to train a Maryknoll Sister, educate her and get her to the missions, if she sleeps on the floor, shivers all night, and ends up with pneumonia? A corpse is of no further mission value.

As we entered our little convent, clean and dry, I found something at least that made it not too comfortable. It was the caterpillar season and the floor was full of black worms an inch long. It's

255

not pleasant to feel them squoosh under your bedroom slippers at night. I could offer that up for Silvestre and his mother.

Caterpillars, bugs, snakes, lizards and rodents often come to visit the Madres. The concrete floor is on a level with the ground outside and the walls, for coolness' sake, are merely slats set at an angle like venetian blinds. This leaves plenty of space for St. Francis' little sisters and brothers to walk in.

On the whole, Siuna is a paradise for God's little creatures. I never saw so many strange birds—wild canaries, solid red birds, black ones with red wings, tiny humming birds who poke their long beaks into the papaya blossoms while their rapid beating wings suspend them motionless in the air. Father Rodrigo had two green parrots and several pigeons. But most impressive is the *lata*, a red parrot-like fellow with long tail feathers. He sits outside our door on a mango tree and squawks his opinion of us in unmistakable terms.

Others of God's creatures are not so handsome. One day, not far from the convent, a big boa constrictor was loafing after a chicken dinner when a load of buckshot rudely terminated his life. The skin, recently evacuated by the snake, was smoked and given to Father Rodrigo, the Capuchin stationed at Siuna. He, in turn, gave it to me. It was a foot wide and nine feet long. And that did not include about 5 feet which was too badly riddled with shot to be useful.

I shared a very small room with Sister Pauline Marie. All my collection of boxes, suitcases, brown paper parcels and shopping bags was there, too. In some eight months of travel, we had acquired quite a number of Would-You-Mind?'s. (Would you mind bringing this to Mexico? Would you mind tucking this into your bags for So-and-So?) My snake was put on top of it all. It was the prize of my collection. Every time I entered the room, the dulcet odor of smoked snake wafted aloft, reminding me that I had a beautiful snake skin to bring back to our Mother General. I don't know what it reminded Sister Pauline Marie of. Probably she remembered with pleasure that I was not to stay permanently at Siuna.

⟡ 24 ⟡

MARIA NEXT-TIME COMES TODAY

We were out mule riding, Sister Pauline Marie and I.

She was on Flor de Cana, a mild creature named for Nicaragua's strongest whiskey. I rode Descanso, which means Rest. He suited his name. Indeed, the words of a Spanish funeral sermon came often to mind, *"O Eterne descanso! O dulce tombo!* (Oh Eternal Rest! Oh, sweet tomb!)" I think Descanso meditated on them twenty-four hours a day.

We were going to Siunawas, a hamlet about three hours away in the jungle. Two of our school children lived there although they boarded with relatives in Siuna during the school year. Sister thought a visit to their home might patch together a better family background for the youngsters.

Sometimes our way led along a good road the mining company was building to connect a new site with the refining plant. More often, the mules went single file in dense jungle, crashing through the undergrowth into mud up to their hocks. But *"no importa"* as Sister said. "We'll be fording a stream soon and that will wash off the mud."

I knew Sister Pauline Marie in the days when she used to pilot something faster than a mule. I watched to see if she would try to get 60 out of Flor de Cana, or if a flaming red flower might remind her of a traffic light and she would draw up from sheer force of habit.

But it's wonderful what mission life does for the nerves. Sister sat her saddle as casually as if she had ridden mules to St. Brendan's school in Brooklyn all through the grades and high school. Flor de Cana flopped his ears contentedly and plugged right along.

A man crouched by a stream was digging up mud from the bottom with a shallow pan.

"Any luck, Eduardo?" Sister asked him.

"My luck is always bad, Madre," he answered. He gazed intently at the mud and then threw it away. "But someday it will change. Alberto's did."

We passed on.

"That's one of our gold-crazy fellows," Sister sighed. "Every now and then, we live through a gold rush. Not long ago, someone claimed to have found gold in the street. Men, women and children dug holes all over our main thoroughfare. Even the kiddies in my kindergarten came with gold dust hoarded in pill boxes.

"The current gold rush began with Alberto's find. The story is that Alberto had a stubborn mule. He picked up a stone and threw it at the animal. That didn't make him budge. He picked up another stone and threw it. That had no effect either. Alberto picked up a third stone but he never threw it. Instead, he forgot all about his mule. He hugged the stone to his breast and ran to the mine's assaying office. The mine pays these independent operators for any gold they are able to bring in. The story says—mind, now, Alberto isn't telling—but the story says that he was paid $238.00 for that third stone. Now, every man in town, including Alberto, is looking for the first two stones. Eduardo is one of the many."

"And in the meantime?" I asked.

"In the meantime, Luisa is scraping every last penny together to keep the family alive until Eduardo makes them all millionaires. We're able to give them clothes now and then and of course the children don't pay anything at school. There's Luisa now."

She pointed to a group of four women waist deep in another stream. It was plainly Saturday bath day. Children were splashing around, sudsing and rinsing, sudsing and rinsing their brown bodies a million times. Mamas, decorously attired in pink slips, were getting a good bath, too. Whenever they could catch one of their own wriggling "brown bares," they started in on the hair with all the vigor that an energetic Mama can put into exercising a scalp.

"Madre Paulina!" they called with one accord.

258

It was a real parent-teacher meeting. What matter that the parents were waist deep in a mountain stream and the teacher was perched on a mule? Parents and teachers talk about the same things, no matter where they meet. These mothers with their black hair streaming wet down their backs had much the same problems as the women whose children go to any parochial school in the States. Sick children, unregenerate husbands, the rent due and nothing to pay it with, and their own personal problems. "The doctor at the mine told me I have TB. How can I spend three months in bed, as he says I should?" They don't, of course. It's much simpler just to live out your short span, knowing that when you die friends and relatives will gladly add your motherless brood to their own little ones.

We did not go into such things just then. It was "Hello" and "Goodbye" and "I hope Juan gets over that snake bite soon. It ought to teach him to come straight to school and not play in the woods on the way."

We emerged from the cool shady forest to the blistering road again. Flor de Cana was in no mood to prove his mettle. He jogged along the dusty road content to show no more fire than a cataclysmic sneeze now and then just to clear his nostrils.

Conversation lagged too. We rode side by side in silence, greeting the passersby with only an uplifted hand. After a half mile or so, a ragged little figure trudged before us, her bare feet kicking up the dust and her dirty little hand brushing the hair from her hot face.

"It's Yolanda!" Sister Pauline Marie exclaimed. "One of my kindergarteners, away out here! Oh, that's right. She lives here and stays with her grandmother in Siuna during the week."

"Yolanda," as we came up to her, "where are you going?"

"There," she said. The brown hand waved off vaguely to the distance.

"How would you like to ride with me?" Sister Pauline Marie leaned over and swung the child into the saddle before her. I was dumbfounded. Where did she learn circus tricks like that? We were in the novitiate together and that, I know, is not a standard part of the Maryknoll training.

259

"Which is your house?" Sister asked her small passenger as we passed one shack after another along the road.

"121 DDT," she said.

"DDT—that's funny," I thought, but I had noticed numbers like that stencilled on every rickety shack on the road.

Flor de Cana liked his extra passenger evidently for he had sprinted quite a ways ahead. I dug my heels into lackadaisical Descanso and caught up.

"What's the DDT for?" I panted. "Is this DDT Boulevarde? I've always had a quite different meaning for those letters."

Sister laughed. "Yours is the right one," she said. "Every year the mining Company DDT's every house for miles around. The stencilled numbers show the order in which they are to be taken. We have no house numbers nor streets nor avenues here; the DDT numbers take their place."

A far-away look came into her eyes. "We're getting so cluttered up in Siuna now. Civilization is closing in on us. Annual DDT-ing, Clean-Up campaigns, the youngsters are getting used to shoes—at least on Sundays. You watch! Sooner or later somebody's going to bring the first bathtub to town. Then you can ring the deathknell of old Siuna."

"A good thing, too," I said.

"Yes, to be sure. But it complicates life. The people in Siuna are getting caught in the Mechanical Age. They drive trucks and operate elevators and know about dynamos and batteries and electric drills. They learn it all at the mine. In the process, they can't help but lose something. Now take Macantaca, on the Rio Grande. For utter simplicity . . ."

During summer vacation at Siuna, the Sisters go to small hamlets on the rivers which drain the eastern side of Nicaragua. Usually a team of two Sisters goes to each station for six weeks or so. A Sister-nurse spends two weeks in each one. The summer before, Sister Pauline Marie and Sister Rose Anna had gone to Macantaca. She told me about it, as we jogged through the humid jungle.

As the crow flies, Macantaca is not so far from Siuna. Maybe fifty miles. But crows are not interested in taking passengers. We first planned to go on horse back. We were to go fifteen minutes by plane to Alamicamba and pick up the horses there. But so many people told us of swamps and quicksands on the overland route, that we decided to go by plane to Karawala on the Rio Grande—not the river between Mexico and Texas, but a little Rio Grande all our own in Nicaragua. It was 225 miles to Karawala. From there we would go by boat to Macantaca, some fifty miles up the river.

These launches run only once in a while. They are always crowded. By the time we came aboard, about thirty people, packed like sardines, were lying on the deck ready for a peaceful night. We stepped over them, looking for some available space. Nothing. Then Sister Rose Anna spied a place on the hatch up front. It was out in the open, unprotected by the little roofing, but we did not care. A beautiful moon, a sky-full of stars—why should anyone want to sleep under a roof? Famous last words!

The hatch was not a Simmons Beautyrest—not even a reasonable facsimile thereof—but we lost no time in getting to sleep. A few hours later: Came the rain. What had happened to the moon and the stars and that oh, so beautiful night? How it poured! I dripped my way toward the few inches of roof that was left for me. Often I have wondered what it would be like to jump into the ocean fully clothed to rescue someone. Now I know, at least, how you would feel when you got back on board. We were wet missioners, but our enthusiasm was not the least dampened. At 5:30 A.M. we left the river launch stepping over the side into a *"gasolina,"* as they call an outboard motor-boat here. This took us up the creek to Macantaca.

For fifteen minutes we were climbing the tiny hill from the river bank to the pueblo. For every two steps up, we slid back one. At the top, some helpful little boys came with sticks and scraped the greater part of the mud from our shoes. Looking a mite more presentable, we entered the *cantina* where Mass was to be celebrated.

Liquor bottles lined the shelves. The people perched on the bar to get a better view of the Mass. Father's tiny missal rested on an empty Bubble Mint can which he had covered nicely. Our Lady of Grace (a tiny plastic statue) reigned from her throne atop a pretty blue pedestal. It had once been a Chase and Sanborn coffee tin. The water and wine cruets were twin toilet water bottles, but you would never have known it.

Then came Mass and Communion. Father Martin, whose parish is this Rio Grande River, celebrated the Holy Sacrifice. How we were to miss it in the weeks ahead! The wetness of the night was forgotten. We felt safe and secure in the Great Mystery before us —a beginning of our work in Macantaca.

We were shown to our quarters. It was one of the best houses in the pueblo—another *cantina,* though. All the places around us were built of bamboo but ours was made of wide wooden planks, set far apart to let in plenty of air. At almost any hour, from sun-up at 5 until late in the evening, we could spot a pair of shining brown eyes at the cracks and hear the familiar call "Ma-dre-ce-e-ta!" Weeks later when we were leaving, one of the neighbors said, "I am going to miss you very much. I have so enjoyed coming over and taking a peek once in a while." We were something brand new to Macantaca. Not a few came to the door saying, "We don't want anything, Madre. We just came to look at you."

There were two rooms in our combination clinic, classroom and living quarters. The large room in front was the width of the house—there was a tiny curtained-off section to the left—and a bar or counter to the right. Someone had thoughtfully put up a heavy sheet in front of the bar right to the ceiling, this made our only hideaway. We had arrived earlier than expected; our good neighbors were still scouting around for furnishings. For the three of us, there was a table, one chair and two *tijeras*—comfortable native beds made of canvas stretched tight across two posts and standing on criss-crossed legs. They get their name from their scissor-like legs. *Tijera* is the Spanish word for scissors.

After the rain-soaked night, we would gladly have fallen into any shape of bed and let the rest of the world go by. But no. There were only two *tijeras* and we were all three too gallant to let anybody else stay up. Anyway, we had visitors all day long. The people were so happy to see us, we couldn't possibly have turned them away.

One of the first to come was Mr. Ping, a Seventh Day Adventist. He proved to be a Fairy Godfather.

"My wife sent me with this," he said, unrolling a mosquito net. It was the first of many such kindnesses.

Little by little, we learned about Macantaca. The name is an Indian word meaning "Going and Coming." The town is built around a lumber company operated by men from Mississippi. There are just three of them to supervise the camp. They were all counting the days until their two-year contract would be up. Our enthusiasm for the place was a deep mystery to them. But there is this difference: We were there for living souls, not dead wood.

Non-Catholics and from Mississippi, the Americans felt pretty ill at ease with us. They told Mr. Ping later that they had never talked to Sisters in their lives before. But, to show their friendliness they sent us a few blocks of precious ice and—of all things!—a lemon pie.

The little pueblo of Macantaca has grown into something of a trading center for people up and down the river. In native canoes (or *pit-pans*) they carry their produce—bananas, beans, rice and a few other fruits and vegetables—to Macantaca and sell or barter them for other items. The pity of this is that there are so many *cantinas* in Macantaca. The farmers spend the few pesos they make on *guara*—a native home brew. We had a *cantina* on either side of the Convent, which was built as a *cantina,* too. I am all for starting some Temperance Leagues here in Nicaragua. Drink is certainly the curse of these poor people.

As we would not be having Mass in the morning, we agreed on a late sleep but our little friends in the pueblo had another idea. Bright and early the next day we heard the call "Madrecita!" Through all the peep holes, wide blades of light were already criss-crossed on the walls and floor. I dressed quickly and opened the door to accept a gift—a beer bottle full of milk. In a little while our breakfast arrived. Life was looking very bright after a wonderful night's sleep.

That morning all sorts of pictures went up on the available wall space. The sheet hanging in front of the bar became the gallery panel for posters of the mysteries of the Rosary. Sister George Francis set up her medicine in one corner of the room. As we put the finishing touches on this glorified arrangement some 25 patients appeared at the door.

In no time at all 72 youngsters swung their bare feet from the benches or sat on the floor. We had religion classes, then some craft work. Sewing for the older girls and woodcraft for the boys taught them how to make their homes attractive. We usually ended with a bit of music. Somedays we had games. But the high point was reached when we played the *discos*—some phonograph records my brother had sent from New York. Mostly nursery tales in Spanish.

Everybody loved them. Red Riding Hood, *Caperucita Roja,* came into her own with Macantaca folk. Not only the children, but big men and women used to come in the evening and beg for Red Riding Hood. One night, as the little girl was strolling through the woods taking her cakes to Grandma, I noticed a giant of a man, very gruff and burly, hanging around the door. He looked sullen to me. "That fellow is up to no good," I thought. "He must be the Big Bad Wolf in person."

I quaked as he came toward me, across the room. His deep booming voice said, "Mam, that was very nice. Will you please make the machine tell about *Caperucita Roja* again? I sure liked that one!"

I was only too happy to oblige. As the little red-caped figure came dancing through the wood, I looked at the Big Bad Wolf. The nicest smile played over his forbidding countenance. He stayed to hear it three times. A few days later, he shyly returned with a watermelon as a gift.

After a while, I felt like the lady in the 5 & 10 who puts on a record for you on request. The people knew our *discos* by heart, but still they asked to hear them again.

We had a play. None of our children had ever taken part in the like before. They had not even heard of a play. Many times during the first rehearsals, I felt that The Histrionic Art, as such, was quite beyond them. We spend hours typing out the parts for the various characters. Then—and only then—we found that, out of the ten children selected for speaking parts, seven could not read a letter. Lucia, our star, a girl of 14, was among the seven. Neither she nor anybody in her house had the faintest knowledge of reading. We had to buckle down to teaching Lucia by rote.

This discovery changed our curriculum somewhat. We started

reading and writing classes and plugged on that until our short stay ended.

Boanerges—yes, that's the name—was one of our dimmer lights. He was seventeen years old but as simple as a child of six. I gave him private lessons in readin', writin', and 'rithmetic, starting with 1 plus 1. He was avid to learn. Never missed a single class. When he could write his name, he confided to us that, just for practice, he had carved it on a couple of trees.

Boanerges was quite a character. He had very long hair pushed behind his ears. One day, I couldn't stand it any longer.

"Why don't you get your hair cut?" I asked him. "It looks quite untidy, Boanerges."

"I like it this way," he answered. "It makes me look like Tarzan."

"So? I never noticed the resemblance, Boanerges. But now that you speak of it . . ." Tarzan-types of movies seem to be the only ones that penetrate to Macantaca. From watching the boys swing on the trees near the river bank, I wouldn't be surprised but what Tarzan has a very good following in the pueblo.

"For all his jungle skill," I said, "Tarzan was a very intelligent fellow, Boanerges. He picked up quite an education for himself, I remember."

I did not succeed in getting the hair cut, but my Budding Intellectual dug into his lessons even harder after that.

A play about Our Lady of Fatima was the "graduation" program. We kept the costuming very simple. Borrowed pieces of material made skirts and blouses. Sister Rose Anna did an excellent job on our "priest." A black kimono was his cassock; one of our habit collars became a Roman collar for him. Maybe the Portuguese would not have recognized him, but our people were enchanted.

Our lovely Lady of Fatima wore a white nightgown. Her mantle was the width of a roll of crepe paper. The silver brocade was made of beautiful metallic paper that said, "Fleischman Yeast" on the reverse side. The little dancers in the plaza wore crepe paper skirts, kerchiefs and big hair ribbons—bows of paper holly ribbon that had come on our Christmas packages from home. Not exactly authentic, but we felt Our Lady would understand. Surely, players on the Great White Way were never more pleased with themselves.

We moved everything out of the big room, borrowed benches from the shacks around, carried in lots of greenery from the river bank, built up a bush around a chair on which Our Lady would appear, and everything was ready.

Then came Fatima! The children did very well. We had strung up a couple of sheets for a curtain; halfway through, the string broke and the sheets collapsed. We finished by holding up the curtain and prompting the players at the same time. We could not find a single child or adult who could read well enough to be narrator so Sister Rose Anna took her place behind the bar (and the sheet) and before each act she read the narrator's part.

The people were very attentive. There wasn't an inch of space anywhere. Both the windows and front doorway were filled. There was only a hairline between the actors and the audience. Since most of them had never seen a play before, it would not have been extraordinary for them to come right up and share the space with the players—especially after the curtain fell.

The play was over two days before First Holy Communion day so that excitement would be out of the way and children could prepare more recollectedly for the great day.

Justo was 18 years old. He required much extra attention. He was working during the day, couldn't read a word, and had too much shame to join the evening classes. We arranged to give him a lesson each evening after Rosary. It was hard going; Justo did not even know his prayers. What a pity! And not an unusual case down here where families break up and move from camp to camp constantly.

We realized from the beginning that the children were too poor to get special clothes for First Communion. We told the mothers, "Just have a clean dress or suit ready." We repeated often to the children that they did not need new clothes—just a clean outfit including a beautiful, bright, shiny soul. As it was, most of the little ones came barefoot, too. This was one group who would not have the distraction of finery! Father had a few old veils that were really old. Sister and I spent hours patching, cutting them up and pulling them together to get enough for the group. Crepe paper arm bands with a little more Fleischman Yeast silver paper decorated the boys.

It was at this late date—just the day before the Grand Finale—that we discovered Maria Next-Time. I have always known that the devil is a very cagey fellow, but only after our little session with Maria did I realize how many tricks he has up his sleeve.

Sister Rose Anna and I thought we had visited every single house in town in making the parish census. We were sure we knew, by name, every one of the five hundred people in town. But Sister was puzzled.

"There are 25 houses on the main street," she said. "And we have only 24 families listed. We must have skipped one."

So we looked again. Sure enough. There was a door which did not seem to be a door and, behind it, a little room. A woman answered the door. She was thirty-odd, which is fairly old here. Thin, spare, nervous, there was something haunting in her eyes. She looked at us and at the women with us.

"What is your name, please?" we asked.

The woman turned and walked back into the room. But she did not close the door on us.

"She is Maria," a neighbor volunteered.

"And do you live here, Maria?" Sister called to her.

"Yes," came a monosyllable.

"Do you live here alone?"

"Yes," she said and, a long second later, "now."

I drew a breath and explained, "Father is coming to Macantaca tomorrow. Many will be going to Confession then and to Communion the next day. How about you, Maria."

"No," she said dully. "I cannot go to Confession."

Then poor Maria began to talk. It had been fifteen years since her last confession; she had lived with many different men, and had "lots of other bad sins." She ended with the cold statement of a fact, "If I die now, I know I go to hell."

Her next door neighbor spoke up. "Maria is always like this. Each time the priest is coming, she tortures herself; but she never gets any nearer to Confession than to say she will go the next time."

"Maria," we pleaded. "Perhaps there won't be a next time."

"My sins are so great that the priest's ear cannot contain them."

"But you are telling them to Christ Himself. Surely they are not too great for Him to hear."

This shook her for a moment. Then she hardened once again.

"Everybody will taunt me if I go to Confession," she said.

We were desperate. Only prayer can help this soul, we thought. I resolved to spend every minute of the afternoon praying for Maria as I worked. As we left the house that the Old Boy had hidden from us for six weeks, I said,

"Why not come to our house, Maria, and wait until everybody else has already gone to Confession? Then I will go over with you and help you. Nobody needs to know a thing about it."

She did not look too impressed with this proposal.

That afternoon we were rushed with last minute preparations for First Holy Communion Day. The little ones came for First Confessions; the ladies in town wanted the things for the breakfast; the older girls were on hand to help; the mothers came to borrow white dresses. But we remembered Maria through it all.

At nightfall, there was a knock at the convent door. In the dark came an unmistakable voice.

"It's Maria, Madre; I have come."

We went across the street to the *cantina* which was serving as Chapel while Father was in town. Two or three people were still in the line. Maria began to get cold feet, even though we stood outside in the dark where no one could see us.

"Oh, Madre," she said, "I think I am getting a headache. My headaches are terrific. I had better go home and try the next time Father comes."

"We have some wonderful headache pills in the convent, Maria. We'll get one for you right away." I dispatched a little girl who happened to be passing.

A few minutes later: "The kerosene lamp is glinting in my eyes. I'm sure it is injuring my sight, Madre, and you know I must sew to live."

Silently, I moved the lamp. One person more, waiting!

"Oh, Madre, I feel faint. I must walk around the block a little while. No, don't keep the priest waiting. I'll go the next time."

I fanned her with a holy card. That last man was in the box! Now Maria really became scared.

"It is impossible to go to Confession, Madre. My rheumatism is so bad that I cannot kneel. Next time, this rheumatic attack will have passed and I can kneel properly."

"Father won't mind if you sit down," I said steering her up the stairs and into the little waiting room. Where, oh, where, was a chair or a bench for her to sit on! I spied one in the corner.

I suppose Father did not know what to think when I marched into his impromptu confessional behind the bar and dropped the bench at his feet.

"She has rheumatism and cannot kneel," was all I said.

Then I left him with Maria.

She was very happy afterwards. At the convent, we gave her remedies for every ailment, ending with Sloan's Liniment for her rheumatism.

The next morning, when it was time to go to Communion, she came over and took my arm. I understood about her rheumatism and gave her gentle but firm escort to the railing. I would gladly have carried her in my arms!

◆ 25 ◆

QUEEN OF MEXICO

So far as I can judge, from the few times I have dipped into such matters, the American Hierarchy have missed quite a trick in not encouraging the liturgical use of fans. As a means of directing traffic in a crowded sanctuary, as well as keeping tempers cool in functionaries who have reached the boiling point of frustration and annoyance, there is nothing better than a high class, dignified fan, preferably one edged with black lace.

Down in Merida, Yucatan, the fan is a definite adjunct to the proper administration of the Sacraments. An old priest, fan in hand, approaches his confessional. As he steps into the box, a crowd of penitent ladies, draped in mantillas, gathers round him. The confessional is built for ventilation, necessary in this hot climate. Two prie-dieus face each other with a chair between. The sides are built up so that the priest cannot see the penitent. But everybody else can.

The other ladies crowd so close that if it were not for a black fan held discreetly over her mouth, the penitent's confession might as well be shouted from the roof-tops.

The old priest, too, makes good use of the simple little paper fan he holds in his hand. As each confession ends, he dismisses the penitent with a wave of the fan and beckons somebody else to take the empty place. Between times he fans himself vigorously. A large picture of Coca-Cola and the words—omnipresent in all Latin America—"Tome Coca-Cola," waves back and forth in his hand, faithfully acting as mentor and instructor. I wonder how many cardboard fans he wears out during one year's confessions. Also it seems that advertising companies ought to do psychological research on the sales-effects of hearing, "Say Ten Hail Marys" at the same time the eye takes in the message "Tome Coca-Cola." Possibly the subconscious mind would link Coca-Cola with the idea of penance; that would be too bad for business.

But this is nothing. A mere by-product of the liturgical use of the fan, you might say. The best person to wield an imperious fan down here in Merida is the Master of Ceremonies in a Solemn High Mass. A flick of his black lace fan in a certain direction sends the deacon on his way. A dainty crack on an altar boy's knuckles reminds him to stop day-dreaming and get busy with those cruets. And when the Bishop starts fuming on his episcopal throne, the agile MC waves the fan for a few seconds at him. He is reconciled once more to sit in majestic impotence watching everybody do everything wrong. A truly great Master of Ceremonies wields his fan like a baton, quieting the growls from the onlookers while he puts the priests through their paces smartly.

In the States, I have watched many a helpless MC going through the antics of making himself understood. He twirls his eyebrows, bares his teeth, beckons subtly with his little finger and, in pantomine, strangles every functionary in the sanctuary. Still he has often to go to bed with an icebag on his fevered brow as soon as the Mass is ended.

The fan in the hands of the laity has good use, too. There was an old lady behind me at Rosary every night who opened her fan for the first Hail Mary of each decade and slapped it shut for the Gloria and Our Father. I thought this was her own private devotion, but one time the priest tried to slip in an eleventh Hail Mary. Old Julia behind me would have none of it. She opened her fan again and whammed it shut against the pew in front of her with a tone which said clearly, "None of that nonsense, Padre. If you can't count to ten, there are some in the parish who can and do." Padre Jaime caught on. He swung into the Gloria just as if it were always said, "Hail Mary, full of. . . . to the Son and to the Holy Ghost."

Yucatan has a character all its own. The Yucatecans do not classify themselves as Mexicans. Indeed, they say, "He is a Mexican," as if they spoke of another breed of people entirely.

The sturdy independence of the barren little nub of land might account for this. It is almost a square peninsula jutting out into the Caribbean, 200 miles wide and 280 miles long. The Spanish never got very far on it. Maybe they didn't want to. But the fact remains that descendants of the Mayas controlled their own land for centuries after the rest of Latin America had absorbed Spanish culture.

It's queer topography. The whole area is limestone rock with a thin covering of coral, weathered sufficiently to be like sand. In this, nothing grows except the omnipresent henequin, a type of sisal. Yucatan supplies more than half of the world's henequin. Small wonder then the land looks a huge spike-bed left behind by a giant fakir of India. The cactus-y henequin grows a single central flower which rises 20 to 25 feet into the air. Neat rows of these spikes slide beneath the plane as one lands at Merida. If you are nervous, you can easily picture the plane impaled on one, like a fly on a pin.

Merida is a city of windmills—all of which come from the Aermotor Company of Chicago. This fact is blazoned on the tail in bold letters. Everyone uses windmills because all the water in Yucatan flows underground. There are no rivers, no creeks, no lakes. The water is underneath and you must dig through solid rock to get to it.

If you have no windmill, you must carry your pitcher to a "cenote." These are deep caves which lead down to an underground river. Friends of ours in Yucatan have one on their property. It's wonderful. You enter a cave and down several steps. What a relief from the torrid sun! There, before you at the bottom step, is a pool of water, crystal clear. I did not know it was water at all until the gardener dipped his hand into it and ruffled the surface.

Because Yucatan is so rocky and dry, you would think that the city would be treeless. Not so. Every street is lined with palms or poinciana. To plant a tree, one must dig a hole in the rock and fill it with soil imported from a distance. Soil sells for 25 cents a bushel. You can imagine how expensive it was to make Merida a tree-lined city. You are grateful to the city fathers, however, as you slide into the shady city from the sun-baked flats outside.

The flats are very flat. Margarito, ten years old, was telling me about the hills on the way to Chichen Itza.

"Hills?" I said. "I didn't notice any at all."

"Didn't you?" he asked, shocked. "Why, there's one place on the road where the hollows are so deep that you can't see a man coming toward you. That makes it a hill, doesn't it?"

Henequin, cenotes, ancient civilizations—these are Yucatan's specialties. There is another which is much more delightful. Hammocks! Every Yucatecan sleeps in a hammock. We have the wrong technique here in the States. Those-Who-Know don't sleep North-and-South in a hammock; they take it East-by-West. When you lie lengthwise, you bend like the letter U. Around 3 A.M., your back is twisted, your blanket is in a lump beneath you and your feet are stone cold and bloodless. But take it straight across or, if it isn't wide enough, on the diagonal and you are rocked in the Cradle of the Deep all night long.

The head of a boys' school in Merida showed us around. He pointed out the dormitory. It was a long, bare room. Each boy had rolled up his hammock and hung it neatly on a hook along the wall. At night, they simply swing them across to the opposite wall.

"Everyone in Merida uses a hammock," Mr. Lopez said. "The boys do; I do; the mayor does; even the Archbishop does. A good hammock costs far more than one of your American beds."

I can believe it. A friend told us that she gave the Archbishop a new hammock costing 700 pesos—nearly $100. Hand-crocheted, elegantly adorned, it was quite a gift. But the Archbishop is the type of person you read about in Second Nocturnes. The same day, he gave that scrumptious hammock to a poor old woman who came a-begging. Our generous friend saw red. Being an old friend, she scolded His Excellency, "I could give you ten hammocks for what I paid for that one. Next time, I'll give you nine and save money."

Yes, the Archbishop has the reputation of giving everything away. He saw me patting a stuffed turtle which reposed on the bottom shelf of his what-not cabinet, a beautiful big thing with flippers and a polished back. I coveted him greatly but had not the courage to come right out and ask for him. "Dear Lord," I prayed, "if You want me to have this turtle, inspire the Archbishop to give him to me." Soon it was time to take a picture of His Excellency. I pushed the table out of the way, adjusted a tiger-skin rug under his feet, fixed a flash bulb in the camera and pressed the trigger.

273

Perfect!! But when I went to turn the film, I realized that there was no film in the camera. I simply was not humble enough to ask the Archbishop to wait a minute until I re-loaded the camera. So I said nothing. Imagine the red-hot coals heaped on my blistered head, when His Excellency said, "Would you like to take that turtle back to Maryknoll as a gift from Merida to Mother Mary Columba?" Would I? I loved him!

With the turtle under my arm, happily waving his fins at the thought of going to the States, we left the Arzobispado and took a bus home while my tortured conscience groaned aloud. To take a beautiful turtle from the Archbishop when I had been so stupid about the picture! There's a current story about a celebrity arriving at the Pearly Gates but hesitating to go into Heaven until the photographers came. Well, I'm thinking he'll wait a long time at the Pearly Gates if he's expecting photographers to get even that close to Heaven.

As I say, it rarely rains in Yucatan. But one day it elected to pour. That was a day at Chichen Itza, seat of the old Mayan civilization which was the glory of Yucatan from 1000 to 1200 A.D. It fell then before the Toltecs who, in turn, were subdued by the Aztecs. Both of these were fearsome tribes. They ruled by force, and offered human sacrifices to their gods. But the Mayas, like the Greeks in Europe, conquered their conquerors by their culture.

Just to make you realize that you are going back centuries into a totally different civilization, the Good Lord put about 75 miles of flat barren country between the really Spanish city of Merida and that of Yucatan's mighty ghosts, the Mayas. A few hours' rolling over the sun-baked land with the hot wind scorching your face, is enough to make the city of Chichen Itza seem a far glimpse of Heaven.

It is a city, indeed. First built in 530 A.D. it was an outpost of the Old Mayan Empire which flourished then to the South. It was abandoned for three hundred years from 668 until 964. Then the Itza tribe returned to build new glory on the ruins of the old. This was The New Empire when three Mayan cities joined hands to rule all Yucatan until 1201. The setting of the two sacred cenotes, the grandeur of the temples, the impressive religious ceremonies, made Chichen Itza the cultural fountain-head of the peninsula.

Over many square miles, great pyramids rise from the flat land. They are tremendous buildings. The Court of a Thousand Columns encloses a central plaza of five acres complete with temples, colonnaded halls, sunken courts, terraces and theaters. The Ball Court, built like a rectangular stadium, has grandstand seats at either end and bleachers on the sides. The acoustics are so perfect that a normal voice carries from one end to the other.

After 800-and-more years of weathering, the stone serpents, the gargoyle heads, the monolith statues are distinct. How were they carved, when the Mayas were totally ignorant of iron?

The biggest pyramid is El Castillo. Its base covers an acre of ground. It is really two pyramids, one inside the other. The smaller enclosed one is much older. It was a shrine for a sort of Judgment Seat which sits alone in a tiny chamber deep in the masonry.

When I think of it now, it's a wonder we did not burn to death, or break our necks, or have a panic and be trampled on. The only entrance to the inner chamber is a small door on the outside of El Castillo. You enter this and immediately you are in complete and absolute darkness. Not the faintest glimmer pierces it. You might just as well close your eyes from this point on. However, you feel your way along this narrow tunnel, touching both side walls with your hands. Then you begin to mount a steep stairway, still in total darkness. After some twenty or twenty-five steps you have reached a landing. Your foot feels no further step; your hands cannot touch the walls. At this point, Carmen lit a match. The sudden flare showed us a tiny cell and in it a bench-like seat of reddish stone, ornamented with lions' heads and feet, and set with colored stones. The match died; we were once more in blackness.

This flashing glimpse into another world was all that was given us. Loud laughter and giggles floated up the stairway in increasing volume. Obviously, a party of tourists was on its way up.

"Oh, it's so dark!"

"Say, where *is* everybody?"

"Is that you, Matilda?"

"Who put the light out!"

Carmen touched my arm in the dark.

"Let's escape! They'll ruin everything."

The two of us felt our way to the head of the stairs and started

275

down. The rises were so uneven, we had to measure each step as we went down. Midway, we collided with the tourist group! We should have known better than to start the descent. For a few minutes there was unutterable confusion. A welter of arms and legs and heads; people pushing up and we pushing down; a child screamed in terror; his mother tried to hush him from a distance; she was several steps apart from him.

At last, it was over. The last tourist had struggled past us and we were free to climb down to level land again. It was good to get out into sunshine—and back into the 20th century.

Sunshine, I said. Brilliant sunshine then. Half an hour later, it was pouring! We were 'way on top of the Warriors' Temple, then. How we got there was a triumph of Mind over Matter. The pyramids are great blocks of stone, not smoothly tapered as those in Egypt are, but in a series of steps each about 18 inches high. These gave one the merest toe-hold. It was as if you put a step ladder against a ten-story building. But Carmen and I let neither age nor rheumatism deter us. Up we went, like Alpine climbers, hanging on to higher steps as we scaled the lower ones. At last we reached the top, 100 feet above the ground. There were some stone serpents up there and a whole temple complete with altar, side courts for priests' vesting and so on. We sat on a very uncomplaining serpent to rest. Then, the heavens opened.

We ran around the top looking for shelter. Nothing. At last we found a pair of steps leading into the interior and ducked down into them. Fifteen minutes of sitting on the steps were enough for a restless soul like Carmen.

"Let's explore further," she proposed.

"It's pretty dark," I demurred. "And there isn't anybody around."

"Are you a mouse?" she asked. "Who's afraid of the dark! There's the head of a ladder over there. I'm going to see where it goes."

We were off. She went down the ladder with me after her. The bottom was absolutely black. Once more, we felt our way along tunnels with nary a gleam to guide us. I only wished I were a mouse, now. There were places where the tunnel wall gave way on one side or the other. We went along several such side passages. Once as we shuffled along the floor, feeling every inch of the way, we came to a spot where there simply was no floor. It ended abruptly. I felt as far down as my foot would reach, but there was nothing to step on. Was this a jumping off place? Was it a well 50 feet deep or only three feet? If we had had flashlights or more matches, we might have found out for posterity to know. As it was we turned back and felt our way to the main tunnel again.

We fell silent, inching our way through the blackness. As for me, my resolution was "sicklied o'er with the pale cast of thought." Suppose there were snakes hiding in the cool darkness? Or scorpions? Suppose the walls caved in, or we found the return way blocked? How did we know what evil lurked in this black labyrinth? Human bones and skeletons. Floors which stopped all of a sudden. A misstep, and one of us might break her leg. THEN, what would I do? But I said nothing. Carmen would be ashamed of me.

Carmen, Ye Bold Adventurer, had stopped.

"Maybe we'd better turn back," she said in a small voice.

At the airport in Mexico City we descended from the plane into a seething pool of photographers, military men, politicians and reporters. All that fuss wasn't for us, of course. Behind us came a contingent of VIP's in Army, Navy and Air Force uniforms. We watched for a while and then went on to the baggage rooms, thinking that we had been given our little dose of excitement for the day.

Then, just as our bags were stowed into the trunk of a taxi, a close-packed crowd of men came toward us. They were pushing along a wild-eyed man in a green suit, some of them clutching his collar, some his sleeves, pants, head, waist so that the poor fellow could do nothing but skitter along with arms outstretched. "*Senores!*" he protested, "*Un momentito! . . . Un momentito, por favor!*" But the police pushed him straight along—right to our taxi.

Sister Victoria Francis was just in the act of opening the door to get into the car. The police brushed her aside. They pushed their prisoner up against the car, then opened the door and shoved him in. What were they going to do? Commandeer the car? But our baggage was in it! I had visions of our belongings going off to some police station. We would never catch up to them again. I tried to get the attention of one of the men manhandling the prisoner. He was stone deaf, so I pounded on his shoulder. "Our baggage is in that car! Let us take it out and you can have the car." He pushed me away with his elbow.

Just then, a police jeep covered fore and aft, top and bottom with steel plates and shatter-proof glass drew up. It was a real armored jeep. The police pulled the prisoner out of our car and put him into this. Then no less than eight policemen piled in with him. If the poor fellow could wiggle a toe, he was lucky. Off they drove. We breathed easier and got into our taxi for a very dull ride to our hotel.

The Maryknoll Fathers were not aware as yet that we were in town. It was just as well. We were only too glad to be "on our own." We both had only one idea. To get to Guadalupe and just pray there.

So, early the next morning, we took a bus for 3 cents each and rode the four miles to Guadalupe. I don't know exactly what I expected. I thought there would be much more in the line of Indians, candles, praying out loud, confusion, people eating lunches right in the pews, ornate but unkempt altars, candle-wax and smoke, and women crawling up the aisle on their knees. It was a surprise to find a magnificent basilica, clean as a whistle, with flowers banked solidly across the sanctuary railing. Beautiful lighting, majestic arches, rich hangings. A modern church, it was, on Grand Central Terminal proportions and style, and jam-packed with people. A Solemn High Mass was going on; the sonorous chant rolled from the choir loft, hidden somewhere miles above us. By standing on tippy toes in back of the silent, reverent crowd, poor little Madres Viejita and Bajita could just about see the priests on the altar.

Madre Viejita's knees gave out and she sat down on a stone bench off to the side. "When this Mass is over and the place clears," she said, "we can move into a pew." It was then past eleven o'clock. The Masses had followed each other since early hours.

But after that Solemn High Mass, there was another and a new thousand-or-so of people were in the pews. And after the second Solemn High, there was a blast of bugles out front. A crowd of workmen, headed by a band, came up the middle aisle. Hundreds of laborers filled in the pews in the sanctuary, dressed only in their overalls and work-a-day clothes. We managed to squeeze into a pew for this affair along with a couple million more people.

Everything was very orderly. There were some few going up the aisle on their knees but they were quiet and kept up a pretty good pace. Many of the men carried lighted candles. Signs here and there directed traffic so that it would flow in one direction. There were so many with missals and prayerbook! Everyone followed the Mass; nobody was gossiping or talking.

It was perfect for us. We sat there for almost three hours just soaking in the atmosphere and praying for everything, big or small, that this world has need of. All that time, Masses were going on at the high altar. A group of farmers brought a huge offering of gladioli. It sailed up the main aisle on the shoulders of four men like a bath-tub full of flowers. Just the day before, a pilgrim group from a little town miles and miles away had brought their annual offering—two tons of flowers! Twenty thousand gardenias—a hundred thousand carnations and other flowers. With these they made a picture on the floor of the basilica, showing the Holy Father standing beside his papal throne. It was a huge thing, covering fully a third of the floor. Can you imagine about one-third of the floor of Grand Central Terminal covered with flowers arranged to make a picture? The people of this village have been doing this sort of thing for twenty-two years now. In 1931, they made a vow to do it every year.

La Virgen of Guadalupe is everybody's mother in Mexico. It is so trite to write, "rich and poor," "young and old," "men and women," "ignorant and learned," but that's what we saw at Guadalupe. Everybody was so intent on prayer that even I, hard-hearted as I am, could not bring myself to take a single picture. I did not want to distract them for even a moment.

After praying and steeping in prayer for several hours, we went across the street to a modest restaurant—not at all fancy—and got a little lunch. Then we began the climb to Tepeyac where Our Blessed Mother revealed herself to Juan Diego. It was a Via Penitencia—steep, rough, hot, and rugged. I was wearing Sister Anton's shoes for I told her I would go there in her shoes, if I could. They are fine shoes; I had worn them all through Guatemala and Mexico. But I must say, they added to the penitencia considerably on that rough climb. At the top we rested in the chapel up there and then came down to the main basilica.

Another bus and we were home from our pilgrimage. By this time, the Maryknoll Fathers had caught up with us. They had read the telegram wrong and were a day late. But we were grateful to have had our day at Guadalupe.

Everybody in Mexico loves the Virgin. I have never seen anything like it. Enroute to the hotel, we shared a taxi with a very sophisticated Mexican, immaculately dressed and spreading a vast aroma of hair oil and shaving cream. He was in the household of a hotel magnate and lived in Los Angeles permanently.

"Mexico City!" he said disdainfully. "I have no interest in Mexico City. I come here for one purpose only—to visit my Mother, my Queen, at Guadalupe. This morning I left Los Angeles by plane and have just now arrived. I will go to the basilica tomorrow; I will talk to my Queen. Then, tomorrow afternoon, I take a plane back to Los Angeles."

We talked about other things and as he left the taxi, Sister said, "We will remember you at Guadalupe tomorrow." "Oh!" he cried with his arms crossed on his breast, "She is my Mother! My Queen!" We left him still in ecstasy, standing on the pavement.

We also had a gay time with a taxi driver. As we walked down the streets, word flew around that two rich Americans were loose. Every peddler in town came up to interest us in bracelets, rings, postcards, Aztec ruins, sightseeing tours, etc. To be rid of them, we hailed a taxi and hopped in.

"Take us for an hour's drive around the city," Sister said.

The driver was splendid. What we liked most about him was his Spanish. We understood every word he said. A marvellous feeling on this last night in Mexico, to feel at home in the language! Like being handed a diploma or something.

It was the eve of Mexico's Independence Day, September 16. Our man had begun his celebration early. This may account for his exuberant patriotism. Every other word was, "*Viva Libertad! Viva Mexico!*"

He gave us a synopsis of Mexican history from Cortez on. His descriptions were graphic. He lifted his hand from the wheel to help Cortez strangle an Indian; he lifted the Cross on high over the